D1784004

Women and Housing

In the context of contemporary economic, political, social and cultural transformations, this book brings together contributions from developed and emerging societies in Europe, the USA and East Asia in order to highlight the nature, extent and impact of these changes on the housing opportunities of women.

The collection seeks to contribute to comparative housing debates by highlighting the gendered nature of housing processes, locating these processes within wider structured and institutionalised relations of power, and to show how these socially constructed relationships are culturally contingent, and manifest and transform over time and space.

The international contributors draw on a wide range of empirical evidence relating to labour market participation, wealth distribution, family formation and education to demonstrate the complexity and gendered nature of the interlocking arenas of production, reproduction and consumption, and the implications for the housing opportunities of women in different social contexts. Worldwide examples are drawn from Australia, China, Great Britain, Hong Kong, Japan, Spain, Sweden, Taiwan and the USA.

Patricia Kennett is a Reader in Comparative Policy Studies and Head of the Centre for Urban Studies in the School for Policy Studies, University of Bristol, UK. She has undertaken substantial research and published widely on issues relating to housing and home ownership, homelessness and social exclusion, citizenship and the welfare state in comparative perspective.

Chan Kam Wah is an Associate Professor in the Department of Applied Social Sciences, The Hong Kong Polytechnic University. He mainly teaches social policy and housing policy. His major research interests are gender studies, housing studies, and social welfare and social policy analysis. Recent publications include: 'Deconstructing the Asian Welfare Model: social equality matters' in *Journal of Asian Public Policy* 1(3), 2008, *The Crisis of Welfare in East Asia* (Lexington, 2007, co-ed) and *Gender and Social Work – Theory and Practice* (Chinese University Press, 2006, in Chinese, co-ed).

Housing and society series

Edited by Ray Forrest,
School for Policy Studies, University of Bristol

This series aims to situate housing within its wider social, political and economic context at both national and international level. In doing so it will draw on the full range of social science disciplines and on mainstream debate on the nature of contemporary social change. The books are intended to appeal to an international academic audience as well as to practitioners and policymakers – to be theoretically informed and policy relevant.

Women and Housing
An international analysis
Edited by Patricia Kennett and Chan Kam Wah

Affluence, Mobility and Second Home Ownership
Chris Paris

Housing, Markets and Policy
Peter Malpass and Rob Rowlands

Housing and Health in Europe
Edited by David Ormandy

The Hidden Millions
Graham Tipple and Suzanne Speak

Housing, Care and Inheritance
Misa Izuhara

Housing and Social Transition in Japan
Edited by Yosuke Hirayama and Richard Ronald

Housing Transformations
Shaping the space of 21st century living
Bridget Franklin

Housing and Social Policy
Contemporary themes and critical perspectives
Edited by Peter Somerville with Nigel Sprigings

Housing and Social Change
East-West perspectives
Edited by Ray Forrest and James Lee

Urban Poverty, Housing and Social Change in China
Ya Ping Wang

Gentrification in a Global Context
Edited by Rowland Atkinson and Gary Bridge

Women and Housing

An international analysis

Edited by Patricia Kennett
and Chan Kam Wah

Routledge
Taylor & Francis Group

LONDON AND NEW YORK

First published 2011
by Routledge
2 Park Square, Milton Park, Abingdon, Oxon, OX14 4RN

Simultaneously published in the USA and Canada
by Routledge
270 Madison Avenue, New York, NY 10016

Routledge is an imprint of the Taylor & Francis Group, an informa business

Typeset in Times and Frutiger by
HWA Text and Data Management, London
Printed and bound in Great Britain by
TJ International Ltd, Padstow, Cornwall

British Library Cataloguing in Publication Data
A catalogue record for this book is available from the British Library

Library of Congress Cataloging-in-Publication Data
Women and housing : an international analysis / [edited by] Patricia Kennett and Chan Kam Wah.
        p. cm. – (Housing and society series)
    Includes bibliographical references and index.
    1. Housing policy. 2. Housing–Sex differences. 3. Sex discrimination against women. I. Kennett, Patricia, 1959- II. Chan, Kam-Wah.
    HD7287.3.W66 2011
    363.5`92–dc22   2010023821

ISBN13: 978-0-415-54895-3 (hbk)
ISBN13: 978-0-415-54897-7 (pbk)
ISBN13: 978-0-203-81893-0 (ebk)

Contents

Contents

Tables

Figures

Contributors

Herng-Dar Bih is an Associate Professor in the Graduate Institute of Building and Planning, National Taiwan University, Taipei, Taiwan. His research interests include gender and space, masculinities, street graffiti and qualitative research methods. Research publications include (with F. T.-Y Wang and D. J. Brennan) 'Have they really come out: Gay men and their parents in Taiwan' in *Culture, Health & Sexuality* (2009); (with Y.-W. Peng, 'Protection? Correction? Or Exclusion? The gender implications of women-only cars in Taiwan' in *Journal of Women's and Gender Studies* (2008, in Chinese) and 'Women and public facilities in Taiwan: Revising policies on public spaces' in *Women & Environments International Magazine* (2006).

Chan Kam Wah is an Associate Professor in the Department of Applied Social Sciences, The Hong Kong Polytechnic University. He mainly teaches social policy and housing policy. His major research interests are gender studies, housing studies, and social welfare and social policy analysis. Recent publications include 'Deconstructing the Asian Welfare Model: social equality matters' in *Journal of Asian Public Policy* (2008), *The Crisis of Welfare in East Asia* (Lexington, 2007, co-ed) and *Gender and Social Work – Theory and Practice* (Chinese University Press, 2006, in Chinese, co-ed).

Yi-Ling Chen is an Assistant Professor in the program of International Studies and Department of Geography at the University of Wyoming, USA. Her previous position was in the Department of Natural Resources and Environmental Studies, National Dong Hwa University, Taiwan. Her research interests are housing policies, gender, urban development, and neo-liberalism. She has published several papers on neo-liberalization and transformation of housing policies in Taiwan and Taiwanese women's housing problems.

Mieko Hinokidani is a Professor in the Graduate school of Life and Environmental Sciences at Kyoto Prefectural University, Japan. She specializes in comparative housing policy and received her PhD in housing and built environmental studies at Osaka City University. She has abundant cross-disciplinary research experience in France, Canada and Japan. Her recent articles deal with issues of governance for local housing programs, housing for the frail and elderly and managerial questions for public housing estates in Japan and France.

Guo Hui-min is a Professor of law in the Humanity and Economic Law College of Northwestern Polytechnical University, and Director of the Women Development and Rights Research Center of Northwestern Polytechnical University. Professor Guo has taught and conducted research on legal studies for 25 years. She is active in non-governmental organizations, and is the vice-president of the Association of Women Jurists in Shaanxi Province, China. Recent publications including: *Study on Women's Labour Rights – a report from Shaanxi Province* (in Chinese, China Social Sciences Press, 2009), *Gender and Labour Rights* (in Chinese, Northwestern Polytechnical University Press, 2005); and more than 20 articles in various academic journals.

Patricia Kennett is a Reader in Comparative Policy Studies and Head of the Centre for Urban Studies in the School for Policy Studies, University of Bristol, UK. She has undertaken substantial research and published widely on issues relating to housing and home ownership, homelessness and social exclusion, citizenship and the welfare state in comparative perspective.

Elizabeth A. Mulroy is Professor Emerita in the Graduate School of Social Work, University of Maryland at Baltimore, USA. Professor Mulroy's research interests include affordable housing and community development, implementation of social policy, women and housing, homeless prevention, and interorganizational collaboration and organizational change. She has authored or co-authored over 50 scholarly journal articles and book chapters, and in 2005 she and co-author M. Back Tamboro received the national Slavin-Patti Award for Scholarly Excellence for their article "Nonprofit organizations and welfare-to-work: environmental turbulence and organizational change" published in *Administration in Social Work*. Professor Mulroy has authored or edited three books, including *Women as single parents: Confronting institutional barriers in the courts, the workplace, and the housing market* (1988, Auburn House), and *The new uprooted: Single mothers in urban life* (1995, Greenwood Press).

Montserrat Pareja-Eastaway is an Associate Professor and has worked at the University of Barcelona, Spain since 1993 researching and teaching in Economics. Her field of interest is focused on housing policy and its social implications. Housing affordability, sustainable housing and urban development and urban regeneration strategies are, among others, key aspects in her research. Recent publications include 'The effects of the Spanish housing system on the settlement patterns of immigrants', *Journal of Economic and Social Geography*, 2009 and (with M.T. Sánchez-Martínez) 'European rental markets: regulation or liberalization? The Spanish case', in *Housing Market Challenges in Europe and the United States. Any Solutions Available*? (Palgrave Macmillan, 2009).

Richard Ronald is a Lecturer in Urban Studies in the Department of Geography, Planning and International Development Studies at the University of Amsterdam. He is also affiliated with the OTB Research Institute for the Built Environment at Delft University of Technology, also in the Netherlands. He has numerous publications on housing, urban and social change in Europe and Asia-Pacific. His most recent books include a monograph, *The Ideology of Home Ownership: the Role of Housing in Homeowner Societies* (Palgrave Macmillan, 2008), and a number of co-edited works including *Housing and Social Transition in Japan* (Routledge, 2006) and *Home and Family in Japan: Continuity and Transformation* (Routledge, 2010). He is currently the review editor of the *International Journal of Housing Policy* and section editor of the forthcoming *Encyclopedia of Home and Housing*.

Ingrid Sahlin is Professor in Social Work at the Department of Social Work, University of Gothenburg, Sweden. Her main fields of research are housing exclusion and crime prevention, with a special focus in both areas on the construction of so-called problem groups. Recent publications include 'Urban definitions of places and people' in *In my Caravan I Feel like Superman* (Feantsa, 2009) and 'De uppstudsiga kvinnorna på Stora fattighuset [The rebellious women of the great poorhouse]' in *Villkorandets politik. Fattigdomens premisser och samhällets åtgärder* [The Policy of Conditioning – The Conditions of Poverty and Societal Interventions] (Égalité, 2008).

Teresa Sánchez-Martínez is an Associate Professor of Economics at the University of Granada, Spain since 1990. The key aspects of her research are housing finance, distributive aspects of public expenditure on housing, housing affordability, social housing, private and social rented housing markets and housing policies from a comparative perspective. She has published numerous articles in specialized journals in the field of housing economy. Recent publications include 'The Spanish financial system:

Facing up to the real estate crisis and credit crunch" in *European Journal of Housing Policy*, (2008) and (with M. Pareja-Eastaway), 'European rental markets: regulation or liberalization? The Spanish case' in *Housing Market Challenges in Europe and the United States. Any Solutions Available?* (Palgrave Macmillan, 2009).

Selina Tually is a Research Fellow in the School of Social Sciences at The University of Adelaide, Australia. She is a geographer with a keen interest in housing and her key area of expertise is Australian women and housing. She has authored a number of commissioned reports in this field, including a recent synthesis report on *Women, Domestic and Family Violence and Homelessness* (2008) for the Australian Government's Office for Women. Dr Tually was also the lead author of the report *Too Big to Ignore Future. Issues for Australian Women's Housing 2006–2025* (2007) for the Women's Housing Caucus of South Australia. Dr Tually's research interests include: women and housing generally, housing needs, housing markets, housing/homelessness and vulnerable groups (including youth, people with a disability and women), homelessness and domestic and family violence; and social inclusion. She has been a contributing author to a number of reports on housing for the Australian Housing and Urban Research Institute.

Ingrid Westendorp is a Lecturer/Researcher in the International and European Law Department of the Faculty of Law, Maastricht University, the Netherlands. Her research is focused on economic, social and cultural human rights and human rights of women. Her publications predominantly concern women's land and housing rights, the connection between domestic violence and the right to adequate housing, and culture and women's right to equality. Her most recent publications include '15 years United Nations Special Rapporteur on Violence Against Women: Lessons learned about domestic violence and the way forward' in *Mimbar Hukum Journal* (2010), '*Vrouwen en huisvesting; een kwestie van cultuur* [Women and housing; a matter of culture]' in Een kwestie van grensoverschrijding; Liber Amicorum P.E.L. Janssen (Wolf Legal Publishers, 2009) and *Women and Housing: Gender Makes a Difference*, (Intersentia, 2007).

Acknowledgements

The editors would like to thank the contributors for their enthusiasm and commitment to this project. We also appreciate their timely and thoughtful responses to our comments and suggestions.

ABS data used with permission from the Australian Bureau of Statistics. Tables and data analysis undertaken by the National Centre for Social and Economic Modelling (NATSEM) and The Association of Superannuation Funds of Australia Ltd (ASFA) used with permission from NATSEM and ASFA respectively.

Every effort has been made to contact and acknowledge copyright owners. The publishers would be grateful to hear from any copyright holder who is not acknowledged here and will undertake to rectify any errors or omissions in future printings or editions of the book.

Abbreviations

ABC	Australian Broadcasting Corporation
ABS	Australian Bureau of Statistics
AC	Autonomous Communities
AHURI	Australian Housing and Urban Research Institute
AONB	Areas of Outstanding Natural Beauty
AR	additional residence (in AuSSA survey)
ARHC	Affordable Rural Housing Commission
AuSSA	Australian Survey of Social Attitudes
BTL	buy-to-let (investors *or* types of mortgages)
CGT	capital gains tax
CLNC	Coleraine/Limavady/North Coast
CPRE	Campaign to Protect Rural England
DCLG	Department of Communities and Local Government (Britain)
ENHR	European Network for Housing Research
EPA	Active Population Survey of Spain
EU	European Union
GDP	gross domestic product
HMRC	Her Majesty's Revenue and Customs (UK tax authority)
HVS	Helford Village Society
ICT	information and communications technology
INE	National Institute of Statistics of Spain
LAT	living apart together (relationships)
LGA	Local Government Area
LME	Lower Mill Estate
MMSH	Malaysia My Second Home (Malaysian government programme)
NAMA	National Asset Management Agency
NATSEM	National Centre for Social and Economic Modelling (Canberra, Australia)
NIHE	Northern Ireland Housing Executive

List of abbreviations

NISRA	Northern Ireland Statistics and Research Agency
NSW	New South Wales
ODPM	Office of the Deputy Prime Minister (became DCLG in May 2006)
OECD	Organisation of Economic Co-operation and Development
ONS	Office of National Statistics
OPSI	Office of Public Sector Information
PIIGS	Portugal, Italy, Ireland, Greece and Spain
PIPWE	Department of Primary Industries, Parks, Water and Environment (Tasmania)
RICS	Royal Institute of Chartered Surveyors
RRS	rural renewal scheme
RV	recreational vehicle
SA	South Australia
SEH	Survey of English Housing
SRS	seaside resorts scheme
SUV	sports utility vehicle

1 Introduction

Women and housing systems

Chan Kam Wah and Patricia Kennett

Introduction

This book aims to highlight the gendered nature of housing processes and systems in an international context. The intention is to explore the dynamics of contemporary economic and social change and consider the implications for the relationship between women and the housing system in developed and emerging societies in Europe, the USA and East Asia. Whilst there has been a growing interest in comparative and international housing studies, the inclusion of a gender dimension is relatively underdeveloped compared to other policy arenas such as employment and education. Housing is often portrayed as a neutral system, mere 'bricks and mortar', that does not preference any one gender. It is assumed that housing policy and urban planning serves the needs of the whole society or community equally, and that the distribution of housing resources serves the needs of the whole family equally. This collection is concerned with exploring and deconstructing these assumptions through an analysis of the housing circumstances of women in developed and emerging societies, at a time of substantial economic and social change. It seeks to promote an approach to housing analysis that reinstates gender sensitivity in international and comparative housing studies. The focus is on the interface between housing and gender and how this socially constructed relationship manifests and transforms over time and space. Housing systems and opportunities are embedded within structured and institutionalised relations of power which are gendered. For example, in many countries the wider context of housing provision has been heavily influenced by attitudes surrounding the male breadwinner model' whereby the male wage-earner provides for a dependent wife and children, supported by the notion of a 'family wage' (Land 1980; Pascall 1997). These and other perceptions reflect the structured and institutionalised relations of power which permeate the policy process and the wider world (Harrison 2001), the nature and dynamics are culturally contingent as will be demonstrated by the contributions to this collection.

This chapter begins by exploring three discourses of feminist housing studies: environmental change discourse, housing welfare discourse, and social constructionist discourse. We argue that adopting a dynamic social constructionist approach enhances our understanding of how gender inequality in the housing system is constructed and perpetuated and how these processes manifest in different ways with varying outcomes in different societies. This is not to underestimate the significance of improving the living environment for men and women in terms of housing and urban planning, nor neglect the need for improving the housing welfare of women. The chapter then goes on to consider the ideology underpinning housing policy and housing services, focusing particularly on the domestic ideal and familial ideology. We conclude by pointing out that the social construction of gender equality in the housing system is not a simple and one-dimensional process, but a complex and dynamic process that varies substantially from one country to another, from one culture to another, and over time. It is these processes, their manifestations and impact that the contributors to this collection seek to highlight. The remainder of the chapter will introduce the country specific chapters in the book.

Discourses of gender and housing

In general we can identify three dominant discourses in the study of women and housing: environmental change discourse, housing welfare discourse, and social construction discourse. These discourses are not mutually exclusive or contradictory but rather reflect different emphases emerging from different academic disciplines, or the development of feminist theory in different historical periods.

Discourse of environmental change

The earliest concern with the issue of gender and housing can be traced to the urban planning profession. Feminist urban planners have long been concerned about how housing design and the living environment create and perpetuate gender inequality (Matrix 1984; Hayden 1980; Coleman 1990). In the late nineteenth century and early twentieth century, long before the professionalisation of urban planning, some female planners had already attempted to develop non-sexist housing projects. For example, in the 1870s Melusina Peirce proposed a 'neighbourhood strategy' in developing kitchenless housing in which housekeeping cooperatives would take over most of the housework. (Hayden 2002: 93). Peirce believed that this improved housing design could reduce women's burden of household chores and liberate women from confinement at home.

The strength of this 'environmental change discourse' is that it demystifies the conception of housing as a neutral entity or the 'bricks and mortar discourse'; and demonstrates that housing and urban design could reinforce women's subordination. Although this approach runs the risk of oversimplifying the complex social dynamic of how gender inequality in housing is produced and perpetuated, In recent decades studies on cities and space have developed a more dynamic analysis on how space is socially produced (Lefebvre 1991) and the relationship between social justice and space (Harvey 2000). The work of feminist geographers and urban planners (McDowell 1999; Massey 1994; Weisman 1992; Darke et al. 2000; Fainstein and Servon 2005; Fincher 2007) has also shed light on the complex relations between gender, housing and space, and contributed to the development of 'social constructionist discourse' discussed later in this chapter.

Housing welfare discourse

The 'housing welfare discourse' evolved from 'welfare feminism' in the 1970s and 1980s. Welfare feminists emphasise the importance of improving social policy and social welfare services for women in order to achieve gender equality (Lewis 1983; Dale and Foster 1986; Hallett 1996). Access to housing resources has become one of the major focuses of social policy studies (Ungerson and Kember 1997; Pascall 1997; Woods 1996). At the same time, in housing studies there has been an increasing number of studies devoted to women's housing issues (Brion and Tinker 1980; Gilroy and Woods 1994), and many housing textbooks now include a chapter on gender and housing (e.g. Balchin and Rhoden 2002; Morris and Winn 1990; Davis 2001).

The strength of the 'housing welfare discourse' is that it calls attention to the neglected housing needs of women. It draws attention to the fact that housing policy and housing services are largely gender blind, and that many women in marginal groups are deprived of adequate housing services. However, the limitation of this approach is that it sometimes tends to over-emphasise the vulnerability of women in the housing system (Ungerson and Kember 1997; Pascall 1997; Balchin and Rhoden 2002). As Clapham and Smith (1990) have pointed out, the over-emphasis on vulnerability seems to imply that the housing problems of women arise out of their lack of ability in solving their problems. Over-emphasis on 'special housing needs' diverts attention from the structural problem inherent in the housing system (Marcuse 1989). As Watson (1986a) has pointed out, this 'add-on approach' to including women on the agenda without challenging the gender blind assumption underpinning the housing system is unlikely to be effective in solving women's housing problems.

Social construction discourse

The rise of the 'social construction discourse' can be attributed to the development of neo-Marxism, critical theory, post-structuralism and postmodernism in social sciences, especially after the 1990s. This development had a significant impact on gender and housing studies (Harrison 2001; Gilroy and Woods 1994; Watson

1988, 1999a; Smith 2005; Chan 1997). Watson (1988:141; 1999a) advocated a 'deconstruction approach' to reveal how gender inequality is constructed in the housing system. For example, Watson and Austerberry (1986) adopted this approach to study the issue of women and homelessness and showed how this issue is marginalised through the gender blind conception of homelessness. Chan (1997) argued that the disadvantaged position of lone mothers in the housing system is not due to their lack of problem-solving ability, but their systematic exclusion in housing policy and practice. The focus of study shifted from what type of housing design is unfavourable to women and what type of housing resource is missing for women, to the question of why is it that gender-blind housing design and housing policy seems acceptable and how is this dominant conception maintained and perpetuated? Poststructuralist analysis pointed out that existing housing design and housing policy is underpinned by hegemonic social practice and discourse which obscures or justifies gender inequalities in the housing system. Power relations between men and women, especially in the housing system, are very subtle. As Foucault has pointed out (Foucault 1980; Smart 1985: 76–80; McNay 1992: 38–40), power is not a static entity or simply an instrument possessed by those in power to oppress the powerless. Power is a social relation developed in everyday social interaction, in which the powerless as well as those in power abide by taken-for-granted social regulations.

Towards a gender sensitive housing analysis

The strength of the social constructionist approach is that it is more sensitive to power inequalities embedded in taken-for-granted social practices, which is effective for unveiling deep-rooted gender inequalities in the housing system. Moreover, in emphasising diversity and difference, it calls attention to addressing the needs of women from different social backgrounds, facing different housing problems in a range of societal and cultural settings. However, in recent decades there has been increasing conflict between postmodernist and social policy analysis (Ferguson and Johnston 2001; Taylor-Gooby 1994). The most important critique has been that by focusing on interpretation and cultural meaning, postmodernism runs the risk of diverting attention from material deprivation. However, both structural and cultural levels are equally important, with no one level more important than the other. In fact, it is problematic to dichotomise material and cultural analysis. McNay (2004), adopting Bourdieu's conception of the phenomenology of social space, tries to integrate objectivist and subjectivist analysis, material and cultural analysis, structure and agency; and argues that gender should be understood as a lived relation.

In this collection the social construction of gender inequality in the housing system is interpreted as a consequence of taken-for-granted cultural and social practices, as well as the material deprivation of housing resources and structural inequalities in society at large. Harrison (2001: 53), adopting a social regulatory framework, pointed out that social structure, institutions, discourse, and ideology are important in constructing the housing experience of different social groups. Thus, in this sense housing design, access to housing resources, and housing ideology are all part and parcel of the social construction process.

Deconstructing housing ideology

Two dominant, taken-for-granted and influential ideologies in the housing system include the domestic ideal and familial ideology. To a certain extent, these ideologies are interrelated, and, as the chapters in this collection demonstrate, are likely to be interpreted in different ways across societies and cultures.

Domestic ideal

Traditional housing design and urban planning is dominated by an ideology of 'domestic ideal', which is build on the patriarchal 'public-men private-women model' (Davidoff *et al.* 1976, Davidoff 2003). Modern housing design emphasises privacy and detachment, which is partly a consequence of industrialisation and urbanisation. Home–work separation becomes the way of life in industrial society, and home becomes the haven to escape from the hostile work environment. This can be coupled with the traditional gender division of labour, whereby men become the breadwinners working outside the home and women become the homemakers responsible for providing a comfortable living environment. However, the quiet and comfortable home, a haven for men, is the workplace for women. Privacy and detachment of home implies isolation and less accessibility to social support, which is especially difficult for women in nuclear families. The problem is further exacerbated by sub-urbanisation, in which housing estates are developed in remote new towns or rural areas.

Another problem with home–work separation or the private-public divide is that housing design and community planning tends to skew toward catering for the needs of work and the public sphere, while neglecting homemaking activities. Housing design is dominated by male professionals that do not fully understand women's work at home (Weisman 1992). This male-oriented housing design can increase women's burden in homemaking, or even cause hazards and threaten the safety of women and children at home. Some geographers and urban planners argue that most transportation services in the community, especially those in remote new towns, are geared towards the needs of commuting to work, while neglecting the needs of women in homemaking such as taking children to school, going to the market, bank, and shopping (Pickup 1988; Coleman 2000; Wekerle 2005). The dominant ideology in housing design and urban planning seems to assume that paid work in the labour market or productive activity is more important than unpaid housework or consumption activity at home.

Watson (1991) questioned the separation of work and home, and pointed out that this does not reflect the reality, but serves to rationalise male domination. Pugh (1997) points out that housing and household economics are playing an increasingly important role in human capital and social capital formation such as performance of paid work at home, self-education activities at home, and new ideas in housing welfare. There is increasing concern that housing design and urban planning should play a more active role in producing a work–family balance environment (Silbaugh 2007). Gibson-Graham (1996, 2003) goes further to deconstruct the capitalist economy from a poststructuralist feminist perspective, arguing that the capitalist logic marginalises women's contribution and other forms of economic activities. In other words, the domestic ideal, home–work separation, the division between production and reproduction underpinning the housing system, are myths reflecting hegemonic patriarchal values and at the same time reinforcing male domination.

Familial ideology

'Familial ideology' is another common belief underpinning the housing system. Very often, housing policy and planning, and the distribution of housing resources are based on the assumption of the 'family as a unit' and traditional gender role differentiation within the family. Here, 'family' is often assumed to be the conventional heterosexual married nuclear family, preferably with children. In this sense, housing policy may marginalise 'unconventional family' types (Watson 1986b). In many societies, if a woman is outside the conventional marriage relationship, living alone, a lone mother, older woman, or a lesbian, she may not enjoy as full housing rights as other citizens, especially in some traditional societies in Asia, the Middle East, or Africa where divorce is still regarded as a disgrace for women. Woman living alone is a group that is easily neglected (Watson 1988). They are not attached to a conventional family or dependent on a man. In many countries social housing policy gives higher priority to family than to people living alone. On average, women have lower incomes than men, limiting opportunities for them to find housing solutions in the private market. Housing wealth is another major problem unfavourable to women. Usually housing property is regarded as 'family wealth'. However, in many traditional societies the man is regarded as the household head, and 'family wealth' virtually becomes men's wealth. Studies on gender and housing wealth have shown that men benefit more than women from homeownership (Smith 1990) and this is true across societies as many of the chapters in this collection will demonstrate. In a nutshell, family and marriage in a patriarchal society could create disadvantages for women (Delphy and Leonard 1992). Housing policy and practice reflects and reinforces men's domination in society at large.

Structures, institutions, and processes function as bearers of gender at the macro, meso and micro levels in a context in which the interrelationships between the public and the private spheres, and between social and economic capital are significant (Dewan 1999: 429). The contributions to this collection will seek to identify the significance of structures, institutions, ideologies and processes for understanding the differential housing experiences for men and women, and for women in different class locations, from different ethnic backgrounds, at different stages of the lifecycle, and from 'non-conventional' family formations. Thus, they will consider the historically and geographically specific relations of power and the connection and intersection between the social relations of gender and other culturally relevant forms of social division such as ethnicity, class, and age, with housing. The collection will provide an analysis of the interface between women and housing and the implications of social and economic change on this relationship in different social contexts. The collection provides a coherent analytical framework for exploring substantively and comparatively the housing experiences of women in their broader context

The first chapter is concerned with addressing more theoretical and conceptual concerns, such as the social construction of gender and housing systems, theorising gender and housing in an international context, gender, power and institutions, and women's rights to housing. In Chapter 2 Ingrid Westendorp considers the international framework and its relevance to women's housing rights. At the international level article 11(1) International Covenant on Economic, Social and Cultural Rights is the most authoritative treaty provision containing the right to adequate housing. While in theory this norm equally entitles everyone to adequate housing, in practice women's different socio-economic position, brought about by gender-based discrimination, hampers their ability to realise this right. In particular, gender-specific cultural habits, such as patriarchy, female exogamy, widow practices and son preference, have not been taken into account, and combined with the prevalence of domestic violence, and the lack of an autonomous right to housing for women, internationally many women are dependent on others for their housing and shelter. For Westendorp, the internationally developed housing rights norm is not compatible with women's socio-economic reality and she provides suggestions and recommendations for adapting and extending the norm in such a way that it encompasses a female perspective.

In Chapter 3 Selina Tually examines the many reasons why Australian women occupy a more vulnerable position in the housing market than their male counterparts. She begins with a discussion of the historical, social- and economic factors that have shaped women's housing circumstances in Australia, focusing on the period since the 1970s when power relations between Australian men and women were challenged through the feminist movement, no-fault divorce was introduced, and the role of women both within society and the family unit itself changed. Moreover, the traditional social norms of 'male-as-breadwinner' and 'women-as-stay-at-home-mother' have largely been reconfigured since this time, allowing and necessitating increased female labour force participation, including among mothers. This chapter goes on to consider the likely future housing demands of women. It points to the much weaker financial position of women relative to men: a consequence of women continuing to shoulder the majority of responsibility for caring in Australian society – for children, people with disabilities, and the elderly – and the effects and limitations such caring responsibilities have (by choice or necessity) on the labour force participation of many women. The discussion notes the effects of structural and institutional factors on the financial position of Australian women and the implications for their housing choices.

These themes are similarly pursued by Elizabeth Mulroy in Chapter 4, who provides a critical analysis of the development of housing policy in the USA and considers a range of differences among women concerning their housing circumstances. She considers issues of housing affordability in the context of gender inequality and a 'blame the victim' mentality that has contributed to the affordability issue for women in the United States.

Montserrat Pareja Eastaway and Teresa Sánchez-Martínez focus on Spain in Chapter 5, and adopt a transversal approach in terms of the application of a gender perspective to housing policy and the housing needs of women. As a relatively young democracy the country has experienced substantial social, political, and economic change in recent years with formal equality between the sexes achieved later than in other European countries. Political mechanisms are, today, stable but long-term problems remain as the almost non-existent welfare state, mainly driven by four decades of dictatorship, has been unable to provide alternative solutions. This has had a major effect on the role played by women in Spanish society along with the longstanding reproduction of the 'male-breadwinner' model in Spain. This chapter focuses on the relationship between the changing role of women in Spain, a housing system dominated by owner-occupation, and a residual public housing sector.

In contrast, in Chapter 6, Ingrid Sahlin focuses on Sweden, a country with a comprehensive welfare state, generally high-quality housing provision, extensive childcare provision and greater gender equality than many other societies. She considers the development of housing and family policies over the last century, and the role of the 'household' and 'family' as central cultural institutions. She concludes by exploring housing policies, tenure and their relationship with class, ethnicity, national origin and type of household, as well as the implications of family change and income distribution for different types of women

In Great Britain housing has become a main source of asset accumulation, cultural capital, citizenship and identity as the notion of home ownership as the 'natural' tenure of choice has been promoted by governments and is a widely accepted ideology in British society. These linkages have been heavily influenced by attitudes surrounding the 'male-breadwinner model' with home ownership traditionally a sphere of consumption from which women have been excluded and unable to enjoy financial rewards to the same extent as men. However, there has been considerable change in British society in recent years particularly in relation to the nature and extent of women's waged work and wealth accumulation, family arrangements, housing opportunities, and the renegotiating of the boundaries of citizenship. In Chapter 7 Patricia Kennett outlines these changes and explores a number of important aspects of women's lives and the implications in relation to housing opportunities, constraints, empowerment, and exclusion.

In Chapter 8 Richard Ronald and Meiko Hinokidani consider the historical constraints placed on women's housing opportunities in Japan, as well as the more recent transition away from the standard family system and the housing implications for women. Recent social changes have undermined the male-breadwinner model and provided some opportunities for greater independence, but have also enhanced inequalities and the vulnerability of many women. Although realignments in approaches to employment, marriage and family formation have begun to reshape women's housing conditions, institutional practices and social policies have failed to keep up with change. The authors specifically consider the unravelling of the male-breadwinner model, nuclear families and corporate paternalism, and how these developments are restructuring the relationship between women and housing with the emergence of new patterns of inequality among different groups of women.

In Taiwan, homeownership has been the dominant housing tenure and housing is a very expensive commodity. The state plays a minor role in the provision of housing and there is little consideration of issues relating to social justice. Since the end of the 1980s, housing policies have been subject to several reforms under the influence of democratisation and neoliberalisation. Although women's status has improved in recent years, patriarchal culture still affects the gender division of labour, women's economic opportunities, and housing conditions. In Chapter 9 Herng-Dar Bih and Yi-Ling Chen explore the housing conditions of women in the above social and economic context and in different circumstances.

As Guo Huimin in Chapter 10 argues, women are supposed to enjoy equal housing rights to men under a socialist system. However, dominated by traditional ideologies, the housing circumstances and needs of women in China have been, and are still largely neglected. This chapter starts with a general description of existing housing problems and needs of women in China, and then turns to focus on a particularly disadvantaged group to show how women's housing problems have been constructed and marginalised. Drawing on recent research, this chapter focuses on the experiences of domestic workers who are lone mothers. This group has experienced the double social exclusion of losing their job, as well as the break-up of their marriage, resulting in unemployment, divorce, and inadequate accomodation. The chapter also addresses the tensions and gaps between women's real needs, protection provided by existing legislation and social policy, the patriarchal attitudes permeating the legal arena, and the implications for women in the the spatial and housing arenas.

In Chapter 11 Chan Kam Wah focuses on Hong Kong, a global city but one still dominated by traditional Chinese culture. He argues that the predominance of patriarchal society combined with liberalist economic values have constrained the opportunities for women in the housing system. He outlines the development of housing policy and gender relations in Hong Kong, and considers social change and power dynamics impacting on women's housing opportunities.

In combination, the contributions to this collection illuminate the gendered nature of housing processes, and the ways in which these processes are constituted, mediated and manifest in different societies.

2 Women's housing rights
Is anything wrong with the international norm?

Ingrid Westendorp

Introduction

Housing is one of the most fundamental needs human beings may have. A home brings safety to one's life and the possibility to retreat from society at large and be oneself. A house protects its habitants from unfavourable climate conditions and offers space to safely put away one's belongings and foodstuffs. An adequate home containing all necessary commodities is a safeguard against diseases and a secure place for children to grow up in. According to international human rights standards, everyone has the right to adequate housing. While this has been accepted worldwide, for many people this right only exists on paper because in practice they are unable to obtain or retain accommodation that fulfils the adequacy standard. The corollary of the right to housing is states' obligation to enable their citizens to realize their housing rights. It is therefore important that states are aware of the main obstacles people encounter in trying to fulfil their right to housing so that they may develop legislation and policies that meet their citizens' housing needs. While both men and women can have difficulties in realizing their housing rights, women face additional barriers that are brought about by gender discrimination and the ensuing different socio-economic position women find themselves in. In view of these circumstances, the question arises whether the international housing rights norm is adequate and suited to take women's perspective into account.

In the first part of this chapter, the development of the right to adequate housing as a human right will be discussed. Emphasis will be put on the interpretation of this right by the Committee on Economic, Social and Cultural Rights, while also attention will be paid to states' obligations. Next, the protection of equality will be examined. The concept of discrimination based on gender will be explained and put in the context of the right to housing. The causes and consequences of the main obstacles why people and particularly women do not succeed in fulfilling their housing rights will be studied in the fourth section. In the fifth section, the existing interpretation of the right to adequate housing will be put to the test by applying it to women's socio-economic situation. In the final section, some conclusions will be drawn.

Development and contents of the right to adequate housing

International recognition of the human right to adequate housing has been developing over the last few decades. Politically speaking, the two World Habitat conferences in Vancouver (1976) and Istanbul (1996) were most important since they drew the attention to the housing crisis and are proof of a worldwide consensus that housing is indeed a human right.[1] Within the framework of the UN the significance of the right to housing was among other actions expressed by the appointment of a Special Rapporteur on housing by the former Sub-Commission on the Promotion and Protection of Human Rights,[2] and the creation of the mandate of the Special Rapporteur on adequate housing by the Human Rights Council.[3] In addition, UN Habitat has shown a growing concern for the housing crisis and is devoting more and more of its efforts and funds on studying housing dilemmas and advising states on solving the problems of homelessness and urbanization.[4] Reducing the number of slums and improving the living conditions of 100 million slum dwellers is also one of the Millennium Development Goals that were adopted by the UN General Assembly in 2000.[5]

Legal obligations for states ensue from the Universal Declaration on Human Rights, particularly art. 25(1),[6] and the various human rights treaties that contain a provision on the right to housing.[7] Women's equal right to housing is specifically mentioned in article 14(h) of the Convention on the Elimination of All Forms of Discrimination Against Women (Women's Convention), though it must be noted that this provision only relates to the situation of rural women. The most important provision on the right to housing is included in the Covenant on Economic, Social and Cultural Rights (ICESCR). Article 11(1) of this treaty reads that 'The States Parties to the present Covenant recognize the right of everyone to an adequate standard of living for himself and his family, including … housing ….' Due to the efforts of housing civil society organizations (CSOs),[8] and the work that has been done by the Committee on Economic, Social and Cultural Rights (CESCR),[9] the right to housing has developed from a rather insignificant element of the right to an adequate standard of living into a fully fledged right that enjoys worldwide recognition.

Already before the CESCR started its interpretative work by adopting two General Comments,[10] it was generally acknowledged, that the right to housing means much more than just having a roof over one's head. This notion was confirmed by the CESCR in its General Comment number 4 in which it is stated that housing should be 'adequate' and that several conditions should be fulfilled.[11]

First and foremost, there should be *security of tenure* which entails that irrespective of the legal basis on which a person lives in a certain house, be it ownership, property rights, usufruct, occupancy rights, access, or even squatting, everyone should be able to peacefully enjoy their housing and be protected against violation of their home by the state or third parties. The main violation in this regard would be forced evictions either carried out or condoned by the state. The Committee regarded this violation as so important that General Comment number 7 is devoted to it. It is concluded that forced evictions are *prima facie* incompatible with the requirements of the ICESCR.

Second, *basic services, materials and infrastructure* should be available. The most important of these services would be clean drinking water and energy for cooking and heating.

Housing should be *affordable*, which requires that the cost of housing should not exceed a certain percentage of the average income level and that it is not so high that it may compromise people's ability to afford other basic needs. Governments should see to it that people who are unable to provide for their own housing, have the possibility to fall back on housing subsidies or other ways that support them with gaining access to housing.

An adequate house is *habitable*, meaning that it offers protection against cold, heat, rain and vermin, and that there is enough space for the people it should contain.

Furthermore, the Committee mentions that housing should be *accessible*, which entails that nobody should be excluded, but that adequate housing should also be available – and even as a matter of priority – for disadvantaged groups such as the handicapped, HIV-positive individuals, the mentally ill and children.

Another aspect determining the adequacy of housing is the *location*. On the one hand, the location should be safe. Housing should not, for example, be built on polluted soil or in disaster-prone areas. On the other hand, an adequate location is determined by the presence of such services as schools, shops, markets, hospitals and day-care centres, and the possibility to find employment in the vicinity.

Lastly, the CESCR mentions *cultural adequacy*, entailing that people should be allowed to use building materials and building styles that express their cultural identity.

The interpretative work that has been done by the CESCR is highly valuable, giving insights into the contents of the right to adequate housing. It is a pity, however, that although the Committee shows awareness of discrimination against women,[12] the wording of the General Comments is gender 'neutral',[13] and the conditions of adequate housing seem to lack a female perspective.[14] It is also unfortunate for the development of the right to housing for women, that the monitoring body of the Women's Convention, the Committee on the Elimination of Discrimination Against Women (CEDAW), has limited possibilities to look into the matter, because the Convention does not contain a specific article on this right. It would be possible, however, for CEDAW to address housing rights or even adopt a General

Recommendation on the issue based on *de jure* and *de facto* equality by using articles 2 and 5 of the Women's Convention.[15]

States' obligations concerning housing rights

States' obligations have been formulated by the CESCR in its General Comment number 3.[16] Because of the nature of the convention, states have been given a wide margin of appreciation and are allowed to fulfil the majority of the obligations progressively. Progress may be determined by financial possibilities and economic development. Some obligations, reflecting the 'core' of the rights concerned, must be fulfilled immediately, however, by taking legislative and other appropriate measures. Core aspects of housing are *inter alia* security of tenure and non-discrimination.[17] For women, the principle of non-discrimination is obviously the most important direct obligation since it is clear that the progressive nature of the right to housing cannot be used as a justification for maintaining inequality between the sexes. In addition, article 3 of the ICESCR, concerning equality between men and women, is regarded as a justiciable provision so that women can rely on it before a court of law.[18]

As with all economic, social and cultural rights, it has been accepted that states have an obligation to respect, protect and fulfil their citizens' right to housing.[19] Respect is shown by refraining as much as possible from interference when people manage to fulfil their own housing rights. This entails, for example, allowing the poor to build their own homes uninhibited by unnecessary bureaucratic rules and encouraging self-help initiatives. The most obvious duty in this regard may be that states should desist from forced evictions.

Protection should be offered in cases when people's housing rights are violated by third parties. Besides protection against evictions and harassment, protection should also extend to keeping the cost of housing within reasonable boundaries.

How the fulfilment of the right to adequate housing should be attained, and the pace of realization is largely left to the states' discretion. From General Comment 4 it has become clear that governments are not obliged to supply all citizens with adequate housing but that primarily citizens are responsible for their own accommodation. It is, however, the state's duty to help citizens who are unable to secure housing by themselves. The existence of large numbers of homeless people in a country may be seen as an indication that the state has not put enough effort into fulfilling its housing rights obligations.

Protection of gender equality

The obligation to attain equality between men and women has been laid down in several human rights instruments such as common article 3 of the Covenant on Civil and Political Rights and the Covenant on Economic, Social and Cultural

Rights,[20] and article 2 of the Convention on the Elimination of All Forms of Discrimination Against Women (Women's Convention).[21] It has been made clear that these articles not only require *de jure* but also *de facto* equality.[22] States seem to think that they have lived up to their obligation of *de jure* equality if they put non-discrimination articles in their legislation and if they abolish discriminatory legislation and policies. This is merely the first step, however. Moving forward will entail introducing new legislation that actively promotes equality between men and women in respect to housing rights. For instance by making co-ownership of land and housing for couples the rule.

In order to move beyond *de jure* equality towards *de facto* equality, it is imperative to achieve a change in mentality that will remove social barriers that hold women back. While in the articles mentioned above *de facto* equality is inferred, it is explicitly mentioned in article 5 of the Women's Convention.[23] According to this, provision states should take all appropriate measures to eradicate prejudice, harmful traditional practices and stereotyping. It is particularly these phenomena that constitute discrimination against women based on gender which is a pervasive and illusive form of discrimination.

In the 1990s, it was gradually acknowledged that discrimination against women is not merely based on sex, i.e. biological differences between men and women especially with regard to reproductive capacities, but also based on gender. Gender is understood as a set of culturally determined perceptions, stereotypes and prejudices that determine women's and men's roles in society.[24] The gendered roles of men and women are not equal, however, but women's role is bound up with the private sphere and subordinate to men's. This makes gender a factor that may unfavourably affect or inhibit the fulfilment of women's human rights.[25]

Discrimination based on gender is the reason that girls and women stay behind in respect to education and job training, that there is an income and property gap between women and men, and that women shoulder the main burden of unpaid household chores. The result is that for many women it is difficult to obtain a well paid full-time job or social status that would allow them to obtain and retain housing independently. In addition, traditional views persist that regard housing as a family right that is bestowed on the male breadwinner since it is perceived as his gendered role to take care of the housing situation of his wife and children. It is therefore understandable, that many women are their whole life dependent for their housing situation on their fathers, partners, brothers, sons or other male relatives, which makes housing a privilege rather than a human right.[26]

Several of the UN organs that have dealt with housing rights in the past fifteen years, have regularly adopted resolutions in which states were requested to realize equality between men and women as regards access to and rights to land and housing.[27] In 2002, the Commission on Human Rights took the initiative to appoint a Special Rapporteur on housing whose mandate specifically included examining women's housing situation.[28] Despite these initiatives, no concrete norms were developed that took a gender perspective into account. It is imperative, however, that states understand that *de jure* equality is insufficient because in many cases it will remain a dead letter. Improvement of women's situation can only be achieved if the unequal socio-economic positions of women and men that are caused by culture, tradition and religion are modified or abolished in order to attain *de facto* equality. This is, however, a delicate matter that needs a pussy-footing approach and that must be accepted by societies from within.[29]

Causes and consequences of homelessness and inadequate housing

The main reason why millions of people are homeless or living in wretched housing conditions is, of course, poverty.[30] Poverty also affects the political influence people may have, leaving them basically voiceless and unable to control housing policies. In many states the poor are marginalized or even criminalized. Slum and pavement dwellers and squatters may be regarded as social parasites while in fact the majority of them will have jobs. Poverty is not gender-neutral, however. Because of an ongoing feminization of poverty, the property gap between men and women is growing and more and more women experience difficulties in fulfilling their housing rights.[31] The unequal property division between men and women is partly due to the fact that in many societies girls and women are deprived of a share in the inheritance. Sometimes it is the law that determines that women do not have the same rights as men,[32] and sometimes it is social pressure that makes it impossible for women to claim the share they are entitled to.[33]

Forced evictions are also among the most important reasons why people become homeless or inadequately housed, because as a rule the evictees will lack the necessary resources to acquire alternative housing.[34] Forced evictions may even increase people's poverty because in many cases all their belongings are destroyed in the process of bulldozing or burning their dwellings. The CESCR defines forced evictions as 'the removal against their will of individuals, families and/or communities from the homes and/or land which they occupy, without the provision of, and access to, appropriate forms of legal or other protection'.[35] The Committee's basic assumption is that evictions are caused by third parties, the state or others, while for women the most important form of evictions may be evictions in the private sphere, at the hands of (ex-) partners and in-laws. Especially in societies that know female exogamy,[36] or that traditionally do not allow women to own land or housing, women may be very vulnerable and dependent on the goodwill of their partners, relatives and in-laws for their housing situation. Evicted women indicate that emotionally they are hit harder by evictions in the private sphere than by evictions by strangers since it is family members and others whom they have known and trusted for many years who leave them homeless and destitute.

Disasters and conflict situations also cause homelessness and inadequate housing circumstances. Natural disasters like floods, mud- and landslides, generally cause more female than male victims because the areas where these kinds of disasters occur, are usually known to be unsafe which will make it cheap to settle there. Especially the economically weakest, like female-headed households, are often left with no other option but to settle in unsafe locations.[37]

While the above mentioned causes of homelessness and inadequate housing are true for men and women alike – albeit to unequal measures – there are two causes that virtually exclusively apply to women. The first of these causes is widowhood. In societies where such cultural habits as female exogamy prevail, women are seldom entitled to their fathers' inheritance because the ties with their blood relatives are severed when they get married. Moreover, it is likely that these women are not entitled to the inheritance of their husbands either and that after his death his possessions will be claimed and divided among his relatives. The in-laws may decide to evict the widow from her marital home and in many cases she will become homeless because it is no longer possible to return to her parental home. In India whole cities consist of widows and their children who stay alive by begging or prostituting themselves.[38] In societies that consider women to be the possession of their husbands, they will be unable to inherit because they are part of the inheritance themselves. In certain communities the custom of *levirate* still exists which entails that the deceased husband's younger brother or another male relative will inherit the widow and marry her.[39] If the woman agrees, she may continue to live in the same house that she shared with her deceased husband. If she refuses, she risks being turned out in the streets.

Finally, worldwide, women become homeless or are inadequately housed because of domestic violence. While different forms of domestic violence exist, the most prevalent one is the battering of a woman by her male partner. The main cause of this phenomenon is the unequal power relation between men and women.[40] A woman who is being battered in her own home cannot feel safe anywhere. The notion of home as a safe haven where a person can live in peace and dignity is totally shattered if a woman has to be vigilant all the time and regularly becomes a victim of violence. For battered women it may be very difficult to leave the abusive situation. Besides psychological reasons – they may still love their partner and believe his assurances of non-repetition, or they feel ashamed and guilty – there are also social barriers because communities may not accept that a woman leaves her husband.[41] Another important factor is the economic dependence of many abused women. If no societal safety net has been created in the form of shelters or housing subsidies, or if the existing services are inadequate to accommodate all women who need help, women have to make a choice between remaining in an abusive relationship or becoming homeless.[42]

Consequences of homelessness and inadequate housing

It goes without saying that homelessness and inadequate housing conditions also have consequences for men and boys, but due to the disadvantaged socioeconomic position of women, there are some consequences that mostly or exclusively apply to women and girls.

More than people who may find shelter in their homes, the homeless are susceptible to abuse by strangers. Besides the danger of physical violence and robbery that are also experienced by men, women run the risk of sexual abuse, falling into the hands of pimps and traffickers.[43] Homeless families in developing states will sooner be inclined to force their daughters into early marriage with a view to having one mouth less to feed. Also, the realization of economic and social rights of girls and women is often inhibited or nullified by homelessness. Especially the education of girls will be curtailed because homeless families tend to favour the education of their sons over the education of their daughters.

Housing that does not fulfil the conditions of adequacy will affect women more and in different ways than men because of the gendered division of work in society. Irrespective of the question whether this stereotypical division of work should be abolished and which role states should play to bring this about, it is a fact that in the greater part of societies in the world, women's life is more home-centred than men's because women take care of the household and raise the children.[44] That is why the consequences of unhealthy living conditions will hit women hardest,[45] and why the lack of services and facilities like drinking water, fuel for cooking and waste disposal will especially cost women more time and energy because they are responsible for performing the household chores.[46] This is bound to remain the case as long as women play a subordinate role in society and are disproportionately burdened with care-taking tasks.

Adequate housing for women

Although the CESCR has confirmed in its General Comment number 4 that women are entitled to adequate housing on an equal footing with men, leaving no doubt as to women's *de jure* equality, it should be examined whether the interpretation of the right to adequate housing is also suitable to achieve *de facto* equality of women as far as this right is concerned.

From the explanation pertaining to the first condition mentioned by the CESCR, *security of tenure*, it becomes clear that the Committee was aware of violations in the form of forced evictions, threats and harassments happening from the *outside* by authorities and third parties.[47] As has been mentioned above, for many women, however, threats and evictions occur from the *inside*. Not all families are harmonious communities where resources are equally shared and every individual's rights are respected.[48] In practice, many women lack the rights and the capacity to act independently which forces them to powerlessly wait and see how, where and for how long they will be housed. States should be made aware of the fact that forced evictions also take place in the private sphere because this requires a different legal and policy approach.[49] If security of tenure is not understood to comprise evictions in the private sphere, the protection of many women's right to housing is seriously lacking.

Due to the gendered division of work, women's lives are in general more home-centred than men's. The *availability of basic services, materials and infrastructure*, the *habitability* of a home, and the *location* are therefore not gender-neutral conditions. If services or infrastructure are wanting or inadequate, this may for instance entail that women have to walk long distances to fetch water, gather fuel for cooking or have to take care of the waste disposal themselves. That is why women's experiences and needs should expressly be the point of departure of any legislative and policy decisions with regard to budgetary decisions and planning in this respect. Authorities, especially at the local level, should therefore be encouraged to actively seek the participation of women in the decision-making process. Home-bound women will sooner suffer from health problems when housing conditions are unhealthy or the location is unsafe. That is why women should be involved as much as possible in house-building schemes. Authorities should be made to understand that the decision where to settle down is bound up with the adequacy of a location. The fact that many women cannot decide for themselves where they want to live is a violation of their freedom of residence.[50] Furthermore, authorities should be held responsible if they allow poor women to settle down in disaster prone areas. In their land policies, states should reserve part of the land for the destitute who cannot afford to live in a safe environment without state support.

The condition of *affordability* seems to have been written from a male perspective. In the Committee's view, housing is affordable when the costs do not exceed a certain percentage of the average income in order to ensure that other basic needs can also be fulfilled. It is therefore presumed that there is a (family) income and that on average this income will be high enough to pay for housing and other basic needs such as food, clothing, schooling of children and transport. The authorities are only obliged to take (financially) care of the housing of those people who cannot possibly afford adequate housing by themselves. It is inferred that this will only be the case in exceptional situations. The income and property gap between men and women is so wide, however, that affordability cannot be determined in a gender-neutral way.[51] In comparison with men, much more women do unpaid work, especially care-giving work, but also unpaid work in subsistence agriculture or in family enterprises. The combination of work and care-taking responsibilities induces many women to work part-time or in the informal sector where salaries are very low and chances for promotion are virtually non-existent. Even in developed countries where girls enjoy equality with boys as far as the right to education is concerned, a persistent income gap remains which is estimated to be 15 per cent. In addition, the group of female heads of household is growing,[52] which means that women who are hardly equipped to take care of their own housing, also have to see to it that their dependents have a roof over their heads. The condition of affordability needs to be reconsidered and redefined in view of women's financial position. If female heads of household are structurally unable to afford adequate housing there is apparently something wrong with the state's housing and housing subsidy policy. Supporting single mothers' housings should be a matter of priority and the rule rather than the exception as long as women are faced with societal barriers that prevent them from acquiring an income that is sufficient to afford adequate housing by themselves.

In the description of the condition of *accessibility* the CESCR lists certain groups of disadvantaged people that should explicitly be included in housing schemes. It should be noted that vulnerable groups of women, such as widows or divorced women are not mentioned. This is probably due to the fact that the Committee already reiterates in article 6 of General Comment number 4 that the right to housing applies to everyone even though the text of article 11(1) of the ICESCR refers to *himself* and *his family* suggesting that women or female heads of household would be excluded. According to the Committee, the phrasing used in article 11 is anachronistic and reflects the situation of the 1960s when gender roles were regarded differently and it was automatically assumed that breadwinners and heads of household were men. Although it is not advisable to rank women in general among vulnerable groups, those categories of women who are not able to cope by themselves should be brought to the states' attention. The fact that women have an equal right to housing is no guarantee that disadvantaged groups among them will automatically be considered and included.

Some aspects that determine the adequacy of women's housing situation are not contained in CESCR General Comment number 4. The most striking is the omission of a condition of *safety and dignity* at home. There is a persistent myth that home is a safe haven while in reality home may be a very dangerous place for women (and children) because they are regularly abused. It is impossible to call housing adequate, even if a house is fitted with all sorts of modern conveniences, if it is unsafe. Guaranteeing women's physical safety inside their homes is connected to privacy protection behind the front door. States are on average very hesitant to violate the privacy of the family, and domestic violence is often characterized as a family affair.[53] It should be clarified, however, that privacy protection in cases of domestic violence is to the benefit of the perpetrator, and that the victim may welcome interference. Human dignity becomes illusory when a woman is constantly abused and humiliated in her own home.

Domestic violence takes place on such a large scale and it is such a structural problem in all countries of the world, that in respect to the principle of *due diligence*, the authorities can be held co-responsible if they do not take measures to prevent this form of violence or fail to protect the victims and prosecute the perpetrators.[54]

Another condition that would be important for women is an *autonomous* right to housing. In many societies it is taken for granted that the housing of women will be taken care of in the context of the family. For women's status and position in the family, it would be better if they are legally entitled to housing as an individual. It seems obvious that for structural solutions, women's socio-economic position must be changed so that women are able to realize their autonomous right to housing in practice and are able to leave inadequate housing circumstances for instance because they are being battered.

Lastly, the interpretation of the right to housing as it exists today is focused on permanent housing. Tens of thousands of people, the majority of whom are women, live in temporary housing conditions, however. While it is impossible that temporary shelter such as refugee camps or safe houses meets all the conditions of adequate housing, it is imperative that some basic conditions are fulfilled. Safety and access to services and facilities that take women's needs into account are among the first that have to be realized.[55]

Concluding remarks

Strong and determined intervention by the authorities is needed in order to achieve equality between men and women in relation to the right to adequate housing. Intervention not only requires legislative measures, but also entails bringing about a mentality change which will make it possible to get rid of the existing unequal power relations and traditional habits and stereotypes that are detrimental to the realization of women's housing rights.

There seems to be nothing wrong with the existing housing right norm; it is the interpretation and implementation that are deficient and that need modification because at the moment women's perspective is insufficiently, if at all, taken into account.

In view of the importance and specificity of the ICESCR, it would seem to be best if the CESCR would adopt a General Comment particularly focused on women's housing rights so that states understand which actions are expected of them.

3 Women and housing
The Australian experience
Selina Tually

Introduction

Australian women generally occupy a more vulnerable position in the housing market than their male counterparts, and female headed households in particular experience significant disadvantage in terms of accessing and sustaining appropriate housing. This chapter examines some of the key reasons why Australian women occupy this position. The discussion focuses particularly on the period since the 1970s, as significant shifts have occurred in power relations between men and women over this time and the role of women within society and the family unit has changed dramatically over this period.

The discussion enunciates why we should address the housing circumstances of Australian women. It points to the much weaker financial position of women relative to men; a fact that remains regardless of exponential growth in women's participation in the labour force and in education, brought about by the demise of the relatively strong male breadwinner model that dominated wage and welfare regulation throughout most of the last century – at least until the late 1960s/early 1970s. The discussion notes the effects of structural and institutional factors on the financial position of Australian women. These factors shape women's housing choices, and especially for the increasing number of women raising children on their own, and for women living alone post-divorce/separation, or after the death of a partner.

Moreover, it is also the case that over the last decade the housing circumstances of many Australian women have worsened. This is despite, until very recently, some of the most prosperous economic conditions in Australia's history and, for the most part, has been the result of rapidly escalating house prices and a decline in available *affordable* housing options, including social housing.

The discussion draws on data and research from a range of sources to understand the housing circumstances of Australian women. This is because there is a dearth of gender-specific Australian housing research. Further, women's housing issues have received minimal attention and academic scrutiny for nearly 20 years; since

1991 when the then National Housing Strategy included a paper on *The Housing Needs of Women and Children* (Cass 1991). Reexamination of Australian women's housing circumstances is thus long overdue.

Background to Australian women's current housing circumstances

A nation of male breadwinners and homeowners

Like many developed nations, Australia's economic, political and social institutions formed around and were shaped by a relatively strong male breadwinner model of economic, social and welfare regulation (Broomhill and Sharp 2005; Gilding 1991; Cass 1998; Murphy 2002). This model provided a strong cultural identity and role for Australian men and women; that is, man as provider (and generally household head) and woman as caregiver. It determined the public and private identities and lives of the majority of men and women throughout the first half of the twentieth century, and, arguably, to varying degrees extending into the period of the post Second World War 'long boom' – from 1946 to the early 1970s (Nolan 2003; Murphy 2002). The model gendered work and wages (through the setting and adoption of a basic wage sufficient for males to support their dependents), and housing circumstances.

Australia's highly unionised labour market and tightly regulated wage system sustained the model. It also ensured continuation of a highly gender-segregated labour market – which remains in many ways even today. The lack of formal childcare and the pro-family and pro-population growth and welfare policies of government during the Second World War and the immediate post-war period also supported women's domesticity. So too did pursuance of full (male) employment as the country's key social and economic policy in the period, and favourable treatment of single income families by the taxation system (Nolan 2003; Murphy 2002).

The widespread adoption of the male breadwinner model in social, economic and housing policy supported and promoted the growth of a strong owner-occupation sector. For many decades, Australia has been a nation of homeowners, with government subsidies and housing assistance programs directed at encouraging home ownership. Since the Second World War Australians have had consistently high home-ownership rates: peaking at 70 per cent in 1961, and remaining relatively stable since (Kryger 2009). Home ownership has been a widely held aspiration: "The Great Australian Dream" (Badcock and Beer 2000), particularly among nuclear families – providing stability and security, declining housing costs over time and generally better housing conditions than in the rental tenures.

Reconfiguration of the nation of male breadwinners and the move towards gender equity?

A number of Australian commentators have noted that the cultural pervasiveness of the male breadwinner model was being challenged (as well as supported) *during* the long boom – largely by state actions (Nolan 2003; also Baker 2001; Broomhill and Sharp 2005). The demise of the model is evidenced by significant growth in female labour force participation over the post-war and long-boom periods (see Table 3.1).

By 1966 the labour force participation rate for all women aged 15–64 rose to 41 per cent (and 49 per cent in 1976), with much of this increase in participation due to the greater involvement of married women and mothers in paid employment. Thirty per cent of married women were in the labour force in 1966 (45 per cent in 1976) (ABS 2007d), and the participation rate of mothers aged 15–64 in 1974 was 41 per cent (Wilson *et al.* 1999: 3–6).

Nolan (2003: 76) notes that after the post-war boom was over, 'the economy could no longer afford the family wage' as the economy went into recession in the mid-1970s and unemployment rates began to rise. Recessed economic conditions saw many more women seek work out of necessity – to supplement their family's wage, or to wholly support themselves or their family.

Other social and technological changes occurring within Australia and internationally over the period of the long-boom also determined women's altered social and economic role. The introduction of the contraceptive pill in 1961, for example, gave women control over their fertility, altering financial and family aspirations. And, the emergence of the women's liberation movement across the developed world throughout the 1960s and 1970s saw many women demand a new role in society (see Summers 2002). This second wave feminism centred on removing discrimination and attaining equal rights in many institutions, including education, employment and marriage. Important legislative changes were enacted

Table 3.1 Labour force status of women, Australia, 1933–1961

Year	Proportion of 15–64 year old women at work (%)	Female workforce as proportion of total labour force (%)	Married women as proportion of female labour force (%)	Proportion of married women at work (%)
1933	27.8	21.8	11.0	5.4
1947	28.4	22.4	19.8	8.6
1954	30.5	22.8	34.3	14.8
1961	33.8	24.8	42.0	18.4

Source: Adapted from Martin and Richmond 1968 in Sheridan and Stretton 2004.
Note: Including full-time and part-time work.

as a result protests of by activists, removing many barriers to women's workforce participation. These included: elimination of the bar on married women being employed in the Commonwealth public service in 1966 (see Sheridan and Stretton 2004); the introduction of no-fault divorce in the Federal Family Law Act from 1975, and recognition of the economic contribution of women's unpaid work in the home in the division of assets at divorce; and the passing of the Commonwealth Sex Discrimination Act 1984 and the Commonwealth Affirmative Action (Equal Employment Opportunity for Women Act) in 1986.

The ultimate result of all these factors – which have both transformed and weakened the Australian male breadwinner model – is that women have gained more control over their reproductive and productive lives. Accordingly, unprecedented numbers of women have become active participants in both education and the labour market (Table 3.2), particularly over the recent three decades.

The number of females completing secondary school, for example, has increased exponentially – from around 15 per cent of students in 1967 to around 80 per cent for full-time female students for the decade from 1998–2008 (ABS 2010: 386-387). This rate has remained relatively steady since the early 1990s, with female completion rates outstripping male rates (ABS 2001:409), and reflects government policies to develop a specialised and highly skilled labour force needed in the new technology-driven global economy.

Following on from the much higher secondary school retention rates, has been a significant increase in the number of women in the population (especially women aged under 45) with post-school education. In the decade to 2005, the proportion of women aged 25–34 with a higher education qualification exceeded the number of men (32 per cent versus 27 per cent), up from 14 per cent for both sexes in 1995 (ABS 2006). And, in 1971 only one per cent of women aged 15 and over had a degree, rising to 7 per cent by 1991 (ABS 1994) and for women aged 15–64 rising to 13 per cent in 1996 (the same proportion as for males), to 18 per cent in 2001 and 22 per cent in 2006 (ABS 2008c).[1]

Table 3.2 shows the sustained rate of women's labour force participation over the last three decades. The data show the clear pattern of part-time female workforce participation, the relative stability in Australian women's full-time labour force participation, and the fact that women comprise two thirds of all people not in the labour force. Table 3.10 confirms these trends for the period 1997–2007.

Notably also, the increased availability of child care places for children under five and for children outside school hours over the last decade or so, has facilitated the increased labour force participation of mothers. So too has the introduction of government subsidisation of child care costs through the taxation system for families earning below certain incomes thresholds.

The changes discussed above have worked together to alter women's roles, aspirations and behaviours with regard to family formation and financial independence. They have also seen Australia move towards gender equity and

Table 3.2 Selected labour force statistics by sex (percentage), Australia, selected years 1978– 2009

	Year								
	1978	1981	1986	1991	1996	2001	2006	2008	2009
Participation rate									
Total	61.7	61.4	61.9	63.7	63.9	63.5	64.8	65.5	65.8
Females	43.7	44.5	47.9	52.2	53.9	55.0	57.3	58.5	59.3
Males	80.1	78.7	76.3	75.5	74.2	72.3	72.5	72.8	72.6
Selected characteristics (15–64 year olds)									
Female workforce as a proportion of total labour force	32.4	33.8	35.3	37.8	39.0	41.0	42.3	43.0	42.9
Male workforce as a proportion of total labour force	60.1	59.9	55.9	53.0	51.9	51.7	51.9	52.5	51.1
Women employed full-time as proportion of all persons employed full time	27.5	28.0	30.1	31.8	32.7	34.3	34.6	35.3	35.3
Men employed full-time as a proportion of all persons employed full-time	72.5	72.0	69.9	68.2	67.3	65.7	65.4	64.7	64.7
Women employed part-time as a proportion of all persons employed part time	78.7	80.1	79.5	77.3	74.8	72.3	71.5	70.6	71.3
Men employed part-time as a proportion of all persons employed part-time	21.3	19.9	20.5	22.7	25.2	27.7	28.5	29.4	28.7
Women not in the labour force as a proportion of all persons not in the labour force	74.4	72.9	69.3	66.7	64.9	62.7	61.6	61.1	60.4
Men not in the labour force as a proportion of all persons not in the labour force	25.6	27.1	30.7	33.3	35.1	37.3	38.4	38.9	39.6
Unemployment rate									

Source: Adapted from ABS 2009b.

more symmetry in the economic and social roles occupied by men and women (Manne 2001; Probert 2002). On this point though, Probert and Manne justifiably note that Australia's shift to gender equity in social and economic spheres of life has stalled – particularly in terms of women's financial position compared with men. The remaining sections of this chapter confirm these assertions; in terms of the impacts of the past three decades of social and economic change on women and their personal and housing circumstances.

Australian women's current personal and housing circumstances

This section follows on from the previous discussion, focusing on the implications of the most recent three decades of social and economic change on women. The section examines two specific areas of importance. First, women's financial circumstances, and, second, the impact of now well-entrenched demographic trends on women. These factors have been driven by changes in women's behaviours around family formation generally and Australia's declining total fertility rate[2] – brought about by women's greater control over their fertility, lifestyle choices and the increasing need and desire for self-reliance and self-fulfilment, manifest in increasing participation in education and paid work.

Economic changes: women's financial circumstances

While it is clearly the case that more women than before are employed in the labour force, it is also the case that Australian women continue to generally have much lower lifetime earnings than their male counterparts. And, given that access to more appropriate and better quality housing is largely income dependent, this issue is of central concern for women and their housing circumstances.

There are many reasons for women's poorer financial position relative to men – these include structural and subjective factors. Prominent is the gender wage gap; a trend that has persisted despite the Commonwealth ruling in favour of 'equal pay for equal work' in 1969 and this being phased in from 1972 (EOfWWA 2009). Additionally, current statistics on average weekly earnings (AWE) confirm the well-entrenched trend that women's average full-time ordinary earnings remain at around 85 per cent of men's (see ABS 2009a; Pocock 1999).[3] Recent analysis of the Household, Income and Labour Dynamics in Australia (HILDA) survey by the National Centre for Social and Economic Modelling (NATSEM) shows a marked difference in wages between women of different generations, with different qualifications and labour force attachment (see Table 3.3).

Part of the disparity in incomes between men and women is also due to Australia's highly gender-differentiated workforce. Women are over-represented in lower-paid positions, as well as the part-time and casual occupations that have emerged

Table 3.3 Gender wage gap by generation and employment characteristics, Australia, 2006

Characteristic	Generation Y			Generation X			Baby boomers		
	Male	Female	Wage gap	Male	Female	Wage gap	Male	Female	Wage gap
	A$	A$	ratio	A$	A$	ratio	A$	A$	Ratio
Bachelor degree or higher	1,020	858	0.84	1,587	1,025	0.65	1,590	1,088	0.68
Certificate/ diploma	825	594	0.72	1,147	693	0.60	1,149	711	0.62
Year 12 or below	670	560	0.84	1,043	601	0.58	1,048	654	0.62
1–34 hours per week	404	374	0.93	462	520	1.13	637	509	0.80
40 or more hours per week (full-time)	988	913	0.92	1,427	1,115	0.78	1,438	1,176	0.82
Public sector employee	764	617	0.81	1,253	733	0.58	1,231	698	0.57
Private sector employee	876	824	0.94	1,209	818	0.68	1,250	956	0.76
Other employee	796	724	0.91	1,108	779	0.70	1,152	763	0.66
All	775	657	0.85	1,231	760	0.62	1,225	784	0.64

Source: AMP.NATSEM 2009 based on calculations from the Household, Income and Labour Dynamics in Australia (HILDA) Survey, wave 6 unit record data, p. 25.

over recent decades in response to economic and labour market deregulation (see Table 3.4), and in jobs that generally do not offer overtime (Doughney *et al.* 2004; Pocock 1999). Importantly, women's lower incomes are also a result of women continuing to shoulder the main responsibility for caring in society – caring for children, people with disabilities and the elderly.[4]

Research on the *Cost of Caring in Australia* between 2002 and 2005 (AMP. NATSEM 2006) reveals the prominence of women among informal carers. Across all age cohorts 54 per cent of carers are female, and women comprise 71 per cent of primary carers – the main carer for a person with a disability. For specific age cohorts, women comprise 60 per cent of carers aged 35–44 and 58 per cent of carers aged 45–54: a good proportion of the working years for most women. Further, nine out of ten primary carers aged 65 and under who are caring for a frail elderly parent, are female (pp. 9–10).[5]

The same research reveals the impact of caring for children on women's paid work – around 50 per cent of mothers whose youngest child is aged under two, and 30 per cent of mothers whose youngest child is aged between five and 11, do not work (AMP.NATSEM 2006: 1). As Australia does not have a comprehensive system of paid parental leave and only a small proportion of women/families have access to such a payment, childrearing generally means a significant drop in income for women and families. The need for paid parental leave however, has been widely debated, with the Rudd Labor government commissioning an inquiry into the need for and cost of such a system in 2008 (Productivity Commission 2008). The May 2009 Federal Budget includes for the first time government-funded paid parental leave – commencing January 2011 (Commonwealth of Australia 2009a).

Women's prominence among carers is of concern in terms of their economic autonomy and position, as '… the fact that more women than men spend more time caring for others penalises them financially, and diminishes their professional experience and employability' (AMP.NATSEM 2006: 2).

Statistics on the incomes of sole-parent households is also an area where significant income disparity is evident (see Table 3.4) – particularly between male- and female- headed households and between sole parents and couple families. The income and financial position of sole-parent households is an important consideration given that 83 per cent of these households are female headed (ABS 2007b), and because sole parents are proven to be prone to housing stress (Yates and Gabriel 2006).

Table 3.4 shows three notable trends for sole parents. First, three times as many female-headed sole-parent families are renting their home than are couple families. This is of concern as many researchers have shown that private renters are considered to be susceptible to housing stress (Yates and Gabriel 2006; Beer *et al.* 2007). Second, the proportion of female-headed sole-parent families purchasing their home is much lower than for male-headed sole-parent families and couple families generally, with female-headed sole-parent families proportionately half as likely to be purchasing

Table 3.4 Selected economic characteristics of families with children aged under 15, Australia, 2003–2004

Household characteristic	Unit	Sole-parent families			Couple families
		Female-headed	Male-headed	Total	Total
Income					
Principal source of income government pensions/allowances	%	63.3	47.1	61.3	8.2
Mean weekly equivalised disposable household income[a]	A$	429	372	534	
	A$	364			
Wealth					
Mean net household worth[b]	A$	123,000	171,000	129,000	471,000
Income and wealth					
Is a low economic resources household[c]	%	49.9	39.6	48.6	11.0
Housing tenure					
Renter	%	65.1	56.4	64.0	21.2
Purchaser (with mortgage)	%	24.7	36.7	26.3	62.9
Outright owner	%	7.7	4.9	7.3	13.5

Source: ABS 2007e: 51 (data analysis from ABS 2003–2004 Household Expenditure Survey and 2003–04 Survey of Income and Housing). ABS data used with permission from the Australian Bureau of Statistics.
Notes:
Data presented excludes families in multi-family households, but includes one-family households with persons other than parent/s or child/ren making up the family.
(a) Data presented is equivalised to account for differences in the number of people (adults and children) in each household. Disposable income is income after tax and medicare levy.
(b) Value of household assets less liabilities.
(c) Households simultaneously in lowest three deciles of both equivalised disposable income and equivalised net worth.

their home as couple families. Third, sole mothers clearly earn significantly less than sole fathers and couple families, and this has flow-on effects for household worth.

The relative disadvantage of female-headed households is also demonstrated by the fact that such households are also the major recipients of both public housing assistance (see Hulse & Saugeres 2008: 8–9) and Commonwealth Rent Assistance (62 per cent) (DFaCS 2005) – the Australian Government's rental subsidy for private rental tenants to improve their housing affordability outcomes.

Women, wealth and housing

While the increasing labour force participation of women has improved the individual incomes of households that include working women, investigation of the wealth circumstances of women over the last 25 years reveals a mixed picture of wealth distribution. Analysis of women's incomes over the period from 1982 to 2005–06, for example, reveals that despite increasing workforce participation, women's share of total income has increased minimally in 25 years – from 31 per cent in 1982 to 38 per cent in 2005–06 (Austen and Redmond 2008).

Moreover, as shown in Table 3.5, data on the average net worth of Australians in 2006 shows that female-headed households are fairing poorly, particularly female-headed sole-parent households. The majority of their wealth is in the family home, its contents and in vehicles; likely reflecting the common pattern of division of assets following divorce. That is, with the family home and most of its contents remaining with the parent with primary care responsibility for the children (Sheehan 2002; de Vaus *et al.* 2007).

Previous analysis of ABS data on wealth by the NATSEM confirms these patterns of average net household worth across generations (see Tables 3.6 and 3.7). [6]

The data in Tables 3.6 and 3.7 shows further distributional inequalities in wealth. For example, female baby boomers living alone generally have lower levels of wealth than their male counterparts, and significantly less wealth than all couple households. The net worth of these households, however, is boosted by the equity they have in the family home – equity that increased greatly since the year 2000 when the most recent house price boom started across Australia. It is also likely that some of the women in this cohort have been widowed and either wholly inherited a fully-owned home or have inherited money (from their partners superannuation and/or from a deceased parent) that they have used to pay off their outstanding mortgage.

Additional analysis of wealth data by generations for Australians by NATSEM (AMP.NATSEM 2007: 17) provides further evidence in support of the disparities in wealth within household types. This data perhaps provides a more accurate indication of wealth – although unfortunately not gender disaggregated. For example, in 2004 for all Australian households average net worth was A$292,500, ranging from an average of A$48,800 for households in the poorest 25 per cent

Table 3.5 Average net worth per person by household and asset type, Australia, 2006

| Household type | Average net worth per person (A$) | | | | | Home equity as % of total net worth |
	Home equity	Super-annuation	Other financial assets[a]	Other wealth[b]	Total net worth	
Couple only	144,390	60,400	113,220	109,630	367,230	39.3
Couple with children	145,780	55,290	103,680	98,570	348,030	41.9
Sole male with children	140,170	51,150	91,510	66,480	298,160	47.0
Sole female with children	92,930	19,060	38,460	59,910	191,300	48.6
Male lone person	133,730	44,940	109,980	130,360	374,070	35.7
Female lone person	204,600	35,810	90,920	91,620	387,140	52.8
All	147,720	53,060	103,840	102,740	354,290	41.7

Source: AMP.NATSEM 2009: 27 (calculations from the ABS Survey of Income and Housing 2005–06 unit record data).

Notes:

Analysis excluded mixed and groups households. Figures have been rounded to the nearest A$10.

The per-person wealth of couple households was determined by dividing the household wealth of couples evenly between partners.

(a) Includes the value of accounts with financial institutions, value of all other property, trusts, shares, debentures, bonds and the net value of incorporated own business.

(b) Includes value of vehicles, home contents and other assets not included in other categories, e.g. value of collectibles.

Table 3.6 Average net worth of baby boomer[7] households by asset type, Australia, 2004

Household type by age of reference person	Average net worth per person aged 45–64 (A$)					Home equity as % of total net worth
	Home equity	Super-annuation	Other financial assets[a]	Other wealth[b]	Total net worth	
Couple only						
45–49	115,100	57,200	67,300	103,400	343,000	34
50–54	139,200	70,400	40,800	136,300	386,700	36
55–59	151,800	81,400	51,800	105,400	390,300	39
60–64	189,200	87,000	67,600	163,400	507,200	37
Couple with children						
45–49	151,300	50,000	36,700	92,700	330,800	46
50–54	168,800	57,400	38,100	90,600	354,800	48
55–59	215,900	87,200	68,400	125,500	497,100	43
60–64	161,100	64,000	58,600	102,400	386,100	42
Sole parent with children						
45–49	151,900	36,600	18,000	94,800	301,300	50
50–54	113,600	41,500	18,000	100,100	273,200	42
Male lone person						
45–49	113,200	43,600	39,700	77,900	274,300	41
50–54	111,500	92,100	50,300	78,900	332,800	34
55–59	148,200	63,400	61,400	90,800	363,700	41
60–64	174,800	88,000	52,900	111,800	427,500	41
Female lone person						
45–49	131,500	39,500	12,600	54,500	238,200	55
50–54	157,000	48,800	37,500	78,100	321,300	49
55–59	202,300	43,400	37,000	80,200	363,000	56
60–64	189,300	24,900	49,500	51,900	315,600	60
All	142,400	49,400	39,300	91,700	322,800	44
45–49	153,000	63,000	39,200	103,700	358,500	43
50–54	177,000	78,900	56,600	108,900	421,300	42
55–59	182,500	76,000	62,700	135,500	456,700	40
60–64	161,000	65,100	47,700	107,300	381,100	42

Source: AMP.NATSEM 2007:23.

Notes:

Due to the small number of sole-parent households with children aged 55–59 and 60–64 calculations were not carried out for these households.

(a) Includes the value of accounts with financial institutions, value of all other property, trusts, shares, debentures, bonds and the net value of incorporated own business.

(b) Includes value of vehicles, home contents and other assets not included in other categories, e.g. collectibles.

Table 3.7 Estimated wealth of Generation X[8] households by asset type, Australia, June 2003

Household type	Estimated value of assets of Generation Xers (A$)					Net wealth	Home equity as % of net wealth
	Home equity	Super-annuation	Cash deposits	Equities	Rental properties (net)		
Couple only	100,200	34,500	8,800	7,400	20,400	171,300	58%
Couple with children	133,000	45,000	3,100	27,500	19,500	228,200	58%
Lone person	49,600	21,000	5,800	4,700	7,600	88,700	56%
Sole parent	77,900	20,200	4,500	4,800	10,100	117,500	66%
All Gen X households	99,300	35,500	5,100	15,500	16,700	172,100	58%

Source: AMP.NATSEM 2003: 9.

of all households to A$701,900 for those in the richest quartile. These differences demonstrate the level of variation between richest and poorest households in each cohort. They also show the importance of housing in wealth accumulation. And, as female-headed households are generally the poorest of all household types, it seems fair to assume that the wealth reality for women is likely to be much worse than the averages presented above.

Another indicator of the inequality in wealth between Australian men and women generally is shown in their average superannuation balances (see Table 3.8). The data show that up until the age of about 25, superannuation balances are largely similar. After 25, the picture varies considerably – demonstrating the effect of having children on the labour force attachment and lifetime incomes of women.

More recent data on superannuation by the Association of Superannuation Funds of Australia (Clare 2008: 21) shows that females continue to have significantly less superannuation than men: A$35,520 compared with A$69,050 for persons aged 25–64 (see also Table 3.11). Current balances are likely to be lower than these figures due to negative returns on funds due to the global financial crisis.

The level of superannuation accumulated by women is an important consideration in terms of wealth in Australia, as this mechanism is favoured by the federal government to reduce the dependence of retirees on the Age Pension[9], and as a means for retirees to improve their incomes and standard of living in retirement. The lack of superannuation is a particular concern then for women approaching retirement with insufficient superannuation or other wealth and/or who are unpartnered.

In discussing women and wealth, it would be remiss not to also mention here that a significant proportion of Australian women (and their children) are living in poverty, struggling to get by on a daily basis, let alone accumulating any personal wealth.

Women, poverty and housing

There is a dearth of research about the financial and personal circumstances of many of the women and groups of women living in poverty in Australia. However, we do know two important things from the general poverty literature that sheds light on this issue for women.

First, we know that poverty is both persistent and pervasive in Australia (SCARCS 2004; Harding *et al.* 2001). Current research indicates that between 10 and 20 per cent of all Australians are living in poverty, depending on the poverty measure used. And, as women account for just under 50 per cent of all Australians living in poverty (Lloyd *et al.* 2004) this means that between one and two million women are in this situation.

Second, we know from poverty research (SCARCS 2004) that certain groups are over-represented among those living in poverty (summarised in Figure 3.1).

Table 3.8 Average superannuation balances of Australians by age, gender and employment status, 2002

	Age cohort	% with super-annuation	Average superannuation balance (A$)					
			Employed full-time	Employed part-time	Unemployed	Not in the labour force	All people with super-annuation
Females	15–24	55.3	7,200	1,000	300	450	4,300
	25–34	82.5	26,900	13,700	2,800	8,100	20,800
	35–44	78.3	53,800	23,500	3,600	13,200	37,600
	45–54	77.0	83,400	43,700	34,500	20,300	67,500
	55–64	53.4	76,800	57,800	30,900	41,800	94,700
	65+	12.6	86,300	79,400	–	13,000	124,300
	Total	61.8	47,200	24,000	6,600	17,000	43,300
Males	15–24	59.3	7,800	1,100	6,400	250	6,800
	25–34	92.2	28,600	14,800	5,100	6,300	27,200
	35–44	91.7	69,600	23,600	28,000	8,900	65,400
	45–54	86.8	122,200	66,700	44,800	43,300	122,300
	55–64	68.8	165,500	160,100	38,900	85,000	183,600
	65+	26.6	74,700	78,00	–	45,900	184,900
	Total	73.6	72,000	39,000	16,700	42,300	78,700

Source: Clare 2004: 4–5, data from unit record file, Survey of Household Income and Labour Dynamics in Australia.

All of these groups, and especially sole-parent families, lone-person households and survivors of domestic and family violence, include significant numbers of women. In fact, domestic and family violence has a significant impact on the housing circumstances of the small but unacceptable number of Australian women affected each year (Tually *et al.* 2008; also Chung *et al.* 2000; Weeks and Oberin 2004).[10] Current estimates of homelessness suggest that some *46,000 Australian women are homeless*: 44 per cent of the approximately 105,000 Australians homeless on any given night (according to the 2006 Census – see Chamberlain and MacKenzie 2008).

Homelessness service providers also point to an increasing number of women (and their children, and families generally) presenting to homelessness services, and a lack of capacity in the sector to deal with increasing demand for crisis accommodation from women – especially those escaping domestic violence (Mission Australia 2007; Robinson and Searby 2006). Of particular concern here

---

- Unemployed people and those reliant on government benefits;
- Low wage earners and low wage families, especially those with poor educational levels. This group includes a rising number of 'working poor' families in financial and housing stress, struggling with escalating housing and living costs and wages that are not rising at a commensurate rate (see Pocock and Masterman-Smith 2006);
- Sole parent families;
- People living alone;
- Older people, especially those renting privately or living alone;
- People with disabilities or long-term illness;
- Young people on low incomes – including tertiary students;
- Indigenous Australians;
- Migrants and refugees from culturally and linguistically diverse backgrounds;
- Larger families (three or more children);
- Homeless people;
- Survivors of domestic and family violence;
- People exiting prison;
- People with substance abuse and/or gambling problems;
- People with mental illness;
- Some people with significant caring responsibilities (such as young carers and grandparents caring for grandchildren);
- People living in tenuous housing arrangements, such as caravan parks.

3.1 Groups overrepresented among those in income related poverty, Australia. Source: SCARCS 2004.

are acknowledged 'blockages' in crisis accommodation services caused by a lack of safe and affordable permanent housing options for women staying temporarily in shelters and refuges. These blockages limit the number of women services can assist/house,[11] placing many women and children in danger.

On the issue of poverty, Lloyd *et al.* (2004) and the Senate Community Affairs References Committee Secretariat (2004) point out that overall levels of poverty among women have decreased in recent years due to increased workforce participation by many sole mothers and the introduction of the Child Support Scheme in the late 1980s. However, concerns over rising living and housing costs and the insufficiency of income support payments (particularly for age pensioners), indicate increasing levels of poverty; a fact many social service organisations have vehemently put forward over the last decade. These concerns have led to the federal government reviewing pensions as a priority (Harmer 2008), and subsequently increasing the rate of some pensions to address levels of poverty and rising living costs for Australian's reliant on government income support payments (Harmer 2009; Swan and Macklin 2009).

On the whole what this discussion shows is that some Australian women are doing well in terms of wealth accumulation. This is certainly the case for many of the 65 per cent of Australian women living in couple families (with or without children) who are purchasing their home or who own their home outright (ABS 2007a). It is also likely among those women who bought into the housing market before the recent housing boom (commencing from mid-2000), and for those entering retirement with a manageable mortgage or no mortgage at all. However, those individuals and households who are not homeowners, who have fallen out of home ownership during their lifetime for some reason (e.g. divorce) and have not accumulated significant home equity, are often significantly disadvantaged in terms of wealth. This is an unsurprising finding given that Australia has long been a nation of homeowners, and home ownership is the main way Australians accumulate wealth (Badcock and Beer 2000). Moreover, having a single income or a drop in household income can and does adversely affect the housing circumstances of many women.[12]

Demographic Trends and their Impact on Women's Housing

Population diversity and demographic change

Australia's female population is a diverse population with increasingly diverse needs – socially, physically, economically, culturally and in terms of housing. It includes increasing numbers of older women and women from diverse cultural and linguistic backgrounds, as well as increasing numbers of Indigenous women[13], women with disabilities, women who are single parents, childless women, divorcees, and women who are not and have never been married. As is noted in this section, this diversity shapes the housing needs and requirements of individuals and women generally.

Five established trends in family formation and family dissolution are also pertinent here; not only because of their impact on women and their housing but as they have shaped Australian society in many ways.

First, an increasing number of women never formally marrying and the accompanying trend of significant growth in the number of people living together as a *de facto* couple before marrying – if they do marry at all. Projections on this trend indicate that 'if 2000–2002 nuptiality rates were to prevail into the future, 31 per cent of males and 26 per cent of females would never marry in their lifetimes' (Jain 2007: 45).

Second, younger women and men delaying both formal marriage and first child birth until they are in their late 20s and 30s (Jain 2007; also ABS 2005c). These two trends are important in terms of women and their housing as formal marriage and childbearing have traditionally been strongly correlated with entry into home ownership (Beer and Faulkner 2009; Winter and Stone 1999) and some research points to younger Australians both delaying family formation and entry into homeownership in order to first establish a career and achieve financial stability (see McDonald and Baxter 2004; McDonald and Merlo 2002).

Third, a large and increasing proportion of women are remaining childless. Statistics on this trend indicate that approximately a quarter of women currently remain childless throughout their life (ABS 2002). This is a significant change from previous generations. For example, for women born in the early 1950s only 11 per cent had not had children by the end of their reproductive life (Barnes 2001: 33). Recent research by Kippen (2006), however, finds that around 16 per cent of women born in 1971 will likely be childless at the end of their reproductive life. She contends that this is because women are recouping some of their postponed or 'missing fertility' from their 20s after the age of 30. Current statistics confirm this, with most births in the country now to women aged 30–34 and in 2007 this age cohort experienced its highest fertility rate since 1962 (ABS 2008a). It is also the case that Australia has experienced a small baby boom since around 2007, spurred on by the introduction of a "Baby Bonus" support payment for new parents in 2004 (replacing a much smaller maternity allowance) to address Australia's below replacement-level fertility rate (Drago *et al.* 2009).[14]

Fourth, sustained high rates of relationship breakdown and divorce. ABS estimates for marriage breakdown and divorce in Australia suggest that around a third of marriages entered into in 2000–2002 will end in divorce (Jain 2007: 45). This compares to 28 per cent for marriages entered into in 1985–1987. Projections on divorce rates into the future predict that in 2025 in the order of 54 per cent of all marriages over time will end in divorce (AMP.NATSEM 2005). This sustained high rate of divorce is of significant concern for women and their housing circumstances, as divorce affects the wealth of women and therefore their housing options. Moreover, many women fall out of home ownership because of divorce (Flatau *et al.* 2004; Beer and Faulkner 2009).

And, fifth, gradually declining rates of widowhood for women (due to the increasing life expectancies of men), and declining rates of remarriage for both widows/widowers and all divorcees (Jain 2007: 45–46). Trends in remarriage are important here as research shows it is a key way divorcees can avoid financial hardship and/or poverty in the longer term and rebuild their wealth (Sheehan 2002; de Vaus *et al.* 2007).

Changes in living arrangements

The result of the five main trends in family formation and dissolution discussed above has been unprecedented growth in the number of households in Australia – with household growth outstripping population growth overall. Such growth in households has been driven by the continuing downward trend in both family and household size.[15]

All types of households have grown in number over recent years (ABS 2004c); however, particular trends stand out as important for women:

- an increasing number and proportion of couple families and households *without children* in the total population (and of partners living in such arrangements);
- a decline in the number and proportion of couple households *with children* in the population (and of partners and children living in this formally 'traditional' type of family/household);
- significant growth in the number of female lone-person households in Australia – particularly in the older age cohorts (including widows, divorcees and women who have not formally married or partnered); and
- growth in the number and proportion of female-headed sole-parent families and in the number of children living in such families.

The clear trend of accelerating growth in lone-person and single-parent households is of particular importance here. These household types are projected to grow most strongly into the future, signalling the continuing decline of the nuclear family household that dominated the Australian social fabric up until the 1970s.

Importantly, *Household and Family Projections* produced by Australia's national statistics agency, the Australian Bureau of Statistics (ABS), point to the dominance of female-headed households among both lone-person and single-parent households over the next twenty years. The projected growth in this household type is a function of structural ageing and older women being more likely to live alone in old age than men (ABS 2004c: 22). The housing needs and demands of women living alone, and especially older women living alone, will clearly be an area in need of specific housing market and government attention.

For sole-parent families, ABS projections anticipate growth in female-headed families from the 700,000 families enumerated at the 2001 Census to between around 900,000 and over 1.1 million families in 2026. Further, female sole-parent families are projected to continue to outnumber male-headed households by a ratio of about 5 to 1; reflecting the fact that most children remain with their mothers post-family breakdown (ABS 2004c).

The implications of changes in living arrangements for housing in Australia generally, let alone for women specifically, have not been widely researched. Current research by the Australian Housing and Urban Research Institute (AHURI) addresses this gap (see Beer and Faulkner 2009; Beer *et al.* 2006), showing that changes in living arrangements and family/household formation and dissolution have worked together to create far more complex, multi-directional and non-linear housing careers and pathways for people than was the case in past generations. It is now more common for women to move into, out of, between and within housing tenures (including home ownership) as a result of changes in personal and relationship circumstances, as well as because of the impact of such changes on women's financial position; i.e. due to separation, divorce, disability and frailty, changes in caring responsibilities, the death of a partner or through remarriage or repartnering. Accordingly, women will clearly need different housing options into the future (and at different stages of their life course), with such options needing to be across all tenures and at a range of price points suited to their financial and personal circumstances.

Population ageing

Arguably the most profound social and demographic change in Australia over recent years, and especially currently, is rapid population ageing. ABS population projections (ABS 2004c) clearly show Australia's population is ageing, and women comprise a significant majority within the older age cohorts. The projections show an increase in the proportion of the population aged 55 and over from 24 per cent in 2006 to nearly 33 per cent in 2025, with women aged 65 and over (past traditional retirement age) expected to increase from 1,496,755 people to 2,653,173 people over the same period – a percentage change of 77 per cent. Within the over 65s population there is also predicted to be a significant increase in old and very old women (over 75s), with there predicted to be almost half as many women aged 85 and over in the population in 2025 as in 2006. The reasons for this demographic picture have been widely discussed and centre on the fact that Australia has experienced sustained low levels of fertility and, correspondingly, increasing life expectancies across the population.

Given the rapid ageing of Australia's total and female population, it is clear that the housing needs of the older population must be a prominent consideration in housing policy and the housing market generally. AHURI (2004) suggest that the housing needs of older Australians must be addressed in a system-wide way, because Australia's population now includes, and will continue to include:

- more retirees seeking housing suited to their lifestyles;
- more frail, very old people and especially older women living on their own, creating a greater demand for housing that incorporates some form of support; and
- substantial numbers of women reaching old age as renters and whose housing choices will diminish as they grow older.

Population ageing also has important social ramifications in terms of the level of disability in the population. Statistics on the prevalence of disability in Australia show that disability, and particularly profound or severe core-activity restriction, increases significantly with age, and for women in particular (see Table 3.9).

The rate of disability among women is pertinent in terms of housing and the likely demands for housing for affected households and individuals. Having a profound or severe core-activity restriction shapes the housing circumstances and choices of people affected by disabilities and their primary carers (Kroehn *et al.* 2007). Given the figures above it is fair to assume that a significant number of baby boomer women (and men) can expect to live with disability in their retirement. This has implications for the design, affordability and location of housing. It also has implications for younger women, as most of the care for people with disabilities is undertaken by women, and such informal care may indeed extend for longer periods as older people live to a greater age. This trend will also clearly drive further demand for formal in-home support services and other government or community-funded and -based services – particularly as the preference among many older Australians (and indeed all levels of government) is to 'age in place' – in their own homes or communities (Department of Health and Ageing 2006; House of Representatives Standing Committee on Expenditure 1982).

Threats and barriers to Australian women's housing

If women are to be economically secure, they must all have the capacity to achieve that security independent of their partners. The reality is that there are no guarantees of lifelong partnerships; the falling marriage rate, rising divorce rate and increased incidence of people who never partner argue for the importance of all women being able to provide financially for themselves. In many families, women are and will continue to be the sole breadwinners.

(Security4Women & Boulden 2004: 10)

It is clear from the discussion above that changes in women's circumstances have presented both opportunities and challenges for women. For example, while it is the case that many women are more economically independent than has been the case in the past, women still earn much less than their male counterparts and this affects their personal and housing circumstances. This is especially the case where women are the

Table 3.9 People with disability by age and sex, Australia, 2003

	Female				Male				Total			
	Profound or severe core-activity restriction[a]		All disability		Profound or severe core-activity restriction[a]		All disability		Profound or severe core-activity restriction[a]		All disability	
Age	No (000)	%	No (000)	%	No (000)	%	No ('000)	%	No (000)	%	No (000)	%
0–4	*15.0	*2.5	23.8	3.9	20.8	*3.3	29.7	4.7	35.9	2.9	53.5	4.3
5–14	42.7	3.3	97.3	7.5	88.1	6.5	169.1	12.4	130.8	4.9	266.4	10.0
15–24	29.8	2.2	124.1	9.0	31.2	2.1	127.2	8.9	60.9	2.2	251.3	9.0
25–34	*33.3	*2.2	142.0	9.7	34.2	2.3	174.1	11.7	67.4	2.3	316.1	10.7
35–44	*51.9	*3.5	206.1	13.9	46.9	3.1	214.2	14.5	98.8	3.3	420.2	14.2
44–54	74.4	5.5	290.3	21.5	57.0	4.2	291.2	21.6	131.4	4.9	581.5	21.6
55–59	46.3	8.3	179.7	31.9	37.1	*6.4	166.9	28.7	83.3	7.2	346.6	30.3
60–64	41.7	9.8	157.1	37.1	32.5	*7.6	174.1	40.6	74.3	8.8	331.2	38.9
65–69	36.7	10.3	137.4	38.6	32.8	9.5	147.2	42.6	69.6	9.9	284.6	40.6
70–74	56.8	17.4	162.9	49.8	34.3	11.6	145.9	49.5	91.1	14.6	308.8	49.6
75–79	62.9	21.5	167.6	57.2	43.5	18.7	139.6	60.1	106.5	20.2	307.2	58.5
80–84	88.7	40.5	150.1	68.6	40.2	27.3	107.4	72.9	128.9	30.3	257.5	70.3
85–89	71.3	57.3	98.3	78.9	26.0	*38.9	50.3	75.0	97.3	50.9	148.5	77.6
> 90	*54.7	*79.1	64.1	92.6	13.5	*59.4	20.8	90.9	68.3	74.2	84.9	92.1
Total	706.2	7.1	2000.7	20.1	538.3	5.5	1957.6	19.8	1244.5	6.3	3958.3	20.0

Source: Adapted from ABS 2004a: 16.

Notes: *Figures include estimates for profound or severe core-activity restriction that has a high relative standard error – of between 25 and 50 per cent and the ABS recommends these figures be treated with caution.

(a) Core activities are communication, mobility and self-care.

sole breadwinner in a household or family; a trend shown above to be much more common now than in the past – because of an ageing population, and new aspirations and behaviours around family formation and high rates of family dissolution. This section considers some of the threats and barriers to women's housing security in Australia at the current time. The discussion emphasises the importance of providing affordable housing across all tenures, and meeting the other housing needs of women given the demographic, economic and social trends discussed earlier.

Affordable Housing

One of the most important threats to women's housing access and security at the current time in Australia is the affordability of housing. The current housing affordability crisis is widely acknowledged and has been extensively studied (see, for example, National Housing Supply Council 2009; Yates *et al.* 2007; Yates *et al.* 2004; Yates and Gabriel 2006; UDIA 2007). It has been an area a focus of AHURI for the last few years,[16] and was the subject of a Senate Inquiry in 2008. Considerable media and political attention has been directed at this issue since the mid 2000s in particular; firstly, because of increasing living costs generally; secondly, with the recent house price boom (2000–current); and thirdly and most recently, with the increasing number of labour force retrenchments due to the generally unstable global economic conditions since late 2008.

In 2008 Australia's housing was proven as more unaffordable than at any time in the 22 years since the Real Estate Institute of Australia started its housing affordability index for monitoring the costs of housing for purchase and rental (Dyett in Australian Broadcasting Corporation 2008). Increasing levels of housing stress among households generally, as well as of mortgage default and foreclosures, highlight the current housing crisis across the country (see Yates and Gabriel 2006; AMP.NATSEM 2008; on mortgage default see Berry *et al.* 2009). And, as women generally earn less than men, and we know that certain household types are predisposed to poverty and poor housing outcomes in terms of affordability (i.e. sole-parent and lone-person households – the majority of whom are female-headed), it is fair to assume that women are overrepresented among those suffering most in terms of affordability, and increasing living costs generally.

Research on housing stress and housing affordability shows the implication of the unaffordability of housing for older Australians (AMP.NATSEM 2008). It shows that in 2005–2006 twice as many households with a member aged over 60 were still paying off a mortgage than 10 years earlier. The same research also showed that a quarter of people aged over 60 in 2005–2006 did not fully own their home, up from 20 per cent a decade earlier (p. 26). The research concluded that:

> The mortgage noose now remains around the household neck for much longer periods of time, with those in their late 40s, 50s and 60s now being much more

likely to still be paying off the mortgage than Australians of the same age a decade ago. If these trends continue, future generations of Australians will be less likely to enter their old age with the mortgage paid off and their home underpinning their financial security in retirement.

(AMP.NATSEM 2008: 28)

Up-to-date economic modelling for the federal government adds further context to this issue. It revealed that some 112,000 households headed by a person aged over 70 were in housing stress in 2007, compared with only 57,000 households four years earlier (quoted in DFaHCSIA 2008a). Again, most of these households would be female-headed and no longer in a position to alter this situation as they are unlikely to be active participants in the workforce. Housing stress then is a real and increasing issue for older women, and one that must be addressed, particularly given the ageing population.

It is also now well-documented that there are few housing options available to older low-income tenants in Australia. As Yates (1991) and Castles (1998) have observed, the Australian welfare system is predicated on the assumption that older persons will be owner occupants and that their tenure will lift them out of poverty in their older age. For an increasing number of Australians though this is not the reality, with many people falling out of home ownership through divorce (Beer and Faulkner 2009; also de Vaus *et al.* 2007), loss of employment or other circumstances. There is therefore a need for affordable housing for older people, and especially for women, who constitute the majority of this age group.

Of course housing affordability is not only about the inability of households and individuals to *enter into* home ownership. In fact, *sustaining* home ownership is one of the biggest challenges facing many homeowners. And, especially currently, when the cost of housing remains high after the recent housing boom (although the value of houses are falling in some regions – though less so than in other developed countries at this stage) and the financial circumstances of households and individuals are more changeable across the lifecourse. Sustaining people in home ownership will continue to be a key challenge for governments and communities now and into the future.

Separation from a significant relationship and divorce have clear impacts on women and their housing. Recent research on the housing careers of women who have been divorced or separated from a significant relationship (Tually 2008) shows that a common story among women who were homeowners when they were partnered was the eventual loss of the family home after initially being awarded it as part of their property settlement at divorce or following separation (also Flatau *et al.* 2004). This was particularly the case if the woman was the partner with primary responsibility for caring for children, and had precarious labour force attachment. Importantly, many women (and some men) in this research also mentioned that they might have been able to keep their home had they been able to access a small loan to get them through the tight financial circumstances they faced immediately post-breakup. Many women stated that they felt locked out of home ownership as a housing option, largely because they had fallen out of home ownership just prior to or during the recent housing boom and have been unable to afford to re-enter the housing market. As high rates of divorce and relationship breakdown are projected to be sustained or increase into the future this issue will continue to be a major factor in the lives of many women, shaping their housing, personal and financial circumstances.

Analysis of ABS data by the newly formed National Housing Supply Council[17] further notes the affordability challenges facing low-income households in particular. For example, in 2006, 60 per cent of low-income households were paying more than 60 per cent of their income in rent, up from 43 per cent a decade earlier. With some 439,000 of such households in housing stress,[18] including 156,000 households paying more than 50 per cent of their income in rent (NHSC 2009: 82, 93).[19]

The housing affordability crisis in Australia also extends to the private rental market. In fact it is among private renters that housing stress is most acute (see Beer *et al.* 2007). The increasing unaffordability of private rental accommodation is of particular concern for women now and into the future, as all indications are that more individuals and households will be housed in this sector into the future. The decline in the number of public housing properties across most jurisdictions in Australia (in line with neoliberal rationalization of government provided-services over the period since the early 1990s),[20] as well as home ownership being unaffordable for an increasing number of people, has assured this outcome for many Australians. Given all of this, other ways of providing affordable housing must be developed and trialled if the social housing sector is not to be expanded to fulfil this role. The National Rental Affordability Scheme may assist in this regard (see DFaHCSIA 2008b). Increasing the supply of affordable housing options though will take many years, consequently, many women and their families will continue to struggle with their daily living and housing costs in the meantime. The federal government's recent commitment of A$6 billion to build approximately 20,000 new social housing properties across the country over the period to 2012 as part of its Nation Building Economic Stimulus Plan,[21] as well as additional funds for maintenance on existing properties (DFaHCSIA 2009), will hopefully go some way to assisting women in particular.

The lack of secure and affordable housing options across tenures is also problematic for women affected by domestic and family violence. This is an important area that must be addressed by policy, especially as there is a risk that incidences of domestic and family violence – and resultant homelessness – may increase among families and couples if further economic and emotional pressures are placed on households. Notably, the Rudd/Gillard government has addressing homelessness and violence against women and children as policy priorities, and significant resources have been directed at addressing these issues (Commonwealth of Australia 2008).[22]

The current housing stock

The mismatch of Australia's current housing stock with the demographic profile and preferences of Australian women is another barrier to women's access to appropriate housing. Evident in this regard is the current and likely increasing future demand for smaller housing from older people, especially older women living alone. Recent research commissioned by Planning SA (the South Australian government's planning department), on the housing aspirations and expectations of older South Australians, for example, revealed a strong preference among the participants in the research (baby boomers and over-65s) for smaller properties that are easier and cheaper to run and maintain than their conventional family homes (Faulkner *et al.* 2007). Such preferences are against the trend in housing over the last 15–20 years generally, which has been towards building larger houses despite the decreasing size of households (Hall 2007; ABS 2007c). Demand for lower maintenance housing is something we may also increasingly see from female-headed households on the whole, particularly given their generally more limited financial resources.

The physical design of housing is another threat to the appropriateness of housing for Australian women: one that will continue to be so given population ageing and the prevalence of disability with age for women. Accordingly, it is necessary that actions are taken by Australian governments and the housing industry to design and build "lifetime" or adaptable housing (see Ward 2005; Herd *et al.* 2003). That is, housing that takes into account the abilities and the frailties of its occupants. Building housing that accords with the principles of Universal Design – "the design of products and environments to be useable by all people, to the greatest extent possible, without the need for adaptation or specialized design" (Mace n.d.) – will assist more people to remain living independently as they age or acquire a disability or disabilities.

The UK Government has recently taken steps to address the design and accessibility of housing for its ageing population; an issue the Brown Labour government recognized as one of the most important challenges to sustainable housing for the twenty-first century. In that country the Brown government released a national strategy to address the increasing pressures on housing, health care and social services of its ageing population (UK DfCaLG, DoH and DfWaP 2008). A major component of this strategy is phasing in "lifetime" design principles for new housing, and extension of government assistance to repair and modify unsuitable private and public housing. Given that Australia is also facing similar pressures on housing and services from older people in the population, the Australian government also needs to systematically address this key issue for (women's) housing. Incorporating Universal Design principles into the Building Code of Australia, reinforced by provisions in building legislation and planning regulations, will greatly assist older people and people with disabilities to live independently in their homes (Ward 2005; Herd *et al.* 2003). However, as most women are currently living in housing that has already been built, attention must also be paid to modifying and retrofitting existing houses.

Conclusion: ways forward?

This chapter has examined key social and economic changes in Australia over recent decades and their implications for women and their housing. The discussion shows that women's altered role in society and families due to such changes has provided both opportunities and challenges. It highlights the need for a number of actions in order to address the generally poorer financial and housing outcomes of women.

First, there is clearly need for more affordable housing options for women. Such options are needed across tenures, and particularly in the private rental market where levels of housing stress are most acute and where most women are likely to be housed into the future because of a lack of alternative options. More affordable housing options are particularly needed for women (and children) who are homeless and/or victims of domestic and family violence. The tightening of credit for home purchase as a result of the current global financial crisis will also drive future demand for an increasing number of affordable housing options.

Second, governments need to ensure that women generally, and single parents and older lone-person households in particular, have appropriate incomes to support themselves and their families – particularly in the face of much higher housing and living costs now than in past years. Further support for women renting privately is also needed – as housing stress is highest in this tenure and rents remain high relative to income. The introduction of a paid parental leave scheme will assist many women (and their families) with managing their financial situation while in the family formation stage of the lifecourse.

Third, there is a need for flexibility in housing options for women, to meet the needs of a diverse population of women whose housing requirements and personal and financial circumstances are changeable across the life course. The discussion notes the need for housing that is adaptable and designed with the abilities and frailties of its occupants in mind. This is an area of importance for women's housing given population ageing and the increasing prevalence of disability with age, and as most older people want to 'age in place'. Furthermore, planners, governments and developers must *recognize and respond* to the housing needs of women. For example, the likely increasing demand for smaller, lower-cost, energy-efficient and lower-maintenance dwellings, located in well-serviced areas of cities and towns.

Fourth, assistance programs must be introduced to assist women to both enter/re-enter *and* sustain home ownership. A small low-interest loan or grant would assist many women in this situation to get over the immediate financial shock caused by a change in their personal and/or financial circumstances or help them back on the track to home ownership and wealth accumulation, if this is what they want and is an affordable option. Home ownership remains the most secure housing tenure for Australians, giving substantial tax and health benefits and offering the lowest lifetime housing costs for individuals. Being an outright homeowner at (and in) retirement also buffers homeowners against high housing costs at a time when their incomes are at their lowest. Actions by governments to ensure as many women are in this position at retirement as possible will thus also reduce the number of women needing housing assistance in older age. Shared equity[23] or shared ownership models offer a potential solution here – like those already offered by some state governments in Australia.[24] These models offer the opportunity for many disadvantaged and vulnerable groups of women to enter into home ownership at a more affordable rate, thereby gaining a share of housing wealth. The benefits and drawbacks of such models for low-income women, however, need to be investigated.

Ultimately, the discussion shows that it is clearly time to reassess, plan for and accommodate the diverse housing needs of women. The stark reality for many women (and their families) is that they will be less economically secure across their lives and into old age if they do not have access to appropriate housing and their housing needs are not addressed in a more systematic way.

Acknowledgements

This paper draws on research by the author and Professor Andrew Beer and Dr Debbie Faulkner commissioned by the Women's Housing Caucus of South Australia in 2007 (Tually *et al.* 2007). This research was funded by HomeStart Finance, the Young Women's Christian Association (YWCA) of Adelaide, the Women's Housing Caucus of South Australia, Shelter SA and the South Australian Government's Department for Families and Communities.

Appendix Table 3.10 Selected labour force statistics by sex, Australia, 1997–2007

	1997	1998	1999	2000	2001	2002	2003	2004	2005	2006	2007
Labour force											
Total participation rate	63.4	63.1	63.1	63.1	63.4	63.3	63.6	63.4	63.9	64.4	64.8
Males	73.4	72.9	72.7	72.3	72.1	72.0	71.6	71.4	71.7	72.0	72.2
Females	53.8	53.6	53.8	54.3	54.9	55.0	55.8	55.5	56.3	57.1	57.6
Females with children aged 0-4*	47.8	48.2	47.1	49.1	49.7	49.2	49.8	47.5	51.3	51.7	51.3
Persons aged 55-64											
Males	60.5	60.4	60.8	60.7	61.0	61.4	62.8	64.0	65.4	66.9	67.9
Females	31.1	31.6	32.0	34.5	36.1	38.3	40.0	41.2	43.7	45.9	48.4
Males employed part-time – of total employed males aged 55-64	13.8	14.8	14.9	13.9	15.8	16.3	17.0	15.8	16.1	15.9	16.9
Females employed part-time – of total employed females aged 55-64	51.2	49.7	51.0	51.3	51.3	52.3	50.9	50.1	50.0	50.1	48.0
Part-time employment											
Persons employed part-time – of total employed persons	25.3	25.7	26.1	26.3	26.8	28.0	28.6	28.4	28.4	28.6	28.5
Males employed part-time – of total employed males	11.8	12.1	12.6	12.6	13.4	14.2	14.7	14.7	14.8	14.8	15.2
Females employed part-time – of total employed females	43.1	43.5	43.6	43.8	43.6	45.2	45.7	45.5	45.2	45.6	44.8
Females employed part-time – of total persons employed part-time	73.6	73.3	72.7	73.2	72.2	71.7	71.5	71.3	71.2	71.6	70.7
Unemployment											
Unemployment rate	8.3	8.0	7.4	6.6	6.4	6.7	6.1	5.7	5.2	5.0	4.5
Males	8.6	8.2	7.4	6.7	6.7	6.9	6.2	5.5	5.1	4.9	4.3
Females	8.0	7.6	7.0	6.4	6.0	6.4	6.1	5.8	5.4	5.1	4.8

Source: Adapted from ABS 2008e: 1112–13.

Notes:

All data are average annual figures as at June 30 each year, except data for labour force participation rate of females with children aged 0-4 and for females employed without leave entitlements which are at June and August respectively.

*From 2001 the labour force participation rate of females with children aged 0-4 includes females in opposite-sex and same-sex couples and sole parents with children aged 0-4.

Appendix Table 3.11 Average superannuation balances by gender, Australia, persons aged 25–64, 2005–2006

Age cohort	Average superannuation balance (A$)	
	Females	Males
25–34	14,060	19,780
35–44	25,580	46,890
45–54	48,250	93,920
55–59	58,760	126,090
60-64	62,600	135,810
Total	35,520	69,050

Source: Clare 2008: 21 from Survey of Income and Housing 2005–2006, confidentialised unit record file.

4 Women and housing affordability in the United States

Elizabeth A. Mulroy

Introduction

This chapter offers a conceptual framework to help analyze the ways in which unmet housing needs have become a contemporary social problem for many American women and their families. We identify a wide range of differences among women concerning their housing circumstances. Trends show that women with access to higher education have entered the labor market in record numbers, earned living wages, and achieved economic security to live out the American dream of home ownership—increasingly as heads of household. Conversely, a number of social, political, and economic forces converged to create a housing affordability gap for others, as evidenced in employment, housing, and racial disparities data. As the 2006–2009 housing foreclosure crisis swept the country and unemployment rose, the plight of very low-income renters emerged. The at-risk among them—with unstable, low-wage jobs and a multiplicity of special needs—are most likely to become homeless.

Whether owners or renters, women, as traditional "keepers" of the house, have long understood the meaning of housing beyond provision of shelter—that it has unique economic, psychological, and symbolic significance with profound impacts on a family's well-being and quality of life. In 2009, data show that overall, America's housing is improving, and the majority of Americans continue to live in affordable housing. However, other studies suggest that it is the housing condition of the most vulnerable women and men among us that is significantly deteriorating. Home ownership has always been important to Americans, and millions of women and men experience the American dream of home ownership, with its promise of physically safe shelter, status, security, community resources, and the chance to build assets. But in 2007, the homeownership rate fell below 68 percent for the first time since 2002.

Housing problems are concentrated among the lowest income households, affect both renters and owners, and have extended further up the income distribution (Pelletiere and Waldrip, 2008). Millions of people struggle to retain their housing as the foreclosure crisis deepens. Between 2001 and 2005 consider these facts:

- the number of extremely low-income renters increased at a faster rate than any other income or tenure (renter or homeowner) group;
- the only significant population shift from renting to owning was among upper- and middle-income households;
- the number of households facing a severe housing cost burden increased 23 percent nationwide.

The increase in severe housing cost burden was primarily due to the addition of more than one million severely cost-burdened renters (Pelletiere, 2009; Pelletiere and Waldrip, 2008).

Gender inequality and a *blame the victim* mentality contributed to a housing affordability squeeze for women. Gender inequality is a powerful attitude and value system that has persisted in social institutions in the United States for hundreds of years. It is perpetuated through institutional mechanisms that ration access to resources, such as full-time living-wage jobs. This chapter will begin by examining macro-systems forces that provide a societal context for understanding women and their housing circumstances in the United States. We then offer an overview of salient federal affordable housing policy and rental assistance programs intended to make housing more affordable to low-income people. The concept of Housing *Plus* Services is then introduced. This is an approach to providing affordable housing with on-site community-based health and mental health services for special populations of vulnerable women. The chapter then summarizes some key elements of the current national housing crisis based on demographic patterns and trends. Societal forces that facilitated a marked improvement for women and their housing circumstance and factors that constrained them are then examined. In conclusion, the cross-cutting effects of specific social policies and social change initiatives will be set forth.

Housing affordability in a societal context

The concept-in-use for defining housing affordability assumes spending 30 percent or less of household income on housing costs. The technical term *housing cost burden* refers to housing costs that exceed the 30 percent limit. "Rental affordability is by far the most common housing problem found among renters" (Belsky and Drew, 2007: 10), and for low-income renters the problem can be severe. The dilemma for very low-income households is that in the private rental market they typically pay more than 30 percent of income for housing needs, leaving insufficient funds to cover a household's other basic needs such as food, clothing, child care, health care, transportation, and education. Housing cost burdens are considered severe when housing expenses exceed 50 percent of income. The problem is three-fold: household incomes of women who are very poor are insufficient to afford safe, habitable rental units; private market rents are generally high; and there is an inadequate supply of affordable units *available* to the extremely low-income household (Waldrip *et al.* 2008).

Affordable for whom?

A central question posed by policy makers is this: How much can a household afford to pay for rental housing that is physically adequate and not overcrowded? Historically left unasked is another question: Are there gender differences between women and men relative to housing affordability? Housing needs of men and women are assumed to be essentially the same. Decades of studies on race and class disadvantage in America have pointed to the debilitating effects of living in poverty (Squires, 2008; Shipler, 2004; deSousa-Briggs, 2005; Kotlowitz, 1991; Abramovitz, 1988; Wilson, 1987; Polikoff, 1978). Recent studies examining the gender wage gap point to *affordability* as a key gender difference; men earn more than women (Institute for Women's Policy Research 2009) enabling them to more likely afford housing of their choice than can women (Jones-Deweever and Hartmann, 2006; Mulroy, 1995; 1988).

Housing scholar Eugenie Birch (1985) and her colleagues measured housing problems in America by examining the quality of individual dwelling units. Using indicators of physical adequacy, the presence of crowded units, and the existence of excessive costs these researchers found that about 33 percent of all American dwellings were problem-ridden dwellings. Forty percent of these housing units were occupied by women who headed households. The most severely impacted women were found to be single parents and the elderly. Poverty was their commonality. Their meager earnings, public welfare assistance, or retirement benefit, if any, could only purchase substandard housing. Limited sources and amounts of income were key factors in creating economic insecurity, a housing affordability squeeze, and a greater likelihood of living in neighborhoods of concentrated poverty.

Today, there are stark differences in income levels among households referred to as low income, meaning with incomes 80 percent or less of area median household income (see Figure 4.1). When data are examined more finely below the low-income threshold, it was found that there is an absolute shortage of units affordable to those in the extremely low income category. That is, "the gap between what the lowest income renters can afford and what is affordable and available to them exists nationwide, and the indications are that it is growing" (Pelletiere 2007: 12).

- Extremely low income (ELI) 0–30 percent of state median family income: National median ELI renter household income $7,644.
- Very low income (VLI) 31–50 percent of state median family income: National median VLI renter household income $18,845.
- Low-income (LI) 51–80 percent state median family income: National median LI renter household income $29,557.
- Moderate income (MI) 81–120 percent of state median family income:National median MI renter household income $44,844.
- Above moderate income (ABI) greater than 120 percent of state median family income:National median ABI renter household income $76,439.

4.1 Income categories by percent of state median family income. Source: Pelletiere, 2007: 2.

A "blame the victim" bias

A pervasive "blame the victim" mentality has prevailed in the United States that assumes people are poor through their own personal fault. If they are very low or extremely low income and need government rental assistance it is assumed that they just don't want to work. In reality such households are likely already working in low-wage jobs, or they are elderly, or have disabilities. The confluence of class and racial discrimination has, over time, facilitated the marginalization and social exclusion of people perceived to be "different": whites from blacks, rich from poor, homeowners from renters, male-headed households from female-headed households. When combined with gender inequality, a stereotypical image of the most "unworthy" poor emerges. They are most likely very low-income women of color who rent. Federal and state housing policies have been enacted to provide rental housing assistance for some of America's lowest income households. Federal housing policies and programs that form the foundation of the federal response will be discussed next.

Federal housing policy and programs

Legacy of housing policy

Housing reformers in the late nineteenth and early twentieth centuries worked diligently not only to improve the provision of decent and affordable housing, but also to develop minimum standards for light, ventilation, fire safety, and sanitation for the hoards of poor people moving into unsafe, overcrowded tenements in the burgeoning cities of industrializing America. Federal recognition of the importance of housing as a matter of public policy, is set forth in the Housing Act of 1949:

> The Congress hereby declares that the general welfare and security of the Nation and health and living standards of its people require....the realization as soon as feasible of the goal of a decent home and suitable living environment for every American family.

Federal housing policy in the United States has traditionally concentrated on expanding home ownership and improving the physical quality of private rental market units. The policy is generally based on a long-standing perception that poor people are responsible for their own plight and on the capitalist assumption that housing production is a private sector responsibility. Many economists and policy makers still term housing problems a personal shortcoming. A review of housing history suggest that a crisis has traditionally been perceived as a personal problem for certain people and not a societal one that merits government intervention (Gilderbloom and Applebaum, 1988)—*until*—the financial and housing crisis of 2008/2009 cut across class and income lines, adversely affecting millions of homeowners, renters, developers, investors, financial institutions, government agencies, cities and towns, the jobless, and the homeless (Joint Center for Housing Studies, 2009).

Local governments have had a role as implementers of public policy. They have long been given zoning powers to separate the poor from the affluent. The U.S. Supreme Court, in a 1926 landmark case, *Village of Euclid, Ohio* v. *Ambler Realty Co.*, determined that multifamily rental housing (which it considered commercial) ought to be excluded from single- and two-family residential districts. Thus, local governments were permitted to embark on exclusionary zoning practices that remain a barrier to siting affordable housing today.

Establishing criteria for housing conditions

The U.S. Department of Housing and Urban Development (HUD) has defined and measured housing need and developed standards to determine housing conditions nationally. Its criteria for housing conditions include: quality, crowding, and affordability. Of these, the quality of housing and incidents of overcrowding have improved over the last 50 years, largely through HUD's regulations and monitoring. The affordability criterion has remained more elusive.

Calculating housing affordability

At its most basic, the federal perspective on housing affordability is the relationship of rent (including utilities) to income. It is used as a gauge to calculate how much an applicant should spend for its subsidized housing. The most common standard for housing affordability in government programs is 30 percent of income. For millions of heads of households, as the cost of market-rate housing has risen, women's historically low wages, underemployment, and levels of public assistance have prevented access to housing that is affordable without rental assistance. Women have been squeezed as the supply of subsidized rental housing decreased since inception of the programs. Housing assistance has never been available to all those who qualified for it and needed it. It is not an entitlement. Even when congressional appropriations for affordable housing were at their most generous, waiting lists were still long—from two to eight years in some cities. This rationing of assisted housing is a serious problem for women. After a tight budget period when no new applications for federal rental assistance were accepted, in February 2009 the vacation city of Fort Lauderdale, Florida re-opened the applications process. By early morning an estimated 2,000 people stood in line to apply, and most were women.

Housing programs

Today governments provide a range of housing assistance through direct subsidies or through tax incentives. The federal government provides a large housing subsidy for the affluent in the form of tax benefits for homeownership. According to Schwartz (2006) fewer than 7 million low-income renters benefited from federal housing subsidies in 2003, while nearly 150 million homeowners took mortgage interest deductions on their federal income taxes. Federal expenditures for direct housing assistance totaled less than $32.9 billion in 2004; however, mortgage interest deductions and other homeowner tax benefits exceeded $100 billion. Most of these tax benefits go to households with incomes above $100,000. The federal government provides subsidies for low-income renter households in three ways:

1 *Support the construction and operation of specific housing developments.* One example is *public housing*, established by the Housing Act of 1937. These units are owned by local public housing authorities (PHAs). In 2004 there were 1,220,937 units of public housing, representing 18 percent of the total federally subsidized rental housing stock. In the 1990s many large, older, racially segregated, and economically isolated high-rise projects that deteriorated into distressed public housing were imploded or torn down. Reform efforts have tried to replace them with small-scale, scattered-site, mixed-income communities (Turner *et al.*, 2009; Mulroy, 1991).

2 *Help renters pay for privately-owned housing through a rental voucher program.* Begun in 1974 as the Section 8 Tenant-based certificate program, it is the most widely known, and became the dominant form of low-income rental assistance. It provided rental assistance directly to eligible households to help them find their own housing in the private rental market. The subsidy is portable and can move with the family when it wants to relocate. There were 1,803,013 units subsidized in the Rental Voucher program in 2004,

representing 26 percent of the federally subsidized rental housing stock. The Section 8 tenant-based program has often been referred to as a "women's program" because nearly three-quarters of those participating nationwide are female heads of household. Despite documented difficulties with its use (such as landlords discriminating against renting to women with children, or not agreeing to federal lease requirements or fair market rent levels) it has generally well-served single-parent families in their search for affordable housing in neighborhoods of their choice (Mulroy, 1988). The Project-based Section 8 program offered deep subsidies to nonprofit and for-profit developers to build new apartments or rehabilitate old ones. This type of subsidy was popular in the 1970s and 1980s and added 1,709,808 units of affordable housing to the stock, benefiting primarily the elderly and the disabled.

3 *Provide states and localities funds to develop their own housing programs.* These formula-driven Community Development Block Grants give states and localities some latitude to use the federal money to achieve locally determined, community-based goals.

There are a number of other federal housing programs, both old and new, that, when bundled together with state programs and local nonprofit organizations offer limited housing arrangements that serve discreet populations such as persons with HIV/AIDS, or a group home for children in the care of the child welfare system.

Program eligibility

From among myriad types of federally subsidized rental housing programs in operation a total of nearly 6.9 million low-income households currently receive some form of rental assistance. Applicants must meet program-specific income eligibility requirements. Most programs restrict eligibility to households whose incomes do not exceed a specific percentage of the median family income for the area in which the applicant household lives. HUD defines the median income for each metropolitan area and non-metropolitan county (called area median income, or AMI) and sets income limits for federal program participation. Therefore classifications of eligibility are determined on a location-specific basis. Income limits for four-person households, for example, are categorized as low income (80 percent of area median); very low income (50 percent of area median); and extremely low income (30 percent of area median). In a recent US Census Bureau report (2003) of extremely low income renters who comprise a "worst-case" sample of renters it showed that families with children account for nearly two-fifths of all "worst-case needs and elderly households for one-fifth". Female-headed households comprise more than half of all worst-case needs and one-person households make up 44 percent. The vast majority of worst-case renters have incomes below the poverty line (Schwartz, 2006).

Who benefits?

Over the past three decades, the public housing and Section 8 programs have targeted and served the poorest families. Female heads of household and minorities have been key beneficiaries. They represent three-quarters of all tenant-based Section 8 program beneficiaries, 70 percent of Section 8 project-based beneficiaries, and three-quarters of public housing residents have incomes of 30 percent or less of their area median income.

The next section introduces the concept of housing *plus* services, a new direction in programming that integrates community-based housing needs with community-based service and treatment needs of women and children suffering from serious disabilities, illnesses, traumas, or addictions.

Housing *Plus* Services

The goal of Housing *Plus* Services is to help vulnerable people living in the shadows of America's society re-enter that society (National Low Income Housing Coalition, 2002). This approach responds to unmet needs of both men and women who have special needs. Demand for these programs currently far exceeds supply. Requests for housing *plus* services come from a wide range of vulnerable populations whose needs are typically heard first at the local community level.

Incarcerated women

Women exiting prison need affordable housing on release, and for a fresh start, the housing is ideally in a different neighborhood from which they came when they entered prison (Mulroy 2002). Many in this population need treatment for mental illness, or addictions, or childhood trauma—or all of the above (Salzman, 2009). Women whose children became wards of the state before or during incarceration and who seek to regain custody on release need education and systems skills to successfully navigate the child welfare and court systems (Figueira-McDonough and Sarri, 2002).

Women veterans

A surge of women veterans have experienced difficulty transitioning from military to civilian life. In 2008 women accounted for an estimated 5 percent of all homeless veterans, or 6,500 former servicewomen, a figure that is 67 percent higher than the number reported in 2004, according to the US Department of Veterans Affairs. Last year nearly 27 percent of women veterans returning from Iraq and Afghanistan reported to the Veterans Administration Boston Healthcare

System that they had been victims of "military sexual trauma" (MacQuarrie, 2009).

Victims of child trafficking and prostitution

In a recent national crackdown by the Federal Bureau of Investigation on child prostitution, 52 children were rescued from "sexual slavery", but according to child abuse experts not one of the victims is receiving the help necessary to overcome the trauma and re-enter society (Markman, 2009). Experts contend that child prostitution victims require intensive, long-term residential treatment in order that they may be given their best chance at recovery. Experts allege that most of the girls have run away and are on the streets because of sexual abuse at home. But only three such programs that deal with the complexity of multi-layered problems are known to exist in the country (Markman, 2009). Types of service needs have been found to overlap among special needs populations. For example, women with a history of sexual trauma, addictions, and mental illness need treatment for all these problems.

In summary, the future status of all housing policies and programs is caught in the vortex of the housing and global financial crisis. Responsive federal, state, and local budgetary cutbacks threaten the viability of many affordable housing programs including Housing *Plus* Services. For a fuller discussion of housing plus services, the typologies outlined above, and specific programs in operation see http://www.nlihc.org/template/page.cfm?id=43.retrieved 12/15/09; Cohen, *et al.* 2004; Cohen & Phillips, 1997). An overview of the 2007–2010 financial financial crisis will be discussed next.

The 2007–2010 housing crisis

Any examination of women and housing today must consider the context of the current housing crisis because such knowledge establishes the baseline of where the nation is—economically, politically, and socially—in terms of sheltering its citizens. The recent confluence of an oversupply of single-family housing, the mortgage market meltdown, a crisis in the escalating number of foreclosures across the country, collapsing global financial markets, and an increased number of job losses in both the public and for-profit sectors created severe housing insecurity and a tumultuous downward spiral for millions of American households—irrespective of their housing tenure as home owners, condo owners, or renters.

Investors, developers. homeowners, and renters affected

The "housing boom" of 2003–2005 gave way to "housing bust" in 2006–2009 as the combination of higher interest rates and higher housing prices pulled down demand. The complexity of mortgage markets in a weakening economy generated diverse types of foreclosures. One type of foreclosure involved investors and speculators who, in the face of declining real estate prices, gave up properties because their mortgage loan exceeded the properties' values. Many of these are multi-family rental properties (five, six, or more units). Renters who lived in these properties found themselves caught in the foreclosure crisis. Thirty-eight percent of foreclosures nationwide and roughly half of the recent foreclosures in Nevada, Illinois, and New York involved rental properties. In Boston, cases heard for eviction due to foreclosure in the Housing Court at least doubled from 2006 to 2007. It is estimated that 45 percent of the housing units scheduled for auction or owned by banks in New England were rental units (Pelletiere and Waldrip, 2008).

In a second type of foreclosure "sub-prime" loans were extended to people with weak credit histories and low credit scores by lenders working to generate higher profits for themselves. The initial intent of federal housing policy was to increase access to homeownership for a wider spectrum of the American population. Unfortunately many of the non-traditional products exploited vulnerable and unsophisticated borrowers in low-income and minority neighborhoods. Loans in the sub-prime market re-set to higher interest rates and higher fees than conventional loans, significantly increasing monthly mortgage payments to levels lower-income homeowners could not afford. Some housing researchers argue that the real problem was not the availability of non-traditional products *per se*, but the lack of financial education on the part of purchasers. There is an "increasing gulf between financial sophistication necessary to navigate the mortgage market and the ability of consumers to do it on their own. …We now know that the primary mistake of many of these households was to trust their mortgage lender, assuming that lenders would not approve loans that carried substantial risk of failure" (Spader, 2008: 38)

A current dilemma concerns foreclosure risk for credit-worthy people with prime loans who have recently lost their jobs, and who, in the current credit crunch of downsizing, outsourcing, and layoffs, are unable to secure new jobs. The U.S. Department of Labor reported that by May 2009 the unemployment rate in the United States reached 9.4 percent; by November 2009 it hit a troubling 10 percent.

In examining indicators of racial inequality, one study found that the housing crisis had a disproportionate impact on people of color. It found that structural inequalities were "deeply embedded into the rules, the histories, and the cultural currents of this country." Discriminatory practices in lending and the impact of foreclosures were traced back to the historical and structural patterns of racism in the US housing markets (Applied Research Center, 2009).

Experts in housing finance, economics, and demography will be analyzing the impacts of these events for years to come. Social scientists and social policy analysts will also be studying impacts through a different lens—one that looks at the relationship between economic insecurity and housing problems. Women search for economic security, but it is elusive for many. Which factors facilitate it, and which other factors make it elusive? What resources are available to women? To what extent have they taken advantage of these resources? What barriers have been encountered, and with what effect? In the next two sections we examine these questions.

Factors that facilitate economic security

A number of trends coalesced over the past few decades that helped to create more ladders of opportunity for women. First, women's educational attainment lead to increased labor force participation. That, in turn, increased opportunities for higher income employment. Second, once in the labor force in increased numbers, low-wage women chose to join unions, resulting in higher pay and better benefits than their non-union counterparts. Third, large-scale demographic changes suggest that household composition has changed dramatically. Women do not necessarily assume early marriage is their best option; they are delaying marriage, remaining single, living with partners, and heading families as single parents. We will look at these trends next and examine their relationship to housing affordability.

Higher education and labor force participation

Middle- and upper-income American women have improved their housing circumstances through access to higher education resulting in jobs with higher wages, and access to benefits such as healthcare insurance and pensions. Today's young and middle-aged women not only are completing higher education in numbers equal to men, but represent 53 percent of all those enrolled in graduate schools across the country (Hartmann *et al.* 2006). Success stories abound about women, irrespective of race, who have prestigious, visible positions in the private, public, and nonprofit sectors of economic activity. Their wages and benefits have provided the economic security needed to buy or rent housing of their choice at a price they can afford. However, women's historically ascribed roles as wives, housekeepers, and mothers—as well as their personal lack of access to capital—constrained women in earlier generations from pursuing higher education or gainful employment.

Benefits of union membership

To what extent does union membership matter to working women, particularly low-wage workers? Unionization matters. It substantially improves the pay and benefits for women workers (Schmitt, 2008). In 2004–2007 the median unionized woman earned $18.77/hour, compared to $13.30/hour for the median non-union women worker. Unionized women are more likely to have health insurance (75.4 percent) and a pension (75.8 percent) than workers not in unions; those in low-wage occupations earn $11.95/hour, compared to $9.00/hour for non-union women; and close to sixty percent of unionized women in low-wage occupations have health insurance, compared to about 25 percent of non-union women in the same occupations (Schmitt, 2008).

Like the workforce itself, the union workforce has changed dramatically in many ways. It's membership is now almost half women. It is older, more educated, and more ethnically and racially diverse than unions were 25 years ago. In 2008 over 45 percent of unionized workers were women, up from 35 percent in 1983. If current growth rates continue, women will be the majority of union workers before 2020. They are also increasingly more educated. Over one-third of union workers had a four-year college degree or more, and almost half of union women had at least a four-year degree.

Diversity has also increased. Unions have incorporated large shares of Latinos, Asian Pacific Americans, and recent immigrants. However, African American women and men represented only 6.6 percent and 6.4 percent of the membership respectively (Schmitt and Warner, 2009).

By 2008, with the decline of the manufacturing sector in the United States and the decline of unionization in the private sector generally, public-sector employees represented about half of the unionized workforce. Among women, public-sector employees were 61.5 percent of union workers, compared to 38.4 percent for men. To the extent organized labor can retain a viable niche in the economy—whether in the for-profit, public, or nonprofit sectors—there appear to be leadership opportunities for women. Such leadership in the labor movement would likely push policy makers toward more work/family benefits that help low-wage workers in particular care for their families. Such policies could include more paid leave, child care provisions, and workforce housing.

Expanded choices in household formation

While higher education, increased labor force participation, and unionization contributed to an increase in economic independence, shifting demographic patterns show the emergence of an expanded set of choices in household formation as well. The most salient for our discussion is the decision not to marry. More partners are choosing to live together without marrying, whether they have children or not. Unmarried partners will head 5.6 million households by 2020, up from 5.2 million in 2005. The decision can be seen across the life span. For example, 7.4 percent of women ages 45–54 were never married in 2000, up from 4.1 percent in 1980. Among younger women ages 35–44 the percent more than doubled to 13.1 never-married in 2000, up from 5.3 percent in 1980 (Joint Center for Housing Studies, 2008).

A second key trend is the decision to live alone. Persons living alone constitute more than a third of all households—a fast growing demographic. While economically independent women can afford to live alone, three-quarters of this demographic group will be senior citizens over age 65, likely more females than males, and many will be frail and poor.

In sum, the facilitating factors identified here suggest that women with higher educations and high-or middle-income jobs are more likely to have economic security; they can choose whether to be home buyers or renters, and whether to live alone or with a spouse or partner. Unionization has helped low-wage workers increase their incomes and improve benefits packages. Increased resources contribute to overall family well-being by increasing total family income. Policy makers, developers, and community planners are challenged to develop a broad range of housing options to meet the changing demographic needs and housing preferences of a more diverse population.

Factors constraining economic security

While many women achieved economic security as described above, institutional barriers in the workplace and in communities played an important role in constraining others. This section examines gender and racial disparities that reflect long-held societal attitudes. It also examines the effects of geographic disparities—the impact of differential wages based on one's state of residence.

Disparities in gender, geography, and wages

Despite important gains in the labor market nationwide with median annual earnings of $31,800, women employed full-time, year-round in the United States earn only 77.0 percent of what men earn. In not one of the country's 50 states does the typical full-time woman worker earn as much as a typical man. At the present rate of progress it will take 50 years for women to achieve earnings parity with men nationwide (Hartmann *et al.* 2006). Moreover, multiple factors converge to determine a worker's wage: what state she lives in, employment in the "primary" or "secondary" labor market, full-, part-time, or temporary status, and family care responsibilities.

Geography of economic opportunity

It matters where women live. There are geographic disparities among states with some state economies more favorable to women than others (Hartmann, *et al.*, 2006). The District of Columbia, Maryland, and Massachusetts in the northeast corner of the country and states in the Pacific West generally have the highest earnings among women in the United States, while women in the Southeast and a group of states in the northern plains and mountain areas have the lowest. The District of Columbia had the highest median income for women at $42,400, while in Arkansas and Montana women earned a median salary of $24,800, the lowest in the nation. However, state-level policies and economic development alone do not determine individual well-being. The effects of global and national economic events and unstable labor markets reverberate at the state level as well. In some high-earnings states such as Massachusetts, the wage gap between women and men is increasing. In 2008, the median weekly earnings of women in Massachusetts who were full-time wage or salary workers were $762.00, or 76 percent of the median earnings of $1,003.00 of men. This is down from the peak in 2004 of 79.3 percent, according to Bureau of Labor Statistics (2009) Highlights of Women's Earnings 2008 (http:/www.bls.gov/cps/cpswom 2008.pdf).

Occupational segregation

Some of the income differences reflect the nature of the economies in those states and jurisdictions, while others reflect *occupational segregation*—the hiring of men in traditionally higher-paying "male" jobs and women in lower-paying "female" jobs. These blue-collar jobs offer low wages, few if any benefits, unstable employment, and few opportunities for advancement (Ehrenreich, 2001). If these jobs are in the secondary labor market the work is often part-time, seasonal, or temporary. Examples of secondary labor market jobs include domestic service, retail, waiting on tables, farm work, or fast-food counter work. The "pink-collar ghetto" of women's service, manufacturing, and clerical work is generally considered part of the secondary sector. By contrast, the primary sector traditionally offers high wages, steady employment, and career ladders with built-in policies for promotion and higher wages.

Historically, occupational segregation kept minority and white women's earnings far below those of white men.

Low-wage work, unemployment, and poverty

The United States, has, as a country, moved into a period of high-wage and low-wage jobs with acknowledgement that the middle class is vanishing. Globalization, automation, privatization, job outsourcing—both domestic and global—as well as other economic forces contributed to a changing labor market where low-wage jobs have replaced domestic jobs that used to support the middle class.

Recently re-calculated data on poverty rates suggest more Americans live in poverty than was originally estimated:

- About 18.7 percent of Americans 65 and older, or nearly 7.1 million people are in poverty, compared with 9.7 percent, or 3.7 million, under the traditional measure. About 14.3 percent of working age people 18–64, or 27 million are in poverty, compared with 11.7 percent under the traditional measure. Many are low-income working people.
- The northeast and west regions of the country experienced bigger jumps in poverty, due to the high costs of living in cities such as Boston, New York, Los Angeles, and San Francisco (*The Boston Globe*, 2009).

What is noteworthy is the rise in working-aged adults who are employed and still poor. These data suggest that earlier calculations may have overlooked millions of people who are poor because the calculations didn't include costs of rising medical care, transportation, child care, or geographic variations in housing costs and living expenses (*The Boston Globe* 2009).

There is no universal definition of low-wage work, but research on poverty sets the threshold for low-wage work in the range of $9.83 to $11.64 an hour in 2006, or for a full-time worker $20,447 to $24,211 a year. About one in three jobs in the United States is a low-wage job (Boushey *et al.,* 2007). Confinement in unstable low-wage jobs creates higher risks of unemployment, explaining the fact that low-income single mothers experience unemployment rates twice as high as those for all female workers (Amott, 1988). Moreover, the persistent gender wage gap—in 2007 full-time, year-round women workers earned only 78 cents for every dollar earned by full-time year-round male workers—means that families relying on women's earnings alone face greater hardships. One out of every eight women who are sole breadwinners in their families is unemployed compared with one of every sixteen married men. Families of single mothers have a high poverty rate even as women's earnings have become increasingly important to all families with children. (English *et al.,* 2009). These are important data for policy makers, given the demographic projection that the "single parent family"—an unmarried householder with minor children (under age 18)—is projected to increase from 11.0 million to 11.8 million by 2020. Eighty-six percent of single parent families are headed by women, and 14 percent are headed by men (Joint Center for Housing Studies, 2008).

Legacy of slavery: racial and class disparities

The stark reality is that compared to other capitalist-welfare states, economic inequality in the United States has been greater, but it has recently risen to levels not known since the 1920s and far in excess of other advanced societies today (Figueira-McDonough and Sarri, 2002). What sets the United States apart is the nation's legacy of slavery, institutional racism, and the marginalization of African Americans particularly low-income African American women who head families. According to McAdoo (2002), African-American women have a special history, a different voice, one that no other group has, in which during slavery, atrocious acts were committed against them through sexual and reproductive bondage. …. On many levels, these memories are still alive today. Exploitation has not stopped, and continues in many forms…White women do not know or even understand the pain many mothers of present blacks underwent" (McAdoo, 2002, p. 88).

The effects of Hurricane Katrina in the Gulf Coast: a national disaster

A harsh example of race, gender, and class disadvantage in the United States today is the account of women in the Gulf Coast region of Louisiana and Mississippi after Hurricanes Katrina and Rita hit the area in 2005. This Southern region of the United States where the storms hit was the bedrock of slavery, and its legacy left a racially divided South (Jones-Deweer & Hartmann, 2006). Before the storm black women in this region were found to have a high likelihood of already being poor. They had lower educational attainment than white women, earned lower wages, and were under-represented in managerial and professional jobs. Roughly 40 percent of female-headed families who were residents of the city of New Orleans and its broader Metropolitan Statistical Area lived below the federal poverty line, exceeding the national average.

Then they lost their housing. The housing stock in the Katrina-damaged area was decimated. Shortly after the disaster it was found that in all the Katrina-affected areas of the Gulf Coast, 302,000 housing units were destroyed or damaged by the storms. Of these, 71 percent were affordable to low-income households, and 30 percent were affordable to very low-income households. Fully 47 percent of the units in the entire Katrina area were rental units (National Low Income Housing Coalition, 2005).

It is not surprising that as the storm hit and in its aftermath, these households, with far fewer resources than other households, would have difficulty escaping the devastation, relocating to unfamiliar new areas, securing replacement housing, and building new lives and communities.

While institutional barriers helped to create and maintain the disparities discussed above, activists across the country worked tirelessly for decades to right many wrongs. Counter-forces were mobilized to make the workplace, the housing market, and other institutions more equitable. We will now look at specific social movements and social policies that produced social change.

Elizabeth A. Mulroy

Social movements, social policy, social change

While individual initiative is important, motivation alone, is not responsible for the improved status of women in America. The positive outcomes experienced by women who succeeded in the workplace and housing market are the result of over a century of large-scale organizing for the rights of women and labor. These organizing efforts compelled economic and social change that swept across institutions of American society over the past 50 years generated by social movements and the effects of social policies they spawned. A few of the significant milestones are discussed below.

Cross-cutting effects of social policies

The Civil Rights Movement worked to promote racial equality and the Women's Movement worked to promote gender equality. Both social movements challenged in seismic ways old class structures, statuses, and roles. The movements framed social problems in new and fresh ways, and advocated for much-needed social policy responses. Tactics of organizers challenged the status quo. While progress has been slow, advances have been made to reduce gender and racial inequality. The landmark Civil Rights Act of 1964 was a federal response to institutional racism as it was manifest in public accommodation. The Fair Housing Act of 1968 focused on the discriminatory behavior of real-estate agents who were found to be steering African American people looking for housing away from white neighborhoods, thereby maintaining racial segregation in the housing market. The sought-after passage of the Equal Rights Amendment to the U.S. Constitution was not ratified by the requisite number of states. However, the Women's Movement helped to generate other legislation that did enhance women's opportunities, such as the Equal Pay Act of 1963, the Equal Credit Act of 1977, the Pregnancy Discrimination Act of 1978, and the Family and Medical Leave Act of 1993.

As with the Pregnancy Discrimination Act, the Family and Medical Leave Act enabled women to retain their jobs after childbirth and increase their years on the job, important factors influencing both wage levels and participation in pension plans. Increased wages and pensions are instrumental in achieving economic security, housing affordability, and family stability.

Passage of the Equal Credit Act of 1977 required financial institutions to not discriminate against women in their lending practices. Historically women were denied access to credit by lending institutions because of their gender. As recently as the 1970s financial institutions maintained stereotypical assumptions that women were not good credit risks because, as presumed stay-at-home housewives, they would not have the financial capability to pay back a loan. With passage of the Equal Credit Act women's financial independence began to increase as banks and savings and loan institutions complied with the law, and lent money to women who needed it for reasons similar to those of men: to pursue a college or graduate school education, technical and vocational training, start a business, expand an existing business, buy a car, or a home. This milestone legislation served a key bridging function that connected women to much-needed capital.

The cross-cutting effects of these social policies facilitated for women the opportunity to build assets, gain independence, help their families live in safe, affordable housing, and in the long term improve their status and role in society. However, as we have discussed above, institutional barriers continue to remain for many who live in poverty or at the margins of society .

Conclusion

This chapter postulates that *housing affordability* is a key concept in understanding why some women in the United States have unmet housing needs and others do not. Our study suggests that opportunity for women's upward mobility lies in the institutions of society; however, just as institutions can be enabling structures, they have for generations served as barriers. We have documented that women with access to higher education, who work in the primary labor market, and/ or joined unions, and moved to or already live in states that are more favorable to women relative to earnings, have greater likelihood of being economically secure. The changing face of labor shows that women, including immigrants and refugees, are advancing their levels of education, entering and staying in the labor force, and joining unions as a way of attaining greater economic mobility for themselves and their families. Women with low educational attainment and low-wage, temporary jobs with few if any benefits, and little financial reserves struggle with mobility (McKernan and Sherraden, 2008). Those who are asset poor have difficulty coping with life events such as eviction or unemployment. They are less able to take advantage of opportunities that lead to positive housing outcomes such as: saving money for a down payment to purchase a home; saving money for first and last month's rent plus security deposit required to rent a larger or more habitable apartment in a safer neighborhood; saving up for tuition money to pay for educational or training programs; or saving to cover family health emergencies or purchase a car to get to a new job.

State-level public policies can contribute to upward mobility. State economies need to monitor the wage gap and invest in ways that improve women's economic mobility. Some states have already increased the state-level minimum wage, though a multitude of more progressive public policy options have been put forth (see, for example, Ross & Waller 2008). The national pinch point for achieving socio-structural change as we recover from the current recession is acceptance of and support for innovative policies and programs that reframe how we finance affordable housing, how we educate urban youth, and how we create and retain jobs in America in family/friendly workplaces. This is clearly easier said than done in a global economy where capital seeks the least expensive points of production.

Deeply rooted, is the need to eliminate gender and racial disparities in American institutions so that all people have the chance to live in safe, habitable, affordable housing in neighborhoods of their choice.

5 Social change and housing systems

The case of women in Spain

Montserrat Pareja-Eastaway and Teresa Sánchez-Martínez

Introduction

Spain has many Southern European attributes, as well as specific characteristics that make it unique. The impact of these peculiarities on housing systems and social transformation has been widely studied (Cortés, 1998; Taltavull, 2000; Allen *et al.*, 2004; Bonvalet *et al.*, 2009; Pareja-Eastaway and Sánchez-Martínez, 2009). Certainly, some factors that involve difficulties in accessing housing and gender have contributed to the singularity of Spain. Formal equality between genders was achieved later in Spain than in other European countries. Since 1975, efforts have been made to avoid any discrimination in official regulations, documents and norms. Gender equality now exists legally and politically. However, in other spheres of activity, especially in labour markets and in certain social behaviour, Spanish women still fight against direct or indirect discrimination (Hidalgo *et al.*, 2007). A new Ministry of Equality was created in 2004 to prevent gender inequality and to promote positive discrimination.[1]

From a political perspective, the fact that Spain is a relatively young democracy and its late EU membership contribute to its distinctiveness. The decentralisation of the political and administrative structure through the creation of 17 Autonomous Communities (AC) is a dynamic process that has not yet been completed. Education and health were immediately transferred to sub-national level, but housing policy initially remained in the hands of the central government. Progressive decentralisation has taken place since then. The ACs have the highest expenditure (around 75 per cent) on housing policies (Sánchez-Martínez, 2002). Each regional government adopts different approaches to solving citizens' problems. In fact, Spain is currently a patchwork of different situations.

The aim of establishing a relationship between housing and gender is to explore a particular case of social inequality (Bosch, 2006). We consider that a transversal approach is required to properly analyse the gender issue. The study of factors that determine the identification of vulnerable segments of society, such as immigrants or poor households, should include the female perspective

(Molina, 2006). Within these groups, which usually encounter problems in the housing market, the particular characteristics of the subgroup of women require specific housing policies.

The aim of this chapter is to describe the transformation of Spanish society in the recent past, with a focus on the increase in social inequality, the changing role of women, and the shift in housing policies from 'bricks and mortar' general subsidies to more focused and targeted help for certain groups. Simultaneously, we will describe lines of policy action and specific proposals for increasing access to housing according to gender.

All that will be exposed in this work takes on greater relevance today, because the real estate sector has slowed down in Spain, stagnant investment caused by tightening credit, fall in housing prices, a slow-down of economic growth and a rise in unemployment. For many experts, the latter is considered the largest risk factor, which constitutes an area of growing concern as it produces access problems for the weakest segments of the population, and within these groups women are going to require specific attention.

The following research questions will be examined:

1 What main social transformations have taken place in Spain?
2 Does Spanish women's access to housing differ from that of other European women?
3 To what extent does the situation of women differ from that of other vulnerable groups in terms of access to housing?
4 What has been done at policy level to palliate housing deficits for this group?

The introduction discusses the theoretical framework behind the Spanish welfare system. A broad overview of the main transformations experienced by Spanish society is then given, with a focus on the gender perspective. The next section deals with housing issues in Spain, and examines the main problems encountered by women. In addition, we discuss how gender issues have gained prominence in the philosophy and conceptualisation of policies since the beginning of the twenty-first century. The main characteristics of the Spanish housing system will also be described, with a focus on vulnerable groups that have particular difficulty in accessing housing. We will explain current mechanisms for addressing the housing problems of women in Spain. The conclusion describes the challenges and lines of action for housing policies and gender issues.

The welfare state and the gender perspective

This chapter explores the role of welfare states in counteracting the negative consequences of an increasingly globalised world. In recent decades, welfare systems have been forced to cope with drastic socio-economic changes, many of which have been generated by changing productive systems, intensified competition among countries and the increasing risk of poverty in a polarised society.

There are growing income inequalities in the world, and states have a diminishing capacity to redress this unbalanced distribution. Welfare provisions might counteract the trend initiated by globalisation and the internationalisations of economic liberalism. Consequently, there is an increasing need to reform, substitute or complement the classical conception of the welfare state. This process is highly dependent on the starting point of each country and its own set of problems (Mignone, 2005).

The combination of market, family and state characteristics in each country contributes to the specific institutional framework required for society to achieve higher levels of welfare (Esping-Andersen, 1990). Many gender experts (Sainsbury, 1999; O'Connor 1996; Moreno Mínguez, 2005) have criticised the typology established by Esping-Andersen, as it does not include gender aspects such as the role of women and family in the social production of welfare, and the implications of women's participation in the labour market.

Later on, Esping-Andersen (1999, 2002) tried to include the gender perspective in his typology by analysing the contribution of welfare systems to the degree of familialisation or defamilialisation. Defamilialisation is defined as the extent of the family burden that is taken on by states, in particular 'the degree in which welfare and responsibilities related to domestic care are less due to the contribution of the welfare state or the market' (Esping-Andersen, 1999: 51). In this context, the gender perspective is particularly significant in Southern countries.

As indicated by various researchers (Ferrera, 1996; Flaquer, 2002), the specificities of public policies, family and personal relations and family culture in Southern Europe have contributed to the definition of a 'Mediterranean welfare model' in which gender relations can explain the idiosyncrasy of a country's welfare state. Spain, like many other Southern European countries, does not fit perfectly into Esping-Andersen's typology. Many authors agree that an alternative model is needed for Mediterranean countries in which welfare services are part of the family system (Leibfried, 1992; Naldini, 2003; Allen *et al.*, 2004). As Mignone (2005) points out, this has the following implications:

- kinship relations are more important;
- young people become independent at a later age;
- the birth rate is declining.

All of these factors overburden women, who are usually the heads of their families and also try to participate full-time in the labour market.[2] Unfortunately, Spanish social policies do not offer much assistance to women to ensure that there is an appropriate balance between family responsibilities and professional careers. Most social policies involve transferring funds to increase the income level of certain groups. They are not based on making personal social services widely available.

The labour market and the welfare state have led to a varying combination of restrictions and incentives for several generations of Spanish women (Valiente, 1993). Thus, the low participation of women in the labour market in comparison to other European countries could be explained by the family, labour and gender policies involved in each country's welfare state (Moreno Mínguez, 2008).

In the young Spanish welfare state, the growth rate in public social expenditure was highest between 1980 and 1991. However, the percentage (22 per cent of GDP) is still lower than the European average (26 per cent of GDP). The greatest expenditure is on pensions, health and unemployment benefits. Housing has been one of the main problems in Spain since the end of the 1990s, and is clearly one of its weaker factors. Huge rises in house prices and an almost nonexistent social sector have created several emergency situations, due to the inability to provide affordable and decent housing.

Certain groups, which coincide with the most vulnerable social segments, have been negatively affected by the real-estate boom and the lack of targeted housing policies (OECD, 2005). As housing policies are an important cornerstone of European national welfare states, different traditions and philosophies influence welfare systems and, therefore, housing interventions (Balchin, 1996). Since the end of World War II and the alleviation of housing deficits by European governments, the approach to housing provision has been much more heterogeneous. There are major differences between countries, as the role of the public sector has decreased and market principles have been reinforced. In particular, historical heritage in the form of public housing stock, and the strategies adopted to deal with this stock, including privatisation, management and maintenance, are extremely diverse. Southern Europe, and particularly Spain, has a different history and conceptualisation of the provision of social housing (Pareja-Eastaway and Sánchez-Martínez, 2009). Under these circumstances, housing affordability is increasingly problematic in the case of women, given their worse socio-economic conditions.

Social change and gender in Spain

Like many European countries, Spain is facing profound societal change and must cope with emerging problems for which it has no past history of public action. This change involves common issues such as a considerable increase in the elderly population, the emergence of a new household composition, new modes of economic production and a diminishing welfare state. However, despite the general framework of *European-ness*, the importance of each country's context and path has led to particular examples and diverse situations (Crouch, 1999). Historical paths and traditions, as well as the embeddedness of local actors and institutional factors, contribute to the formation of different urban trajectories and, particularly, to urban dilemmas (Marcuse and van Kempen, 2000).

In 2000, Spain's population rose to above 40 million inhabitants distributed within 504,782 sq km. Population growth is one of the lowest in Europe. It stood at 0.096 per cent in 2008, mainly because of the low birth rate (less than 1.38 per woman in 2006). Consequently, the ageing Spanish society has become a government target for social policies, especially those related to health care and pensions. Even housing policies have been considered in an effort to improve the situation of older people. Differences in age and gender are quite evident in Spain (see Figure 5.1). There is a higher proportion of elderly women than men, whilst the opposite is true for lower age ranges.

The consequences of this phenomenon are clearly related to the feminisation of elderly people, who are one of the most vulnerable groups in terms of housing access, social isolation and the risk of social exclusion.

Household size and composition

Since the beginning of the 1990s, the sizes of Spanish and Irish households were among the highest in the EU (EU15). However, new member states from Eastern Europe have even bigger households. The downward trend in household size in Europe is mainly due to the huge increase in the number of individual households. they represent over 70 per cent of all households in Sweden, Finland, Germany and

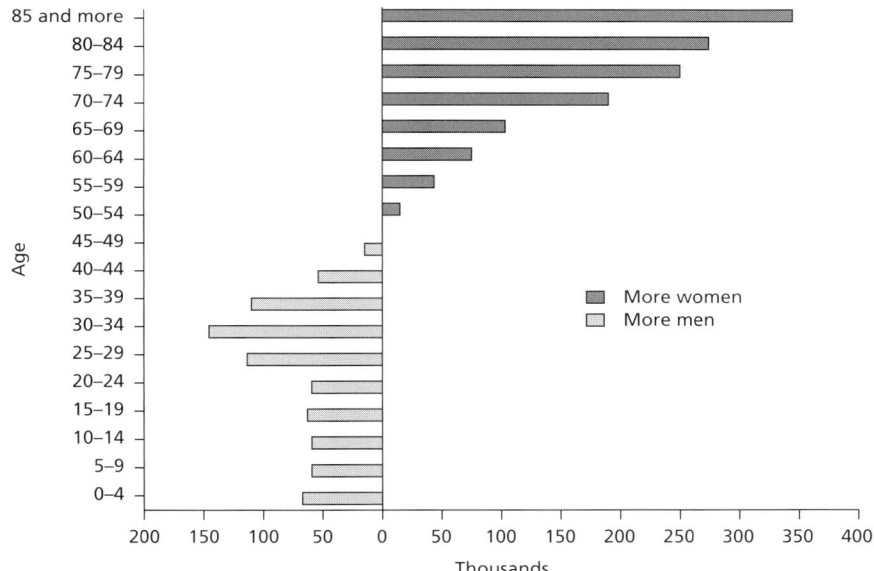

5.1 Differences in numbers of males and females by age group (in thousands) (2008). Source: National Institute of Statistics of Spain (INE): INEBASE, Revision of Padrón Municipal, May 2009.

Denmark. However, in Spain, less than 20 per cent of all households are individual (INE, Household Budget Survey, 2006).

Household size clearly influences the amount and characteristics of housing demand over a certain period of time. However, in addition to larger household sizes, other variables need to be taken into account to understand the relationship between household composition and housing need. These include young people's emancipation, the residential independence of elderly people, and new forms of co-habitation (i.e. living apart together). In these aspects, Spain has certain characteristics that determine its divergence from other European trends.

One of the main consequences of late emancipation in Spain is the delay in maternity. Maternity frequently coincides with marriage and the formation of a stable household (Leal, 1997), which also influences the drop in fertility rate (Figure 5.2). According to Eurostat statistical data, Spain has one of the lowest birth rates in the European Union. The number of children per woman was 2.8 in 1975 and dropped to 1.38 in 2006.

The rise in single adult households with ages between 35 and 55 has an enormous influence on housing demand and rented housing in particular. Uncertainty about household projects usually leads people to temporarily rent dwellings until decisions have been made, especially in terms of location and size. Certainly, more rented housing is occupied by single adults (either separated or divorced) than by

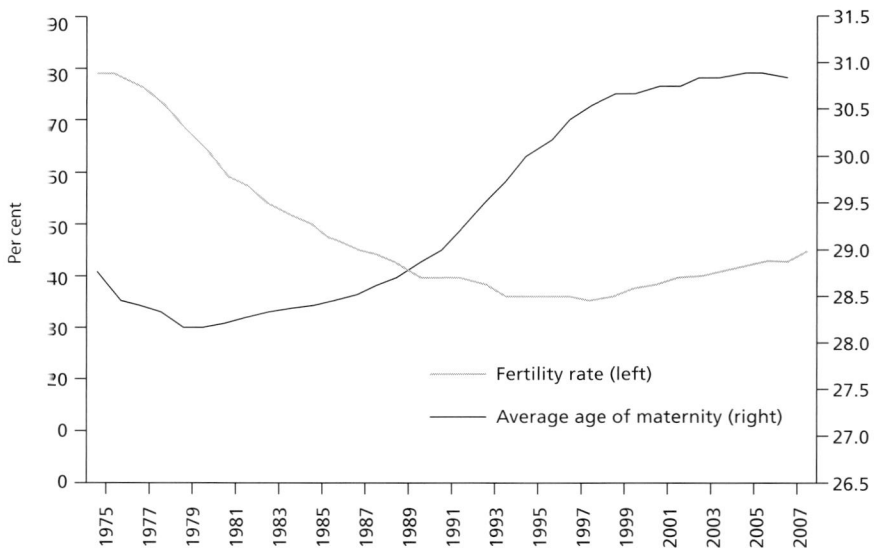

5.2 Age of maternity and fertility rate in Spain (1975–2008). Source: INE, Census of Population and Housing (several years) and estimates of the INE.

other groups. As we will see later on, this issue affects women who are heads of households in particular.

In addition, a considerable change is taking place in Spain in values and other aspects that are related to understanding of the family. The number of separations and divorces has increased significantly in recent years.[3] The Divorce Law, which was passed in 1981, and the incorporation of women into the labour market are two of the main factors behind the increase in the number of single parent households since the beginning of the 1980s. According to the Continuous Survey of Family Budgets (National Institute of Statistics, 2007), households made up of an adult plus one or more children now represent 7.3 per cent of total households. Previously, a traditional and conventional family model prevailed, because of social and religious attitudes. Spain has one of the lowest rates of single-parent households in Europe, although this rate has increased considerably since 2005. In the last few years, from 80 to 90 per cent of single parent households were headed by women. The identification of civil status is a good indicator for analysing and determining reasons for single motherhood. Separation and divorce are the main causes of this new family situation, followed by widowhood, which was the principle reason in the past (See Table 5.1).

With respect to age, it is remarkable that most heads of single-parent households were under 45 in 1996 and 2008. Women were the heads of around 90 per cent (in both years) of the single-parent households. This percentage decreased as households aged. Most single-parent households had only one child, and this percentage increased over time (68.3 per cent in 2008 against 64 per cent in 1996). The larger the family size, the higher the probability that a women is the head of the household.

The absence of a partner has a major impact on the participation of women in the labour market, especially when they are fully responsible for their children. This is a forced situation, as women in such situations cannot choose whether or not to work. The urgent need to receive a salary puts them in the precarious situation of maintaining a double working day (at work and at home), due to the lack of services that support and facilitate the work–life balance. As a result, living conditions for such women are harder than for others. Therefore, single adult households that are managed by women are the group that is at greatest risk of social exclusion.

The arrival of immigrants

During the 1980s, low numbers of immigrants played an import role in bringing the Spanish economy in line with the European context. Immigrants were mainly highly skilled workers who helped international branches of companies to set up businesses in Spain. Immigrants tended to be middle to high-income families, with no housing problems. By the 1990s, the situation had changed dramatically: immigrants came to Spain for economic reasons, in the search for better social conditions and an

Table 5.1 Single parent households, absolute numbers and percentages (1996 and 2008)

	Single-parent household (000s)		Of which percentage are women	
	1996	2008	1996	2008
Total	287.6	451.50	86.23	86.07
By marital status				
Married	25.9	93.70	58.48	92.64
Single	17.2	50.50	96.14	79.01
Widowed	93.1	52.20	80.77	77.20
Divorced	151.4	255.00	91.15	86.90
By age				
Under 45 years	173.5	301.20	90.37	89.04
45 to 59	100.1	148.80	82.52	80.38
60 and over	14.0	1.50	61.43	53.33
Number of children				
1 child	18.0	308.30	86.3	85.01
2 children	84.4	114.40	85.5	88.29
3 children	15.7	26.60	87.9	87.59
4 children and over	3.5	2.20	98.2	100.00
Economic activity				
Active	–	395.20	–	84.94
Employed	–	325.70	–	83.88
Unemployed	–	69.50	–	89.93
Non-active	–	56.30	–	94.14

Source: INE.

improvement in their economic situation. According to Spanish data (INE), in 1998, foreigners represented less than 2 per cent of the total population, while by 2008 the percentage had reached almost 12 per cent (See Figure 5.3).

In most cases, immigrants come to Spain for reasons related to the labour market. Broadly speaking, immigrants are either employed mainly in the service and construction sector or are highly qualified and attracted by the job opportunities offered by companies in Spain. Spain is seen as a gateway to Europe by many immigrants from less-developed countries. However, Spain's openness to external markets also attracts transnational companies, which tend to set up branches in Madrid and Barcelona. This situation brought the first flows of qualified workers to these cities.

According to Pajares (2009), there is a noticeable difference in the reasons given by male and female immigrants in residential permit applications (see Table 5.2). Work is the main reason for remaining in Spain that is given by men, although this figure dropped considerably in 2008. In contrast, women's reasons for requesting residential permits are more balanced between family regrouping and work, both of which increased considerably in 2008.

Immigrant numbers increased from 719,647 in 1998 to 4,473,499 in 2008. In 1998, 48.18 per cent of immigrants were women. This figure dropped to 46.03 per cent in 2008. Table 5.3 shows that more immigrant women have participated in the labour market since 1999 (from 35.41 per cent of the labour force to 42.19 per cent in 2008). Female immigrants work mainly in the service sector, usually as

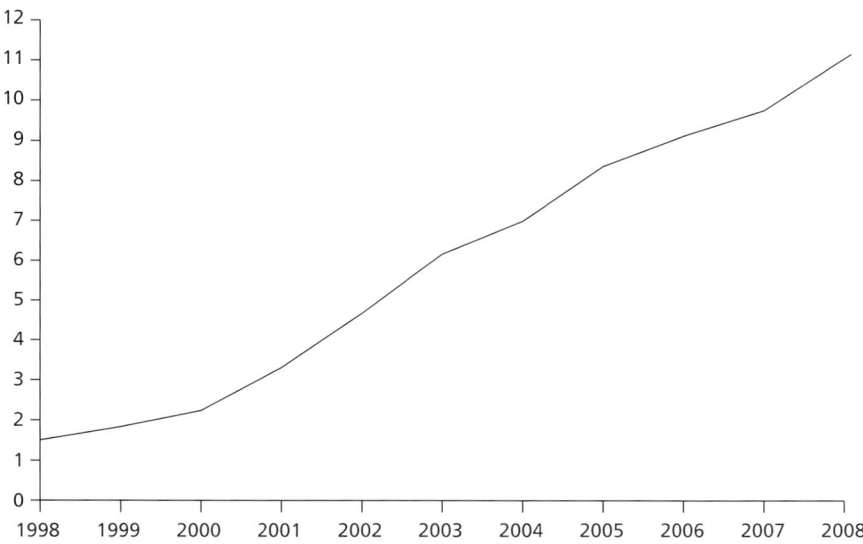

5.3 Percentage of immigrants in total population (2001–2008) Source: INE, Census and Padrón (several years).

Table 5.2 Reasons for requests for residential permits within the number of visas awarded (2007 and 2008)

	Total		Family regrouping %		Work%		Study %	
	2007	2008	2007	2008	2007	2008	2007	2008
Men	138,727	128,825	28.5	32.0	58.3	51.3	12.2	15.4
Women	142,026	159,315	42.0	39.0	38.5	40.7	18.0	18.7

Source: Pajares, 2009.

domestic workers or in care services, where they provide care for elderly people and children. More than a third of immigrant women come from Latin America. The relative weight of female immigrants from Latin America is higher than that of men (54.21 per cent in 2008).

Until quite recently, the living conditions of immigrants in Spain were not known about for several reasons: first, and most important, the irregular situation of many immigrants hindered data collection. Official sources only tend to consider legally registered immigrants, which masks the real flow of arrivals. Second, when immigrants obtain Spanish nationality, which usually occurs once they have found employment, they no longer count as foreigners. This means that their situation cannot be followed up. In addition to the reduction in arrivals since 2005, other problems now characterise this group, particularly in relation to the effects of economic crisis.

In Spain, housing prices are extremely high in urban areas that contain well-developed industrial or service sectors. Insofar as immigrants must live next to their place of work, they have high housing costs and, all too often, find themselves living in marginal neighbourhoods. However, immigrants who live in rural areas and work in the agricultural sector face a better housing situation. Prices are considerably lower than in the cities, and the quality of dwellings is often higher, as they may be in better condition than in urban areas.

As a general rule, it is important to stress the low level of urban segregation in Spain, given the structure of the housing system. The dynamics that affect neighbourhood change and patterns of segregation in Spain respond to the combination of certain variables that directly affect the housing system. Various historical processes and traditions related to housing intervention in the residential real estate market have determined differing future scenarios in terms of housing policy. Structural change in the socio-demographic composition of society influences patterns of housing policy design. This, together with the global trend of economic liberalisation, forms a reference framework for the analysis of the relationship between housing policies and welfare measures. Urban segregation and social exclusion takes many forms and occurs in private owner-occupied neighbourhoods: combating it is a hard issue for policy-makers. As Pareja-

Table 5.3 Working immigrants[a]: age, sector and country of origin (1999 and 2008)

	Working immigrants (000s)		Of which women (%)	
	1999	2008	1999	2008
TOTAL	334,976	1,882,224	35.41	42.19
By age				
Between 16–29 years	101,058	550,717	35.50	42.10
30–45	171,228	978,499	34.30	40.70
45–59	56,312	324,846	36.20	43.80
60 and more	6,378	28,162	28.20	39.90
By sector				
Agriculture	46,515	225,690	8.20	25.21
Industry	28,358	153,094	19.04	24.27
Construction	33,295	270,109	4.80	4.63
Services	226,179	1,233,328	47.59	55.75
Unknown	629	3	23.53	33.33
By country of origin				
Europe	136,071	699,401	38.47	40.86
Africa	101,239	324,014	15.12	21.68
North America	3,943	7,197	44.05	46.19
South and Central America	61,713	710,680	60.55	54.21
Asia	28,835	136,607	37.17	35.16
Oceania	357	836	36.97	33.73
Stateless and others	2,818	3,489	35.33	36.89

Source: *Anuario de Estadísticas Laborales*, Ministerio de Trabajo y Asuntos Sociales.
Note: a Contributing to social security.

Eastaway (2009) points out: 'Spain does not have large areas where social housing is predominant. Although this might create problems of affordability, especially in the initial phases after their arrival, immigrants are forced to look for other shelter alternatives within the existing housing system' (Pareja-Eastaway, 2009, p. 531).

As with gender, the implications that arise from low levels of residential spatial segregation in Spain and the lack of social housing point to the relevance of other factors – social, demographic and cultural – as key elements of integration, as much for immigrants in general as for women. Thus, immigrant women present a varied array of behaviour and attitudes in relation to the host country or neighbourhood with which they deal, above all, with respect to their origin and socio-cultural habits. In this sense, the housing system does not act as a differentiating element, but rather facilitates the integration of the feminine collective, leaving their possibilities of connection with the host culture to other activities which concern women (i.e. taking the children to school, going to the doctor, using public spaces). This is what the welfare state should stress: the specific improvement of the channels of integration for women.

In addition, there is a hidden housing demand, which is higher than the existing direct demand, as two or more families live together in many foreign households. As soon as their working (income) conditions improve, immigrants will probably move out from these overcrowded dwellings.

Changes in the labour market

With respect to the economic cycle, the unemployment rate reached its highest level in 1994 (24.5 per cent) and then dropped until the beginning of 2000. Due to the consequences of the economic crisis, there have been in the first trimester of 2009 over 4 million unemployed people, which represents 17.36 per cent of the active population (National Institute of Statistics (INE), Active Population Survey- Encuesta de Población Activa (EPA), first trimester 2009). The figure is slightly higher for women (18.01 per cent). Spanish, Greek and Italian women have the lowest participation rate in the labour market in Europe, with the exception of single mothers, who are the most active group in Spain.

The dynamics that have affected the role of women in Spanish society are remarkably distinct from other scenarios. Spanish women entered the labour market later than women in the rest of Europe, as the 'male breadwinner' model was maintained for longer than in other countries. Women's decision to participate in the labour market has affected fertility rates enormously (which are now the lowest in Europe) and strengthened family ties, given the lack of public child care. In addition, the arrival of (women) immigrants, especially from Latin-America, has reactivated the participation of Spanish women in the labour market, as domestic activities are now mainly performed by the newcomers.

As seen in Figure 5.4, employment rates are lower for women than for men, and female unemployment is higher and more sensitive to the economic cycle. As shown, the labour market situation has worsened since 2007 as a result of the severe crisis affecting the economy in general and the Spanish property market in particular.

Although the female activity rate has increased considerably in the last three or four decades, women participate in a segmented labour market, as they are underrepresented in long-term contracts and overrepresented in temporary jobs, the informal economy and unemployment (Valiente, 1998). In addition, there is considerable gender variation in the population that works full-time or part-time, as shown in Figure 5.5. About 11.3 million men work full-time, whilst only 6.5 million women are in full-time employment. In contrast, there are a higher number of women in part-time employment (2 million) than men (0.5 million).

When we analyse why people decide to work part-time, 30 per cent claim that it is to take care of young children, the elderly and the disabled or because of other household responsibilities. Around 97 per cent of the people who give this reason for part-time work are women (See Table 5.4). This confirms the unequal allocation of household responsibilities between the genders in Spain. It also highlights the number of women that abandon the labour market for family reasons, and the high number of women (3.3 million of 9,770,000 inactive women in 2007) that declare themselves non-active and do not look for a job or require leave because of their

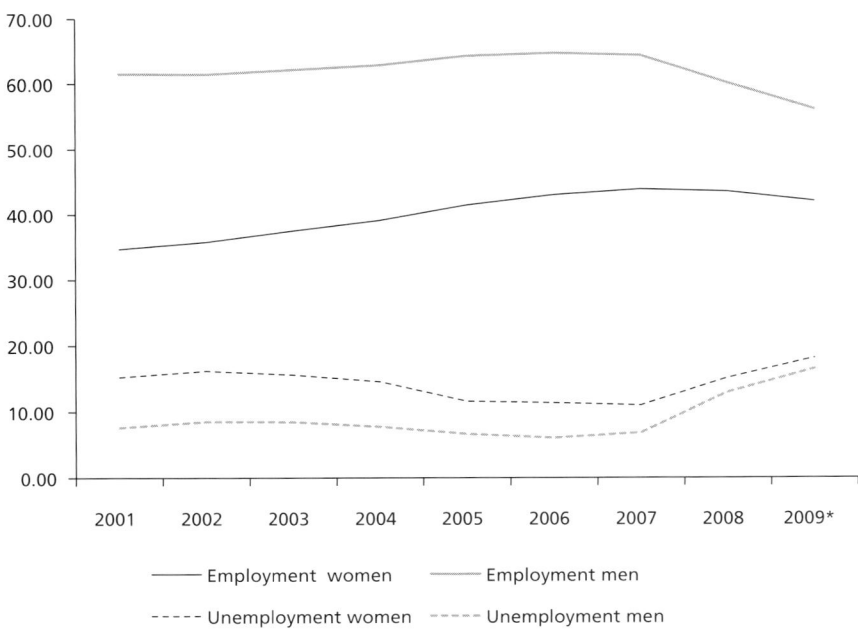

5.4 Employment and unemployment rates by gender (2001–2009). Source: INE, Active Population Survey – Encuesta de Población Activa (EPA), (several years). Note: Data from 2009 to III quarter.

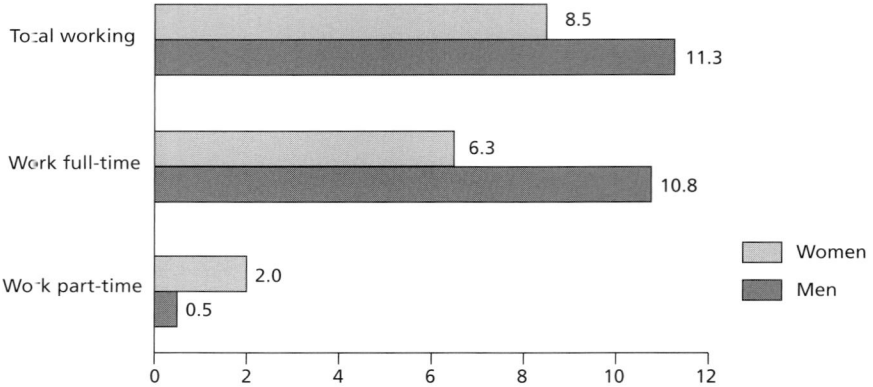

5.5 Employed population by gender and working time in millions (2008).
Source: INE, Active Population Survey – Encuesta de Población Activa (EPA),
(several years).

household responsibilities. Certainly, kinship relationships (and duties) in Spain limit labour opportunities for women, as the availability of social support services is still limited.

On average, Spanish women earn 20 per cent less than men, which is above the European average (15 per cent). Salary differences are higher in the private labour market and lower in the public sector. The wage gap varies with age, and stands at as high as 36.2 per cent for older women. As in many other European countries, differences progressively increase with the level of education: the higher the education, the higher the wage difference between women and men (see Table 5.5).

Economic discrimination occurs in women's active lives and during their retirement. If we analyse the pension system for retired people and widows in Spain, differences are, on average, between 30–35 per cent. The difference is particularly notable for elderly women, as widow pensions,[4] which represent 82 per cent of the total number of pensions, have the lowest standards (INE, Population and Housing Census, 2001).Therefore, many elderly women have extreme economic difficulties (see Figure 5.6).

In summary, in addition to the lower economic capacity of households maintained by women, there is noticeable discrimination, as they earn less than men for the same type of job.

Risk of social exclusion

The right to decent housing is usually included in developed countries' constitutions. When this requirement is not fulfilled, social inequality arises, particularly among the most vulnerable groups. In Spain, housing problems greatly affect young people, immigrants and other weak demand segments. It is important to assess gender in this

Table 5.4 Labour market and kinship duties (2005–2007)

	Number (000s)			Of which percentage women		
	2005	*2006*	*2007*	*2005*	*2006*	*2007*
Abandon work for family reasons	241.5	272.6	237.3	96.07	95.82	94.73
Not active, as they care for children, adults or disabled people in the household	3,586.0	3,370.0	3,444.0	97.80	97.04	96.46
On leave to care for children	18.9	20.2	33.0	95.30	95.33	94.06
Employed part-time, as they care for children, adults or disabled in the household.	566.2	574.8	653.0	97.60	97.20	97.20

Source: Encuesta de Población Activa, INE, Active Population Survey–Encuesta de Población Activa (EPA), (several years).

Table 5.5 Average hourly earnings of women relative to men, 2002 (%)

| | By age | | | | By education level | | |
	<30	30–39	40–49	50–59	Low	Medium	High
EU25	92.0	80.1	69.6	97.2	86.8	75.2	68.6
Denmark	86.4	84.2	82.7	78.0	84.8	80.5	82.7
Germany	90.5	78.3	72.5	67.6	82.0	79.6	74.0
Greece	95.2	86.4	74.0	61.7	74.4	78.8	69.7
Spain	88.4	83.6	72.9	63.8	75.1	72.0	70.5
France	99.3	88.8	79.8	74.2	91.2	89.6	68.8
Italy	93.0	87.2	80.9	72.8	83.0	82.2	65.2
Netherlands	84.6	88.8	71.3	69.5	80.0	76.0	80.9
Portugal	94.5	83.9	74.9	74.0	79.4	79.2	75.0
Sweden	92.0	87.7	83.5	80.5	87.5	85.7	77.2
United Kingdom	87.2	75.2	62.8	58.7	73.8	73.1	72

Source: Eurostat, (2005). Gross Earnings in Europe. Main results of the Structure of Earnings Survey 2002.

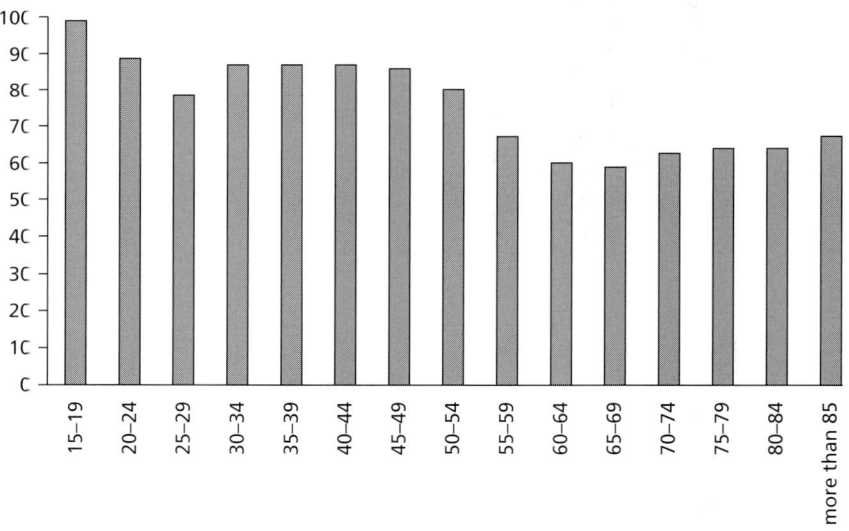

5.6 Average monthly retirement and widows pension of Spanish women with respect to men by age (in percentages). Source: Ministry of Labour and Social Security (2006) and own calculations.

context. The gender perspective is not usually included in traditional approaches, even though it represents one of the most evident situations of social exclusion, given the higher unemployment rate, lower income and greater job instability that directly affect women. In Spain, there is a certain degree of feminisation of poverty, particularly in later life and in single parent households. In fact, higher proportions of elderly women aged 65 and over live in households at risk of poverty[5] than their younger counterparts in most EU states (Eurostat, 2008). As Figure 5.7 shows, in 2005 an average of 21 per cent of women were at risk of poverty compared to 16 per cent of men. There was a higher risk for women once they reached 65. The proportion varied across countries, but in the Spanish case, it stood at around 32 per cent.

Spain has a paradoxical combination of quite a large share of the population who are close to or below the poverty line, but relatively low levels of social exclusion (measured by the number of homeless people, crime rates, infant mortality rates, one-parent and one-person household rates). Two facts may explain this situation. First, solidarity within the family in Spain may lessen the impact of unemployment and job instability (Leal, 2005). The persistent lack of a welfare state has been mitigated by family, and especially by women. This may be a reason for the low fertility rates. Second, protection and social welfare systems have developed in recent years, although social expenditure per capita is still under the European average (Navarro, 2000). Additionally, the housing system that promotes the ownership of social housing could be considered a key element, in terms of the low level of social exclusion.

Social exclusion negatively affects the following groups: households led by women with children in their care; elderly women living alone, usually in sub-standard housing; separated or divorced women; abused women; and immigrant

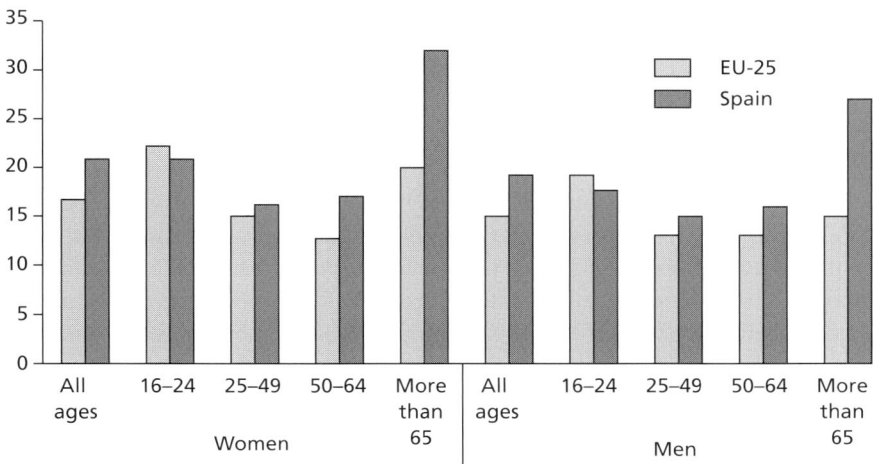

5.7 Risk of poverty in Spain and EU25, by sex and age (2005). Source: Eurostat (2005).

women. In general terms, their situation is usually characterised by the following aspects:

- a lower economic status, given that women receive lower income than men for the same jobs;
- a worse labour market situation, in which they suffer from discrimination that varies according to the economic activity;
- less social and cultural capital;
- fewer possibilities for enjoying leisure time; care of the sick, childcare responsibilities, as well as the management, undertaking and organisation of domestic aspects of life are often exclusively carried out by women.
- they mainly live in urban areas, and have family support to help them to combine work and family obligations.

Their situation is worsened by the narrowness of the Spanish housing market, in which owner-occupation is predominant, rented housing is scarce and social public housing is almost non-existent. Therefore, socio-economic groups that find it difficult to buy a house or pay the rent are faced with considerable distress.

In 2005, a study was conducted by the Sociological Research Center (CIS) that identified the main reasons for social discrimination in Spain, apart from economic reasons. Table 5.6 shows that gender is still one of the main reasons for discrimination in the Spanish population.

Housing system and gender in Spain

Housing systems involve various aspects that are directly or indirectly linked to gender issues. Access to a decent house, mobility within the residential market and the right to adequate housing are some of the critical issues in which gender might play a key role. In this section, we will focus on the difficulties in accessing housing that are encountered by certain groups. Thus, we will increase our understanding of this topic, which is a problem of social inequality (Bosch, 2006).

Spain still has certain unsatisfied segments of demand. In some cases, this is due to the impossibility of buying or renting a house (i.e. young people), in others it is the result of low standards of housing consumption. Young people, elderly people, single-parent households and immigrants are some of the most significantly affected groups. As gender issues are defined throughout this chapter as a transversal characteristic that affects all of the aforementioned groups, women, in all possible situations (for instance, immigrant women or women as the main breadwinners in a household) may be in situations where there is a risk of social exclusion. Simultaneously, women are likely to encounter the main difficulties in accessing housing.

Spain is well-known for the uniqueness of certain attributes of its housing system: the predominately owner-occupied housing market, the scarce supply of

Table 5.6 Reasons for discrimination (2005)

	From 18 to 25 years	From 26 to 40	From 41 to 60	61 and above	All ages
Disabled	3.8	2.5	5.3	2.9	0.6
Not enough education	3.1	3.2	5.6	0.7	4.3
Old	0.9	0.6	2.1	13.8	4.5
Unimportant person	7.0	5.4	4.8	3.8	5.0
Skin color	9.2	5.3	5.4	3.9	0.5
Poor	4.1	7.8	6.1	8.2	6.9
No friends	13.9	12.4	6.4	3.9	8.6
Immigrant	11.5	11.9	11.1	8.0	0.6
Woman	12.1	17.1	11.9	4.1	11.4
There is no discrimination in Spain	3.2	4.2	5.0	5.3	4.6
None of the above	26.4	23.4	27.2	27.9	26.1
Do not know	4.2	3.8	7.3	11.6	0.9
Did not reply	0.4	2.4	2.0	1.9	0.9
Total	100,0	100,0	100,0	100,0	100,0

Source: Sociological Research Center (CIS) (2005).

public housing, and the huge increase in housing prices since 1999, are some of the most frequently analysed and researched aspects (Pareja-Eastaway and San Martin, 2003). These singular features provide a somehow incompatible arena in which social relations take place and evolve. Thus, low rates of household mobility, youngsters leaving home later in life and powerful social and family ties might be understood as direct consequences of such a peculiar housing situation.

Changes in the work history of individuals with higher levels of economic instability or even a slight decrease in their income level will frequently affect general household consumption and, in particular, could lead to an undesired change in their housing situation. However, according to European Community Household Panel (ECHP) results analysed in Pareja-Eastaway and San Martin (2003), the changes in employment in Spain were more noticeable than variations in household structures. The relative importance of ownership was highlighted. Once a household acquires a home, it offers its members permanent shelter, in better or worse conditions, regardless of the household structure.

In Spain, residential and job mobility is far below the European average.[6] Data reveals a lower percentage of households changed their jobs in Spain than in the rest of Europe during the 1990s. In this period, Spain was characterised by low economic growth and moderate job creation. The number of households that changed jobs and moved to another house stood at 11.5 per cent in Spain, which is a similar percentage to the European number (12.8 per cent). Low job mobility is one of the main structural problems in the Spanish economic system (Barceló, 2006). Cultural linkages and the high cost of moving, particularly in terms of housing, are the main reasons for the lack of labour mobility.

The rental sector in Spain is usually associated with less solvent demand segments that are unable to access owner-occupation for economic reasons. Hence, the percentage of households that are led by women is higher in this regime (Bosch, 2006).

Considering age, the percentage of young people (between 16 and 29 years old) living in rented housing is higher than other age groups. Temporary and insecure jobs as well as low salaries are the main reasons for this situation. Young women encounter even more difficulties in accessing housing, as they leave the parental home earlier than men. A higher percentage of young women opt for rented housing (38 per cent against 29.1 per cent for men) (See Figure 5.8).

In the remaining age groups, the percentage of rented dwellings is higher when the household is led by a woman. However, in the case of separated or divorced people, a higher proportion of men live in rented dwellings. This situation is understandable, as children in Spain are usually cared for by their mothers, who keep the parental home.

The elderly also have problems in accessing housing, due to a combination of poverty and the low quality of dwellings. Elderly people tend to have a precarious economic situation,[7] which restricts their ability to fulfil their housing needs. This situation particularly affects women, as they have a longer life expectancy and a higher risk of poverty. In fact, women live in the oldest segment of the housing stock, which is also the most deficient. As Table 5.7 shows, a higher proportion of elderly women (10.4 per cent) than men (9.31 per cent) live in sub-standard dwellings. In addition, women face the usual problems encountered by the elderly population, such as accessibility and mobility, mobbing – understood as the landlords' strategies, legal and illegal, to evict tenants who pay very low rents – difficulties in paying the rent and isolation when they are disabled.

The group of women who are heads of household is also at risk of residential exclusion. The risk is due to discrimination against women in the labour market, as explained above: they have lower salaries, distinct participation in the labour market (lower number of working hours), higher unemployment rates and difficulties in achieving a work–life balance. As we will explain later, Spain does not provide enough public support for the care of children and other dependents or direct subsidies to fund extraordinary expenditure for extra family burdens. The situation is even more dramatic for single parents, as they only have single income sources. Given the scarcity of affordable dwellings (rented or owner-occupied) and the lack of public (social) housing stock in Spain, these groups have more residential problems than in the rest of Europe, in which one of the main clients of social housing are single parent households.

Other groups of women that require special attention, given that they are at high risk of social exclusion and have difficulties in accessing the labour market and,

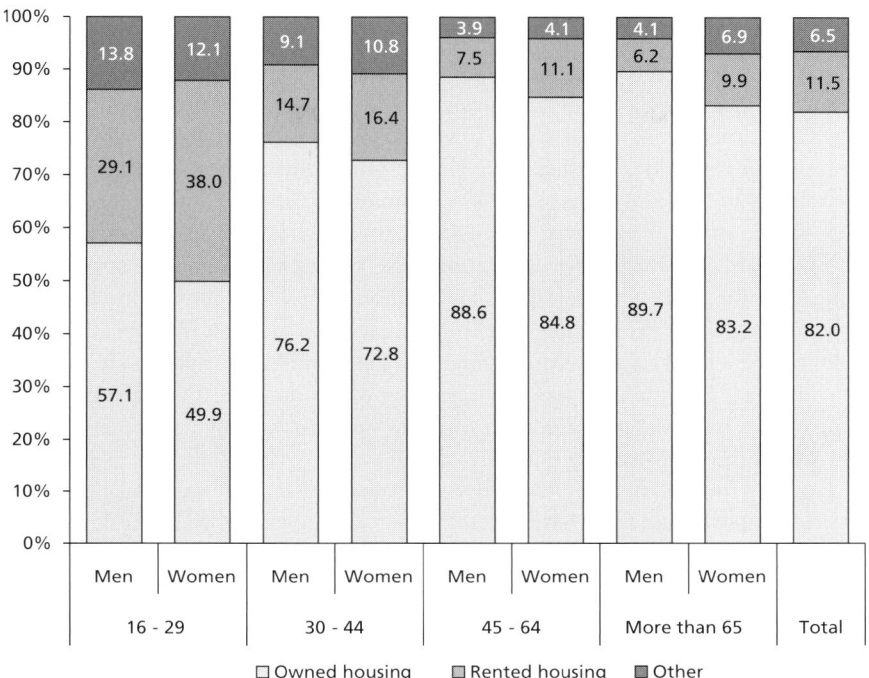

5.8 Tenure by gender and age (2004). INE, Living Conditions Survey (2004).

Table 5.7 Housing quality, age and gender (2001)

	Total population (%)			65 or over (%)		
Housing quality	Men	Women	Total	Men	Women	Total
Sub-standard/highly deficient	7.98	8.07	8.02	9.31	10.04	9.73
Good	91.6	91.5	91.55	90.27	89.5	89.83

Source: INE, Population and Housing Census (2001).

consequently, decent housing, are victims of gender violence (abused women), immigrants, ex-prisoners and prostitutes. Abused women urgently need available housing in which to stay and recover before they can continue with the normal course of their lives, usually far away from their town or city of origin. They also need to achieve economic and residential autonomy, in order to live without their former partners. A law was passed in 2008 that establishes the following: "abused women will be considered a collective of priority in facilitating their access to social housing" (Organic Law 1/2004, BOE 313, pp. 42173). [8]

Montserrat Pareja-Eastaway and Teresa Sánchez-Martínez

Housing policies and the gender approach

As a starting point, it is of critical importance to understand that from the end of the 1980s, a dynamic process of decentralisation of housing and urban policies took place at national level, with a shift to lower tiers of government, that is, autonomous communities and local authorities. The responsibility for housing policy was completely transferred to autonomous communities. However, given the key role they play in the whole country, the national government still defines programmes in which direct subsidies for the acquisition, rehabilitation and construction of rented dwellings are considered, while the autonomous communities are in charge of managing these programmes, as they receive applications for subsidies from potential beneficiaries and decide which ones are suitable. In addition to national programmes, ACs draw up their own housing programmes. Consequently, public expenditure is considerably decentralised towards ACs, which spend around 75 per cent of the total housing budget.

Housing policies in Spain have played a role in the current imbalance in tenure (Pareja-Eastaway and San Martin, 2002). In fact, strategies to cope with affordability problems have allowed the development of a large real estate sector, as a result of 'bricks and mortar' subsidies. From the mid-1990s, a shift occurred from support for supply to more direct aid for demand. At the beginning of this change, support was offered to a wide spectrum of potential beneficiaries, including low- and medium-income households. Currently, both national and regional plans offer a set of housing programmes to facilitate housing access, especially for certain groups. The last National Plan for Housing and Rehabilitation (Plan Estatal de Vivienda y Rehabilitación – PEVR, 2009–2012) increases the potential beneficiaries of public housing support by taking into account new groups that are in highly vulnerable situations.

The following groups have priority access to social housing (Vivienda de Protección Oficial, VPO)[9] and additional support: elderly and young people, abused women, single-parent households with children and other groups that are defined as at risk of social exclusion, which are selected by each AC. Consequently, the strategy behind the PEVR considers as a key line of action an increase in the stock of rented, social dwellings, that are either new or second hand, renovated or requalified[10].

The gender perspective is included in the following issues:

- priority access to social housing (VPO) and direct subsidies for certain groups, including single-parent households and abused women;
- direct subsidies (up to €12,000) for certain groups, including single-parent households and abused women.
- protected rented dwellings for vulnerable groups, residential areas with group facilities, services and rent that is under the market average;
- protected rented dwellings under the Special Regime, for low-income households, and certain groups, including single-parent households and abused women.

In addition, the 17 Autonomous Communities have included the gender perspective in their programmes, mainly by focusing on *ad hoc* subsidies for the vulnerable groups (i.e. elderly people, single-parent households and abused women, among others) that are considered by national programmes.

Spanish policies clearly stimulate new subsidies for the particular problems of women. However, certain groups still deserve more attention (elderly women, immigrants or prostitutes). The success of initiatives is limited by the existing housing supply, in particular, the almost neglected public and rented housing sector. Although the main objectives of national and regional plans focus on stimulating the rented sector, the visible outcome is still poor. However, the current economic crisis and the particular situation of the construction sector in Spain might contribute to promoting the rented option, private and public, to solve the problem of the huge amount of unsold housing.

However, housing policies on a single basis do not solve the precarious situation of many women. Following the EU's Fourth Action Programme for Gender Equality (1996–2000), Spain has improved its support for women during maternity leave and has also facilitated direct support for working women living with dependant people (elderly or disabled). The Dependency Law, Law 39/2006, is a relatively recent example of the public authorities concern with the need to regulate and ameliorate family burdens for women.

To sum up, an integrated approach is needed to strengthen the positive outcomes achieved by a change in the direction of housing policies. Collectives that are in the greatest need for support, in particular, women, need to be specifically targeted.

Conclusions

The institutional changes that Spanish society has been experiencing for more than three decades during long-standing economic growth are reflected in the current situation of families and households. Although the situation follows the general trend observed in other European societies, differences can be found, as a result of the specific characteristics of the country.

Regulatory measures to eliminate gender discrimination have been introduced in Spain since the beginning of the democracy, due to the increase in social awareness of gender equality. Such measures are having positive effects, but are still insufficient.

The following objectives need to be met: to attain conciliation and co-responsibility in society, to make domestic, family and productive activities compatible, and to follow an equal pattern with respect to gender, with no creation of undesired labour costs and no impact on generational replacement. To achieve this, three areas of responses to the changing situation need to be mobilised: the public sector (through policies and a legal framework to facilitate gender equality), companies, and social attitudes, especially with respect to breadwinners.

With respect to the first area, in spite of advances in the legal framework, Spain continues to have a structural deficit in services that is directly related to child care, both in terms of day-care centres and pre-school education. To eliminate gender inequalities in opportunities, flexitime and suitable work schedules need to be consolidated, care services for children and dependent people need to be enhanced, and tax incentives introduced for second household incomes. With respect to the second area, companies have not yet fully explored all the possibilities that the legislation offers. Thus, many working women cannot gain access to them. In Spain, a stagnant, traditional, catholic culture prevails, together with gender discrimination. Precarious work and living conditions affect women more than men, as they are less employable, are at greater risk of unemployment and a higher proportion of them work part-time. In addition, they are subjected to wage discrimination and occupational segregation.

Finally, the third area, society, requires long-term adaptation and lacks an immediate reaction to current events and transformations. The huge impact of female participation in the labour market, which has changed women's role from housewife to household income earner, has had many effects that are already noticeable in Spain. They relate to the delay in maternity age, the decrease in the number of children and the upward trend in separations and divorces. This has occurred in a context of generational change, since young women now have better access to a high level of education, which suggests that parents (and society) have marked preferences for equality. However, this trajectory will only be achieved in the medium to long term.

Certain groups of women in Spain belong to the group that has the highest probability of living with symptoms of social exclusion. In recent years, a process of poverty feminisation has taken place in Spain. Single-mother households, immigrants, abused women and prostitutes are some of the highly vulnerable groups that have difficulties in terms of the labour market and in housing access. As a result, the housing conditions of these groups are usually sub-standard and located in the most deprived neighbourhoods.

In order to progress in the inclusion of the gender perspective in housing policies in Spain and to raise social awareness of this problem, a more integrated housing policy needs to be developed. As a first step, it is essential to increase the public rented housing stock to meet the aforementioned needs of all underprivileged socio-economic groups. This process requires time, public resources and collaboration between the three tiers of government, that is, national, regional and local. In addition, nonprofit organisations, foundations or cooperatives could be used as housing suppliers. This might aid the public role of providing affordable and suitable housing for all.

Current efforts to increase and improve housing subsidies and grants to facilitate housing access directly affect women. Positive discrimination could be established in favour of these groups, by giving them priority as beneficiaries of public housing and as recipients of direct public aid. However, it should be stressed that the isolated positive action of housing policies in favour of women might not be completely successful if it is not accompanied by other related measures concerning integration into the labour market, the provision of adequate services, and direct intervention regarding their integration into the closer social community.

6 Women's housing in Sweden

Ingrid Sahlin

With its nine million people, Sweden is generally regarded as a relatively wealthy nation with high housing quality and gender equality, compared to most other countries in the world. However, this country has not always had such a position, and it is also an assumption that is increasingly being questioned. From the late nineteenth century up to the present time, national and local housing policies have emerged, flourished and faded away, somewhat parallel to the development of public housing. Charities and poor laws have been supplemented or replaced by social services and social securities, which have grown in scope and strength, stabilised, matured but then somewhat declined. The establishment of a comprehensive welfare state from the mid-nineteenth century on encouraged and enabled gender equality and the public sector constitutes an important labour market for women. Some basic elements in family policy were formed in the 1970s and still work to support for families with small children. Along with the historical development of society, women's position in the family and in the home, as well as on the markets for labour and housing, has changed dramatically – although in different ways, depending on class, generation, national origin, family situation and urbanisation.

After an outline of the development of housing and family policies during the past century, I will provide brief accounts of 'household' and 'family' as central cultural institutions, as well as present the Swedish forms of tenure and how they relate to class, ethnicity, national origin and type of household. The third section deals with recent changes with regard to housing, family, income distribution, and benefits and social insurance for parents and children. In the fourth section I discuss threats and options regarding access to housing and security for women in different situations. In order to better illuminate historical change and contemporary varieties I will especially highlight the housing situation of single women in different stages of life, and mothers in different classes and family situations.

Historical background

Housing was, for a long time, inseparable from work and family[1] and, conversely, only unemployed people were regarded as homeless. The one who employed a worker or a servant was also expected to house the employee and his family, if it was a man, whereas female servants often had to leave their masters' house when and if they got married or had children. From 1847 on, secularised poor boards were responsible for housing poor people without a family or an employer, and towns and cities began to establish poor houses. Women made up the majority of their residents (Engberg 2005), and taking care of or nursing other paupers in the same room was sometimes a condition for their access (Sahlin 2008). Some charity associations offered special housing to poor widows of civil servants or well-off citizens (*pauvre honteux*) (*Nordisk Familjebok* 1888: 917–18).

Sweden was industrialised rather late, compared to many other Western countries, but the process took off in the latter part of the nineteenth century. Although the industrialisation involved many small towns and rural areas, it also caused domestic migration and urbanisation. Many industrialists built houses for their workers, but since others failed to live up to this moral duty, homelessness, overcrowding and unhealthy housing conditions became growing problems in the cities. In the big cities some philanthropists built model rental houses for disciplined and decent working-class families, while emergency shelters were established for single men. By the end of the nineteenth century a for-profit rental housing market emerged (Wallengren 1994). However, the shortage and deficiencies of housing for poor workers prevailed.

The emergence of public involvement in housing for families

The central state long refused to take any action with regard to the growing housing problems. Nevertheless, as poverty and disorganisation was increasingly seen as a source of political and social unrest, they gained political weight (Sheiban 2002: 138). In 1890, the royal government established a committee to seek measures to promote owner-occupied housing for workers (*Egnahemskommittén*). Its ultimate purpose was to counteract emigration to the United States, but also to make workers less inclined to strikes, protests and political opposition. Mortgages and house ownership *per se* were supposed to affect their worldview and endorse contentment; 'a settled, independent stock of workers always constitutes a safe and reliable element of society', wrote the committee (quoted in Eriksson 1990: 348).

Faced with increased overcrowding and homelessness in the beginning of the twentieth century, and especially during the depression in the 1930s, municipalities sometimes arranged emergency housing for homeless families, and Stockholm City started to subsidise permanent housing for poor families. However, the actual allocation of the dwellings in these 'cheap houses' was the target of criticism as it:

> … failed to reach down to the strata of society which are most needy in economic terms, and on whose behalf these houses were in fact constructed and the subvention admitted. The rents have turned out to be too high … In fact, these dwellings are inhabited by a relatively well-off population.
>
> (Myrdal and Myrdal 1934: 137)

On the other hand, where towns and municipalities did succeed in housing poor families with many children, the dwellings tended to be of poor quality and severely overcrowded (ibid: 138). This dilemma has remained a leitmotif of Swedish housing policy, which so far has abstained from any 'social housing'.

The Union of Housing and Family Problems

By the 1920s and 1930s, women in the cities usually left working life when they got married, or at least when their first child was born. However, for unmarried, divorced and widowed women it was difficult to support a family.

> Achieving a regular paid work was not easy for the single mother. If she got one, she had to count on women's wages – not wages for male breadwinners. If she had children, it was not easy to take a work. If she could not let her child to a relative or neighbour, there might be a place in any of the city's nurseries – but the nursery, in contrast to the *kindergarten* of the bourgeoisie, was stained by poverty, as it was intended for 'poor and working mothers'.
>
> (Franzén 1992: 325f.)

In an even worse situation were those women who had nowhere to live. In the 1930s, there were some shelters designated especially for women in Stockholm. According to Franzén (1992: 255) their aim was to save 'poor child-bearers', 'single women', and 'women looking for work' from 'the dangerous city'. These target groups also indicate that a mother without a husband, a working mother, and a single woman looking for work were all to some extent regarded as urban anomalies in a time where working class women were expected to find housing either through marriage, a position as maid or with their original families. But this would all change in the decades to come.

National democracy was adopted in 1921, when women, too, could vote for the parliament (men had achieved this right three years earlier), which gradually broadened the scope of parliamentary issues. In the beginning of the twentieth century and especially in the 1930s, social engineering was introduced as a new view on planning and politics, while the ideas of social hygiene encouraged thorough planning, control and rational organisation of homes and family life in order to make the current and future population clean, strong and healthy (see, e.g.,

Schmidt and Kristensen 1986, Nilsson 1994). In this context, a new, radical view on housing and planning emerged.

Although it had been acknowledged already in the nineteenth century that the wealth and health of families and children were closely related to their housing situation, these two problem areas were not theoretically and politically married until in the 1930s, through the writing and thinking by the Myrdals.[2] While Gunnar Myrdal was a political economist, Alva Myrdal was primarily interested in social policy and family issues. In their book on the population crisis (*Kris i befolkningsfrågan*), they claimed that a contemporary drop of the birth rate was to a great extent due to deficient housing – too small, unsound and overcrowded dwellings – and the fact that women through childbirth had to leave the labour market and became tied to the home, unless they could afford to employ nannies and maids. The declining birth rate was interpreted as a result of planning for fewer children, since many families had started to use contraceptives and (illegal) abortions. This trend would not stop, claimed the Myrdals, unless the living conditions of families improved. They provided a very engaged description of the socially deprived life of the modern 'miniature family' with only one or two children. The upbringing situation was said to be 'pathological', and the life of a housewife 'unreasonable', and even 'unbearable' when housework was being rationalised (Myrdal and Myrdal 1934: 303).

Many of the suggestions and recommendations in the book were realised in subsequent legal reforms, such as (universal) child allowances, free school meals, free medical care, public day-care for children free of charge, subsidised rents, and improved dwelling standards.[3] In 1935–45, a number of multi-dwelling houses were constructed with special state subventions and the flats let with subsidised rent to families with three or more dependent children (SOU 1935:2). Like their municipal forerunner, however, these houses for large families (*barnrikehus,* also called *Myrdalshus,* Myrdal Housing) were criticised for either being of too low quality and stigmatising, or failing to reach the target group. Many of them were built and managed by a new kind of public company, the prototype of the municipal housing companies (MHCs), which later on were established in all municipalities and today control all public housing in Sweden.

Swedish housing policy 1945–1990

From the late 1940s up to 1990 – the age of maturing modernity in Sweden – a comprehensive, general housing policy was developed and implemented, based on growing state subventions and extensive municipal control over planning, construction and allocation of housing. It was designed by a team of scientists (including Gunnar Myrdal) working closely with the Social Democratic government in the Housing-Social Committee (SOU 1935:2, SOU 1945:63, SOU 1947:26). A main ambition was to avoid the kind of stigmatisation associated with selective social housing. In the years 1946–47 the conditions for MHCs were settled, and the municipalities were obliged by law to plan for and provide housing for their inhabitants. In addition, state subsidies for housing construction and tenure neutral housing allowances for families and pensioners were introduced.

Many thoroughly planned neighbourhoods, still appreciated by their residents as well as urban planners, were built in the 1950s, but the shortage of housing prevailed. The large-scale, industrial production of one million dwellings on virgin land that took place between 1965 and 1975 did manage to eradicate homelessness and unhealthy housing conditions and to modernise the housing stock. However, the resulting new neighbourhoods were questioned from the start, and became the target of severe, lasting disapproval. This was especially the case for large residential areas with high-rise multi-dwelling houses in the outskirts of the big cities. Thousands of households moved there from inner city blocks under demolition and mixed with migrants from other parts of the country or the continent. Despite repeated rebuilding, these residential areas are in many places still regarded as unattractive and periodically dogged by high vacancy rates. They are to a growing extent inhabited by immigrants, and although they originally housed workers, the rates of people who are unemployed or dependent on social welfare are often high – and increasing, since the segregation has amplified in recent years (NBHW 2006).

The development of a family policy

At roughly the same time as the general housing policy was modelled, a new family policy was outlined, although it was not introduced until in the 1970s. Echoing the Myrdals, Swedish family policy has aimed at improving the living conditions of families in order to affect the birth rate, which has indeed been more stable and higher than in many other European countries (Social Insurance 2008). The focus of reforms has shifted from housing and child allowances in the 1930s and 1940s, to public day-care and separate income taxation for married people in the 1960s, in order to enable and encourage mothers to return to the labour market after having a child, while later reforms have comprised right to parental leave from employment and, importantly, social insurance during such leave after child birth. Nowadays a father is granted a certain quota of the time with parental insurance. This makes it possible for both parents to keep their employment and income while one of them stays at home with their child, until it can be left in public day-care, which the municipality is obliged to arrange.

Institutions and identities

The household and the family – ideals and reality

Housing is tightly connected to the idea of a household, which, in turn – at least during the twentieth century – has been very closely related to the nuclear family. This was not always the case, though. In the nineteenth century, the households of craftsmen and farmers often included youngsters from other families, who worked as servants or apprentices, while working-class urban families, in order to afford their rent, often had single lodgers in their home. More often than men, unmarried women stayed with their parents or their siblings' families, sometimes for their whole life.

Despite this tradition and the fact that of all households today, only a minority comprise a couple with children (who may not be their common offspring), the nuclear family with husband, wife and only common children has come to symbolise the modern household. Also many same sex couples strive for a traditional family life with marriage, children for whom both parties have legal custody, and a conventional family life style. Almqvist (2004) claims that the ideal of a single-family house has grown even stronger among Swedish women lately. Taken together with the increasing proportion of owner-occupied flats, and the fact that the tax regulations favour owner-occupation to renting, such tendencies might be viewed as a sign of a wish for an extended private space, but also of a possible return to traditional gender roles.

This is a paradox in view of the widespread single life. One fifth of all women aged 30–40, a quarter of those aged 40–64 and more than a third of those 65–74 years old live as singles (Statistics Sweden 2008: 19). In fact, less than every fifth household corresponds to the nuclear family which is obvious from Table 6.1.

Table 6.1 Types of household in Sweden in 2008 (children: 1–17 years)

Type of household	%
Cohabiting with children	18
Cohabiting without children	28
Single women with children	4
Single men with children	2
Single women without children	19
Single men without children	17
Other family units	13
Total	100

Source: *Statistics Sweden*, 2010: 16.

Besides that less than half (46 percent) of all households comprise couples, most of these have no children at home and many are not married, at least not when they start to live together and before they have children. In 2005, women were on average 32 and men 35 years old when they first married, while the corresponding mean age for childbirth was 29 and 31, respectively. By the age of 35, only 47 per cent of all women were married (Social Insurance 2008: 5).

There was always a tiny proportion of people preferring collective (non-institutional) living, but except for regular flats shared by poor students or special student housing, specially designed 'collective housing' often include self-contained flats, while the communal areas are confined to rooms for meals and activities.

Tenure, class and national origin

Housing is tightly related to class. Not only the size and comfort of the home, but also its location and tenure has much to do with the income, employment and resources of the household. Families with several children have, in general, fewer resources than couples without or with only a few children, and single parents are on average substantially poorer than other kinds of household.

There are four official kinds of tenure in Sweden: 42 per cent of all dwellings are owner-occupied (single-family houses), 17 per cent are private rental and about 16 per cent public rental, while 20 per cent are owned by tenant-owners societies (TOSs) (Magnusson and Turner 2008: 281). Although a TOS is the legal owner of an estate, each member has an exclusive right to dispose of a specific flat (for which a monthly fee is paid) and this right can be sold on the market to the highest bidder and be used as a security for house loans. In attractive sites, especially in big cities, the prices of such dwellings can be very high.[4]

The Tenants' Act does not distinguish between different kinds of landlord. Rents for flats in private and public rental houses, which are almost exclusively mult -dwelling ones, are settled in negotiations with the Tenants' Association at a similar level; MHC rents are related to the 'use value' of the dwellings and based on the real cost plus a determined profit of public housing, and the private rents determined accordingly. Although it is generally considered cheaper in the long run to own one's home, public rental is the most common form of tenure for low-income people and for households receiving social welfare, especially in metropolitan areas (Magnusson and Turner 2008).

There is an obvious inequality between different kinds of household, since single-parent households – the great majority of which are female-headed – live in high-rise, multi-family and rental buildings to a much higher degree than do couples – with or without children (Table 6.2).

Half of all single parents with three or more children live in multi-dwelling housing with three or more storeys, while only one third live in detached houses, which is where three quarters of couples with the same number of children live.

Table 6.2 Number (in thousands) and share (percentage) of households (heads 16–74 years old) in Sweden living in single-family houses, terrace houses or in multi-dwelling housing of 1–2, 3–4 and 5+ storeys, respectively.

Family type	Number (in thousands)	Single family	Terrace house	1–2 storey	3–4 storey	5+ storey	Home for elderly etc.
Single without children	2109	33	7	11	30	16	3
With 1 child	126	26	8	13	37	15	2
With 2 children	92	29	16	13	30	11	0
With 3+ children	28	32	5	13	42	8	0
Cohabiting without children	2322	55	9	7	19	11	0
With 1 child	645	56	12	5	15	12	0
With 2 children	895	68	15	4	8	5	0
With 3+ children	349	74	7	4	9	7	0

Source: Statistics Sweden (2009: 232), Table 10.2.

Most flats in multi-dwelling houses have only two or three rooms, besides the kitchen. Put differently, the distribution of housing only partly reflects the size of the households; to a much higher extent it seems to mirror class and the uneven distribution of wealth and income between families with two breadwinners, and single-parent households.

We also know that many parents with several children are immigrants living in overcrowded rental flats (Popoola 1999). Immigrants in general more frequently live in high-rise buildings and less often in single-family houses and terrace houses than people born in Sweden (see Table 6.3). However, the housing situation for people from other Northern countries, Great Britain, Germany and the United States is similar to that of those born in Sweden, while people who migrated here from Africa live far more often in high-rise buildings in 'million-programme housing' (Sahlin 2005).

Since the early 1990s, most municipalities expect their MHCs to be run in a business-like manner, which is why the responsibility to accommodate households that fail to get access to regular housing has shifted to the social services. Hence, they rent houses, flats or rooms and sublease them to homeless clients on special terms, with special rules of behaviour and without security of tenure. This system has given rise to a fifth kind of tenure, comprising a 'secondary housing market' (Sahlin 1998). Today, a minimum of 11,000 flats are sublet in this way (NBHBP 2003). On a given night in 2008, women made up the majority (52 per cent) of the residents in such temporary housing which was not associated with treatment or care (NBHW 2009: 37, 119). These figures do not include dwellings and rooms sublet to new refugees, nor accommodation for asylum-seekers. By January 2010, 35,073 asylum-seekers were registered with the Migration Board, which housed 15,760 of them in reception centres (Migration Board, www.migrationsverket. se). Refugees without documents and asylum-seekers, who choose not to stay in reception centres, mostly stay with relatives in already overcrowded dwellings.

Table 6.3 Percentage of inhabitants aged over 18 born in Sweden or abroad, respectively, living in various types of housing. Average 1999–2001 (excluding persons living in institutions)

				Multi-dwelling housing		
	Number (in thousands)	*Single-occupancy*	*Terrace house*	*1–2 storey*	*3–4 storeys*	*5+*
Born in Sweden	6,085	51	9	8	22	10
Born abroad	755	28	9	10	33	23
Total			9	8	23	11

Source: ULF surveys. Special reworking by Statistics Sweden (Sahlin 2005).

Another form of tenure is institutional living, especially for elderly people in need of care and people with intellectual disabilities. Former care institutions have been transformed into special housing with services, where residents pay a monthly rent for their rooms, although such housing is allocated according to the need for services and care. Women make up the great majority (70 per cent) of the residents aged 65 or more in special housing for elderly people, but only 40 per cent of tenants in special housing for disabled people younger than 65 (NBHW statistics).

Recent changes and their impact on women's housing situation

In recent decades welfare policies have been de-stabilised in Sweden, while housing policy has virtually vanished. Gender equality remains high on the agenda but the possible progress has slackened in an age where state funding and involvement in private lives are contracting for ideological as well as financial reasons.

Housing policy and housing market changes since 1990

In 1991, a new conservative government implemented a 'system shift' through deregulation and withdrawal of state expenses in housing. The housing ministry was closed down, allocation and provision of housing were de-regulated, rents increased, municipal housing assignment agencies closed and subventions for construction were severely cut. A serious financial crisis in the early 1990s aggravated the situation on the housing market, and for many subsequent years, Sweden's rate of housing construction was the lowest in the OECD (Sahlin 2001). The Social Democratic government in power from 1994–2006 did little to restore housing policy; a part of its saving programme entailed that housing allowances were reduced continuously from 1997.

Because of the previous success of, and consensus on, the modern Swedish housing policy and the role of the MHCs, the latter's *raison d'être* had not been detailed in the law. Since the early 1990s these companies fail increasingly to house the most vulnerable groups, but the political resistance towards 'social housing' prevails.[5] The fact that the MHCs nevertheless house a higher proportion of low-income residents and vulnerable groups (Magnusson and Turner 2008) could well be interpreted as a market effect; some – but far from all – of the estates of the MHCs belong to the locally least attractive ones. Because of a low rate of construction, population growth and demolition of hard-to-let real estates, the vacancy rate has been very low in all kinds of housing in recent years (NBHBP 2009).

Stimulated by permissive legislation, favourable taxation and a mutual expectation of profit, approximately 115,000 rental dwellings – most of them privately owned – have been converted into TOS-housing between 1990–2007 (Statistics Sweden,

2008:139). Since 2006 the conservative national government and the municipal majority in Stockholm have encouraged tenants in MHCs to organise TOSs and buy their homes. As could have been expected, poor tenants cannot buy, and tenants in estates in bad conditions do not want to. Hence, there is a risk of a gradual residualisation of public housing in less attractive sites, while in the central parts of the cities a great share of previously rental housing is now owned by TOSs. In addition, we are witnessing a gradual growth of owner-occupation on the housing market.

Social security and benefits for families

Regardless of income, parents of all children – up to the age of 16 or until they leave compulsory school – are entitled to *child allowances* of 1,050 SEK/month and child; for the second child an extra 150 SEK is added, and for the third one 454 SEK more. Families with four children get 1,614 SEK more than the basic allowance per child (Social Insurance, http://www.forsakringskassan.se/privatpers/fora_der/barnet_fott/barnbidrag). There is also a right to public day care for children 1–12 years old (when they are not in school) at a fee, which is income-related up to a limit. Children start school at 7; at age 6 they are entitled to three hours per day in preparatory school free of charge.

In recent decades Swedish family policy has been aiming at increased gender equality among parents. Irrespective of whether they live together, both parents are responsible for their children. If they do not cohabit, they mostly share the formal custody for their children, who still tend to live most of the time with one of the parents, most often the mother. If the other parent cannot pay *maintenance support*, Social Insurance can give an advance and/or a supplement up to a limit (presently 1,273 SEK per month and per child) until the child is 18 or, if still in education, 21 years old. This benefit – in most cases eventually recovered by the parent who failed to pay in time – somewhat reduces the financial gap between single parent families and families with two breadwinners.

Through *parental insurance* a parent who stays at home with a newborn child is entitled to 80 per cent of the usual income (up to a limit) for 13 months, but through collective bargaining agreements many get more, e.g., state employees are entitled to 90 percent of their usual income during parental leave (Social Insurance 2008: 13). A fixed, low sum per day is offered for another three months. The days with insurance can be split over time, to enable part-time work for several years, as an alternative. Parents are supposed to share these 16 months as they like, but each parent has to use at least two months, or they will be lost. The aim is to increase the likelihood that fathers take parental leave for each child. On average, men have used up only 20 per cent of the days with parental insurance for a child, although the share is slowly growing (Social Insurance 2008: 15). Reasons claimed for this outcome are that the father is more needed at work, that the mother is more keen to stay home and that the financial loss for the family is greater if the father takes parental leave, since he earns more (ibid.: 15). Yet another benefit is *temporary parental insurance*, which makes it possible for a parent to stay home from work with 80 per cent of the salary when a child is ill and cannot attend day-care.

Housing allowances used to be an important instrument to ensure access to decent, regular housing for poor families and to enable them to keep their homes. This was due to the fact that they covered a large part of the rent (or the interest for mortgages) for low-income parents. However, after a revision of the legislation in 1997, ever fewer households are eligible for this benefit. In 2008, only 142,800 families, of which 64 per cent were single mothers, got such benefits (Social Insurance, statistics, 2009). Pensioners with low pensions have another kind of rent allowance, while young people with low incomes may get a smaller allowance. Low-income people older than 28 without children and not being pensioners are not entitled to housing allowances, but if they receive social welfare, this includes moderate housing costs.

Income distribution and labour market situation

In Sweden, the labour market participation rate among women is approaching that of men. In 1970, the share of women aged 20–64 in the labour force was 60 per cent, of men 90 per cent. In 2007 the proportion was 81 and 87 per cent, respectively (Statistics Sweden 2008: 7). On average, however, women earn only 84 per cent of men's salary. If the figures are adjusted to take account for differences in education, working hours etc., women still earn only 92 per cent of men's wages or salaries for full-time work (Statistics Sweden 2008: 80).

Despite maintenance support and housing allowances, single-parent families are in general poorer and have lost ground especially since the policy shift and recession in the early 1990s (Gähler 2001, Fritzell *et al.* 2007). Single fathers on average have higher incomes than single mothers, and if allowances and number of children are taken into account, the disposable income of single-mother households was only 80 per cent of single-father households in 2006 (Statistics Sweden 2008: 83).

Unemployment is currently growing in Sweden and is expected to continue to grow in 2011. In September 2009, the rate of unemployed people 15–74 years old was 8.3 per cent, (higher – 8.4 pecent – among men, than women – 8.1 per cent) (AKU September 2009). In particular, jobs have vanished in the private industrial sector, where predominantly men are employed. It is expected that when the current crisis matures, cuts in the public sector – where women make up the majority – will follow.

Impact on women's housing situation

Taken together, the current policy and market situation have diverging consequences for women's housing. High-income couples will probably take advantage of the current housing market situation, and home-owners in general have benefitted from the reduction of the interest rates that has been an important means to counteract the crisis. However, since housing costs have risen, the housing shortage increased and the income gap widened, it is more difficult for singles in general, and quite hard for low-income people living alone to find an affordable rental home. Owner-occupation or TOS-housing, at least in the bigger cities, are out of reach.

It is precarious to sort out gender differences in the impact of recent and ongoing changes. However, Lauster and Fransson (2006) studied the relationship between marriage and home ownership in a Swedish town and how it changed between 1975 and 1990. Whereas married couples traditionally live in single-family houses and singles in rental, multi-dwelling houses, the authors found that by the end of the period studied, more singles and co-habiting couples lived in owner-occupied housing. Although such housing often requires two wages, the importance of a second income seemed to grow for men but decrease for women (ibid.). In the article, these findings are understood in the light of the 'second demographic transition', whereby fewer people marry (but still cohabit) and have children. The authors relate these tendencies, in turn, to post-materialistic and individualistic values and increased gender equality (ibid.).

In the previously common system of rental housing allocation according to waiting-time and need, single mothers often got precedence in the waiting lists because of their limited options for buying an owner-occupied home and because of the public obligation to strive for good living conditions for all children. However, where there is no housing queue, there is no precedence, and landlords may prefer as tenants people in a better economic situations. The reduction of housing allowances works in the same direction.

In a report on women, exclusion and homelessness, Sahlin and Thörn (1999) concluded that single mothers were both winners and losers in the Swedish housing market of the 1990s. They did lose financially and in terms of unemployment in the financial crisis at the beginning and middle of that decade, and they suffered from the reductions of social benefits from 1997 onwards. On the other hand, among homeless people, they are still often favoured as vulnerable by the social services. Increased targeting of social security benefits, such as housing allowances, tends to favour single mothers, but this group's dependency on such benefits has also made them vulnerable to cuts and saving plans in the public budget.

Women's housing access and security

In this section I will discuss, first, low-income single women – whether young, old, homeless or housed – without children at home, and then mothers, cohabiting or single, and with or without financial resources. Regardless of their income, marital status and type of household, a general distinction can be drawn between those who already have access to a good-enough dwelling, and those who do not. A final subsection deals with women's lack of safety in their neighbourhoods.

Single women

The focus here is on three different groups of single women and the potential problems they might experience on the housing market: first the young student, or the young working or unemployed woman who must or wants to leave the parental home but who is not yet established on the labour market; second, the single older woman with only a low pension. A third 'type' is the literally homeless woman.

Studies show that girls tend to leave their parental homes at a lower age than do boys, and that both sexes leave home earlier if the parents have separated. (Bernhardt *et al.* 2005). The gender difference regarding the age of leaving home is declining, though (Statistics Sweden 2009). While the median age for women leaving home is now close to 21, the corresponding age for men is close to 22. By the age of 30, 99 per cent of the women and 97 per cent of the men have left their parents' home (ibid.).

As many beginners in the labour market cannot find work other than temporary work, they are often rejected by landlords, who usually demand stable employment as a condition for regular tenancy. Likewise, they will probably be rejected because of too low or uncertain income if they apply for bank loans. Owner-occupied housing is therefore, in general, not available to them. More women than men study at universities and colleges – in 2007/08, 66 per cent of the students were women. While many have to find other solutions, a proportion of them get access to special student housing. A young woman leaving home may also borrow or sublease a flat and possibly share it with one or more friends. Especially in the big cities, her uncertain situation in the labour market and lack of references to previous regular housing may entail several years of moving around between friends and temporarily borrowed or subleased flats. However, this situation for young single women is not gender specific, and is shared with their male peers.

The older single woman, in contrast, has on average a less favourable situation than men of the same age. Pensioners often want to remain in the flat or house where they lived when they were still working, and widows try to stay where they used to live with their late husbands as long as it is possible, but they may not afford it. Due to possible disabilities, and health mobility problems, old people of increasing age may need – and be offered – a more comfortable flat with access to an elevator, public transportation and health care in the near surroundings. Medical reasons to change flats are still respected in many towns and cities. It is also an advantage to have a rental flat, since tenants are entitled to change flats if they have good reasons for it and both of the landlords concerned accept it.

Today, half a million women who are 65 years old or more live as singles in Sweden; the corresponding number of men is only 214,000 (Statistics Sweden 2008: 87). Besides their number, single female pensioners differ from men of the same age with regard to income. Since men usually had paid work for more years and higher wages, thus their pensions are on average considerably higher. Out of 778,000 pensioners with only minimum pension, 80 per cent are women. On the other hand, this implies that more women than men receive housing allowances for pensioners; of 408,566 recipients of this benefit in December 2008, 72 per cent were women (Statistics Sweden/Social Insurance). Still, their disposable income is significantly lower than men's (Table 6.4).

Women live longer, and of 81,500 pensioners 90 years old or more, 73 per cent are women (Statistics Sweden/Social Insurance 2008). Hence, it is a common scenario that elderly women take care of their husbands when they are old and sick, while the women themselves are left alone during their last years in life.

A third 'category' of single women from a housing perspective is *the homeless woman*. Thörn (2001, 2004) analysed images of homeless women and found that these are more stigmatising than are those of homeless men. She noticed that homeless women often underlined in the beginning of an interview that they were *not* prostitutes, as if they expected the researcher to suspect that. This has to do with norms attaching women to home and family and connecting homelessness with being a 'public' woman, that is, a prostitute. Thörn traces this stigma to the cultural association of women and femininity with homes, which, in turn, is regarded as a vehicle for controlling women. Hence, women without a home are viewed as sexually uncontrolled, which reinforces the deviant feature of women's

Table 6.4 Disposable income for single pensioners aged 65 and over by age and gender (2006)

Age	Income (in 1000 SEK)		Number (in 1000s)	
	Women	Men	Women	Men
65–69	132	154	77	55
70–74	126	129	83	43
75–79	119	126	103	48
80–84	108	116	116	27
85+	118	128	109	34
Total	119	130	498	214

Source: 'Household finances' in Statistics Sweden 2008.

homelessness in public opinion. On the other hand, their traditional obligation to take care of families, housework and home decoration and the risk of being oppressed by men make women ambivalent towards the family-home idea. Thörn found that while men talked of home as a place for a family, women tended to speak of it primarily as a place they could master on their own, where they could be alone, close a door and keep other people out (see also Rosengren 2003, cf Woolf 1929).

A final remark is that homeless women, in order to get access to shelters and supported accommodation, are often expected to break relationships with boyfriends; there are only very few places where a homeless woman is allowed to let a boyfriend stay overnight, and homeless shelters in general do not allow couples to stay together. Hence, the woman who was not single when she became homeless is made single to fit the provisions for homeless women (Sahlin and Thörn 1999, Löfstrand and Thörn 2004, Löfstrand 2005).

Mothers

In practice and in general, women – whether married, cohabiting, divorced, widowed or single – bear the main responsibility for their children. For cohabiting or married women, this means that they are more likely than their male partners to work part-time or stay home with infants or sick children. Even if divorced parents mostly have joint formal custody, children still usually live primarily with their mothers.

As mentioned above, *single mothers* are on average poorer than cohabiting or single women or single fathers. In a qualitative study of informal networks of single mothers in quite deprived residential areas, Gardberg Morner (2003) found that being poor and alone responsible for children took considerable time. To be able to take part in school meetings, food shopping, medical consultation etc., single mothers need help with babysitting and practical arrangements for free. These wants lead to a time-consuming system of exchange of favours and services among women with similar needs. This, in turn, requires living in a neighbourhood with other single mothers and a certain stability that allows neighbours to get to know and trust one another, i.e., a viable local community. Local social authorities may offer 'contact families', who can support single mothers through taking care of their children for a while now and then. However, according to Regnér (2006), a common condition is that the single-mother family is defined as being 'in trouble' or 'in need' – not only of time and relief. Constructing the single-mother family as problematic *per se* is not helpful, '[w]ith the nuclear family as the norm, the burden of a lone parenthood will increase' (Regnér and Johnsson 2007: 319).

A great share of the *married or cohabiting women* in Sweden live in owner-occupied single-family houses, which most people consider to be ideal housing for families with children. Still, it is at odds with the image of modern women, since it tends to imply more involvement in home-making and family life. In her dissertation, Almqvist (2004: 21) set out to explain why the dream of a house of one's own is so alive in Sweden, in spite of the aim of housing policy during the welfare state to build dwellings for families with children in multi-family houses, and of the struggle by the women's movement to emancipate women from the home. The conclusion was that women display ambivalence: On the one hand, single-family housing tends to reinforce traditional gender roles and, consequently, women's subordination; on the other hand, a house of one's own is the answer to several needs with the modern individual, such as a free zone of independent power, a place to control and a space for receiving guests and expressing one's taste and style. This relates, Almqvist claims, to a perceived need to get away from the modern, urban life, but at the same time to a late modern urge to constantly change one's image and environment. In this way, owning one's house has an emancipating quality (ibid.).

Swedish tax rules favour home ownership as opposed to renting, since the interest on mortgages can be deducted from the income before taxation, and real-estate taxes are limited. However, unemployment and illness comprise real threats to all those homeowners who have substantial mortgages to pay. Unemployment benefits today cover only a small share of the work income for most people, and only a limited number of days. Although the National Bank in spring 2009 reduced the interest rate to close to zero in Spring 2009 as a part of the financial crisis policy, it is often sufficient that only one of two breadwinners loses their job to make it impossible to pay mortgages for a house or a TOS-flat. This risk is especially high for people who bought their home recently, since the crisis was preceded by booming house prices (NBHBP 2009). For the same reason a woman is often not able to remain in an owner-occupied house in the case of divorce, but has to move to a cheaper and probably smaller home, if the ex-husband claims his share of its value.

Finally, *mothers of many children*, whether living with a husband or not, are vulnerable in the housing market. Families with several children are often expected to move to single-family houses. However, many immigrant families cannot afford this, due to unemployment and/or low wages and lack of capital. Since they also tend to be disfavoured by landlords and dependent on a relatively low rent level, they are often referred to the big residential areas formed within the 'million programme', where most flats still have only two or three rooms besides the kitchen.[6] Severe overcrowding is a great problem in many such areas (Popoola 1999). The situation is further aggravated by the fact that some landlords – not least MHCs – set up limits for how many children an applicant household may have. Even if the young family with only a couple of children does find a flat, it may therefore be impossible for them to move to a larger one when the number of children grows.

Of special relevance for women and housing is the existence of homeless single mothers and homeless two-parent families with many children (today often immigrants) who are not accepted at all in the housing market, including the MHCs, for instance, due to previous rent arrears. These are often placed in overcrowded flats without tenancy rights in bad environments, sometimes in barracks or low-quality hotels (Knutagård 2009). The actual number of families in this situation is not known. According to the NBHPB (2009: 28), more than half of the municipalities reported lack of housing for immigrant families with many children in January 2009. In Stockholm City (dnr 3.1-0333/2009), the social services in September 2008 mapped 160 homeless families; 66 per cent of these came from countries outside the EU.

Unsafe housing environments

In recent years, the meaning of 'safe housing' has been re-directed from targeting tenure, the home situation or security against burglary or fire, towards focusing on the streets and open space surrounding the home. In Sweden, attention has been paid to security against assault and theft, and also to sources of fear in public space and in the neighbourhood, regardless of whether they indeed increase the risk for crime, such as poor streetlighting, undergrowth and pedestrian tunnels. Surveys, information campaigns and programmes to enhance local safety are continuously being initiated by MHCs, NGOs, central and local authorities and researchers. The police are another important party in such endeavours, as are private security firms and insurance companies. Since safety rating is also taken into account in negotiations on rents and housing companies' interest rates, security work has become financially resasonable for property owners and women's sense of fear or insecurity has gained new attention.

Studies show repeatedly that women are more afraid than men to be outdoors at night and more often refrain from going out at night due to fear (Brå 2007, 2008, Listerborn 2002). Only 9 per cent of men but 34 per cent of women 16–79 years old feel unsafe when walking outdoors late at night, while 17 per cent of men and 42 per cent of women avoid being out due to fear of crime (Brå 2007: 86). Being old, immigrant, of low education and living in a city are other factors connected with a high degree of insecurity and fear of crime (Brå 2007, 2008). However, people's housing situation in terms of housing type, tenure and residential area has proven to have an independent effect on felt safety. Hence, regardless of sex, age, origin, own income and exposure of crime, people renting their homes in high-rise buildings in poor neighbourhoods tend to feel more insecure when being out at night (Brå 2008: 8, 35, 54). While only 4 per cent of men 25–64 years old living in single-family houses are afraid, the rate of women aged 65–79 living in multi-dwelling houses is 55 per cent (Brå 2007: 73, 86).

Conclusion

Many features of women's situations are related to the social development, the production system, the degree of urbanisation and social relations of power, including those related to gender. Hence, they are shared in common by many countries. Other qualities may be specific for a nation state, a region or a 'welfare regime' (Esping-Andersen 1990), while yet other traits are formed by the road taken at historical crossroads of national housing policy (Bengtsson *et al.* 2006).

Housing was long seen as integral in work relations. The home could be part of a workplace (or vice versa), and servants and apprentices were included in the master's household. Unmarried women often remained with their parents or lived with relatives. The status of single mother was, for a long time, unacceptable, and women had lower wages and substantial difficulties in supporting themselves and their children independently.

The general connection between women's situation at home and in the labour market, public health, demographics and the housing supply was first articulated by Alva and Gunnar Myrdal in 1934. In the late 1940s, the Housing-Social Committee presented a new, comprehensive and modern housing policy, which was realised after World War II, thrived in the 1960s and 1970s and survived up to the 1990s. Its corner stones were state subsidies for municipality-planned housing construction, a large public housing sector constructed and managed by MHCs, organised housing allocation and tenure-neutral housing allowances. This strategy was less selective and targeted than policies in other Western countries and became an important dimension of 'the Swedish model'.

Although some benefits were introduced earlier, a corresponding comprehensive family policy was realised from the 1970s on. Besides a great expansion of public day-care for children, parental insurance was introduced, which enables mothers *or* fathers to stay home from work with newborn children. In the course of the twentieth century gender equality grew formally and substantially also in other spheres of society. However, women still have lower wages and as a result lower pensions than men, they still do most of the housework and more often than men take care of children after a divorce.

While the family policy has survived and been improved piecemeal in recent decades, with an even stronger emphasis on encouraging fathers to take their part of the care for children, housing policy was abolished in the beginning of the 1990s. Since then higher house prices, de-regulated allocation of rental housing, declining housing allowances and a growing share of owner-occupation have contributed to increased housing shortage, ethnic and socio-economic segregation, inequality and polarisation regarding space and quality of housing, and to persistent homelessness.

In considering the consequences of the market and policy situation for women, it is necessary to distinguish between different classes, generations and family situations and sometimes also between women born in Sweden or abroad. Among single women, the young ones share their housing problems with younger men, while women pensioners on average are poorer, older and more often living alone than male pensioners. Single mothers often face financial problems, while poor mothers with several children may suffer from overcrowding or homelessness, due to lack of flats with sufficient space and affordable rents. Women who have migrated from countries outside Europe are especially vulnerable to this situation, whether they are married or not, while co-habiting couples without children in general are better off in terms of housing.

Single-family, owner-occupied homes were once subsidised in order to pacify the protesting working class. In the past 40 years, this kind of housing has been favoured by tax legislation and general inflation tendencies and has become the norm for nuclear families. Although it tends to reinforce traditional gender roles, many married women display a dedicated attraction to the single-family house, which gives space for privacy as well as identity expression. Less than one in five households in Sweden is a two-parent family with children, while two in five homes are single-family, owner-occupied housing. Whether it signifies inequality or deficient allocation mechanisms, it is remarkable that in most of these homes there are no children, while on the other hand, half of the single-parent families with three or more children and an even higher proportion of immigrant families with many children live in high-rise, multi-family houses. An additional aspect of women's housing is fear and insecurity in the neighbourhood. Poor, old, immigrant women in rental housing exposed residential areas are especially vulnerable to fear of crime.

For women in these different situations, their level of income is decisive for their position on the housing market. Some housing problems are shared with men with low incomes, others are specific to women, such as being a poor pensioner or a single parent, or a fearful immigrant woman in a deprived neighbourhood. For women in these different situations, their level of income is decisive for their position in the housing market.

7 Women, housing and citizenship in Great Britain

Patricia Kennett

Introduction

The last forty years has been marked by considerable change in British[1] society for both men and women as the decline of the male breadwinner model has been replaced by a change in the nature and extent of women and men's waged work, family arrangements, housing opportunities and the form and content of citizenship. This major shift occurred in the 1980s, from an era in which housing interventions were an integral part of the post-war settlement to one in which home ownership has become the dominant tenure and housing a main source of asset accumulation, cultural capital, citizenship and identity. This chapter will consider the changing context and gendered impact of housing policies, as well as the different housing needs of men and women. It will begin by outlining the changing nature of housing provision, particularly in relation to tenure and government policy and provision. It will then go on to explore the relationship between the economic resource position of women in the sphere of production, her responsibilities in the sphere of reproduction or 'home and caring responsibilities', and the social and cultural conventions and sanctions that structure women's housing choices. It will conclude with a consideration of the opportunities and challenges that this creates for women in meeting their housing needs.

The changing policy context

In Britain, one of the major housing development of the post-war period was the building of estates and new towns which became emblematic of the changing conditions for the reproduction of the workforce and the emerging model of mass consumption and Keynesian welfare capitalism. This, according to Campbell 'was the form in which later modernism rearranged the landscape of most British cities' (Campbell 1993, p. 13). It also represented the government's role in elevating the home ideal and reinforcing the exclusive private sphere of the family. Whilst in 1918, 76 per cent of households rented from private landlords and 23 per cent of households were home owners, by 1953, 50 per cent of households were private renters, 32 per cent were home owners and 18 per cent were social renters (see Table 7.1). Between 1945 and 1952 over 80 per cent of all new dwellings were built by local authorities (Malpass and Murie 1987). This was stimulated by a trebling in subsidies compared with 1939, under the 1946 Housing (Financial and Miscellaneous Provisions) Act. The public sector stock in the period 1945–1956 almost doubled as a proportion of the total stock. However, access and quality of housing built during this period, 'reflected the political and economic power of organized skilled labour – the better off working class, as distinct from the poor' (Malpass and Murie 1987, p. 74). For the poor to be incorporated into the home ideal they had to meet certain criteria relating to personal decency and the acceptance of established behavioral norms. Issues relating to gender, class, marital status, ethnicity and sexuality were major considerations in how home was defined and who was able to gain access. Women and people from ethnic minorities were unlikely to have equal access to the capital through which the suburban home ideal could be achieved, and were likely to be denied access to local authority waiting lists (Rex and Tomlinson 1979; Castles and Kosack 1973; Henderson and Karn 1987).

Whilst in 1946 the vast majority of local authority dwellings were houses, by the mid-1950s the situation had changed markedly (Dunleavy 1981). As the 1956 General Housing Subsidy was phased out government aid was to be focused on slum clearance, whilst at the same time the emphasis was placed on inner city redevelopment with subsidy per dwelling replaced by those per acre (Hay 1992). Conservative government policy from 1951 thus combined a commitment for 'unfettered' private enterprise to concentrate on 'general needs' housing, whilst also promising the delivery of 300,000 homes per annum. These factors contributed to an increase in high rise as a proportion of the local authority stock from 15 per cent to 26 per cent between 1960 and 1966 with production usually undertaken by national contractors. The importance of these figures is perhaps increased when regional concentration is analysed. In the assessment made by Dunleavy over 92 per cent of high rise stocks were in conurbations or in free-standing county boroughs (Dunleavy 1981, p 59).

As a visible and prominent entity, high rise production reinforced the commitment to mass housing, served to legitimate the institutions of the Keynesian welfare state and support the hegemony of the post-war settlement and the home ideal. On the new estates the allocation of local authority housing mainly to married couples supported the development of a suburban life-style accompanied by the move towards a more fragmented, home-centred culture, based on patriarchal social relations (Eisenstein 1979; Walby 1989), and the 'family' wage as working-class living standards rose. Married women were unable to take out a mortgage in her own name and a single woman required a male guarantor (Land 2009). In post-war Britain, the importance of women's role as wives and mothers was enshrined within the Beveridgian settlement in which women were treated as dependents

Table 7.1 Trends in tenure 1918–2008 (all households, England)

Year	Owner occupiers			Social renters	Private renters			Total %
	Own outright	Buying with a mortgage	All	All	Unfurnished	Furnished	All	
1918			23.0	1.0			76.0	100
1953			32.0	18.0			50.0	100
1971			51.0	29.0			20.0	100
1981	25.0	32.0	57.2	31.7	8.6	2.4	11.1	100
1988	25.9	39.7	65.7	25.2	6.5	2.6	9.1	100
1991	24.8	42.8	67.6	23.0	6.4	3.0	9.4	100
2001	28.8	41.5	70.4	19.5	7.4	2.7	10.1	100
2003	29.7	41.2	70.9	18.3	8.0	2.8	10.8	100
2005	30.3	40.3	70.7	17.7	8.8	2.9	11.7	100
2008	31.1	37.3	68.3	17.7	10.4	3.6	13.9	100

Sources: Derived from ONS (2009a) Table S101 Trends in Tenure.

for the purpose of social security entitlements up until the 1970s and the passage of equal opportunities legislations. A range of legislation was introduced during this decade, including the 1970 Matrimonial Proceedings and Property Act, the Divorce Law Reform Act and the 1977 Housing (Homeless Persons) Act through which local authorities were made responsible for re-housing homeless families, particularly single mothers. This indicated a shift away from dependence on the male breadwinner model and on marital status as the pre-eminent determinant impacting on women's position in the family, labour market and the housing system (Land 2009). As Land (2009) argues 'Her dependence on her husband had been reduced as her claims on the state, at least as a mother, had increased' (Land 2009, p. 2). However, since the 1980s the specific social and economic conditions have represented a retreat and transition from the broadly 'inclusionary' principles of the past. This has been evident with policies to erode state responsibility (and thus increase reliance on families and private markets), transformations in family arrangements and the nature and extent of men's and women's waged work, and the 'remoralization of citizenship based on labour market participation' (Innes and Scott 2003, p. 1). These developments will be outlined in the next section of this chapter.

Demographic, household and labour market change

In 1971 in the UK people living in couple families with dependent children accounted for more than one half (52 per cent) of all households, compared with around one-third (36 per cent) in 2008. 25 per cent of households in 2008 were couples without children, compared with 19 per cent in 1971. The proportion of people living alone doubled between 1971 and 2001 and has remained constant ever since. Between 1971 and 2008 the proportion of lone-parent households increased to 11 per cent (ONS 2009a). Marriage rates reached an historic low of 270,000 in 2008, whilst cohabiting has grown exponentially, trebling over the last 30 years.[2] For same-sex couples aged 16 and over the Civil Partnership Act 2004 came into force in December 2005 in the UK enabling them to obtain legal recognition of their relationship. The total number of partnerships formed in the UK since the act came into force in December 2005 up to the end of 2008 is 33,956. 47 per cent of all people forming a civil partnership in the UK were female (see Table 7.2) (ONS 2009b).

There has been a vertical and horizontal shift in the populations structure in terms of an ageing population, declining mortality rates and lower fertility rates and the growth of single parents and step families (Griggs 2010). The number of people aged 90 and over in Great Britain increased from around 125,000 in 1971 to around 417,000 in 2007. In 1971 there were around 96,000 women and 29,000 men aged 90 and over in Great Britain. By 2007 these numbers had increased more than threefold to 311,000 women and 106,000 men. Projections indicate that by 2031 there will be more than 1.1 million people aged 90 and over in Great Britain, 715,000 women and 480,000 men (ONS 2010).

Table 7.2 Sex and marital status of household reference person by tenure

	Male					Female					Total %
	Married or civil partner	Cohabiting	Single	Widowed	Divorced or separated	Married or civil partner	Cohabiting	Single	Widowed	Divorced or separated	
Owned outright	47	2	5	6	3	9	1	4	18	6	100
Buying with a mortgage	48	10	7	1	4	11	4	6	1	7	100
All owner occupiers	47	6	6	3	4	10	3	5	9	7	100
All social rented sector tenant	18	5	11	4	8	6	4	15	13	16	100
All rented privately	22	11	20	1	8	5	5	16	4	8	100
All tenures	39	7	9	3	5	9	3	8	9	9	100

Source: ONS (2009a) Table S107 Sex and Marital status of Household reference person by tenure

The proportion of births outside marriage now stands at 45 per cent, three times higher than during the mid-1980s. In 2008 one-person households and lone-parent families accounted for almost one-quarter of the proportion of the population living in private households in Great Britain (ONS 2010).

As in other societies there has been a long-term trend towards increasing participation by women in the labour market, with rates increasing markedly in the UK during the 1980s. In 1984 labour market participation rates by women stood at 66 per cent and by 1990 had reached 71 per cent. Men's economic activity in contrast declined during the 1990s to reach 84 per cent by 2001, having remained constant at 88 per cent during the 1980s. In 2008, 11.7 million men (an increase of 6 per cent since 1998) and 7.3 million women (an increase of 18 per cent since 1998) were in full-time employment (ONS 2009a). Table 7.3 gives an indication of the ethnic composition of the UK population and the proportion of men and women in each ethnic group in 2001. As the table shows, the proportions are fairly evenly distributed within and between ethnic groups in terms of the gender composition. However, when we look at economic activity rates by gender and ethnic group for the UK in 2000, as in Table 7.4, the picture is more disparate. Clearly economic activity rates for all ethnic groups are lower than for the white population, with substantial variation between ethnic groups. There are a number of explanations for these differences relating to access to opportunities, discrimination, levels of education, language ability and cultural differences (Cabinet Office 2002, 2003; Modood *et al.* 1997).

A major factor impacting on the labour market is the changing nature of the economy in the UK. Processes of deindustrialization have seen a transformation in the labour market structure with a changing emphasis from manufacturing to service sector employment, from male manual jobs to service sector and white-

Table 7.3 Ethnic origin by gender (%): UK, 2001

Ethnic origin	Women	Men	Base
White	50.6	49.4	54,539,000
Mixed	51.4	48.6	5,048,000
Asian or Asian British	49.1	50.9	2,156,000
Black or Black British	53.1	46.9	1,160,000
Chinese	48.7	51.3	184,000
Other ethnic group	45.2	54.8	250,000

Source: ONS 2001(a) taken from Izuhara and Kennett (2003); *Base: All persons.*
Note: Percentages are row percentages.

Table 7.4 Economic activity rates, by gender and ethnic group (%): UK, 2000

	Women	Men
White	74	85
All ethnic minorities	55	76
Black	67	80
Indian	62	79
Pakistani/Bangladeshi	31	72

Source: ONS 2001(b) taken from Izuhara and Kennett (2003); Base: All persons of working
age (women 16–59; men 16–64).

collar work (traditionally women's work). Occupational segregation in the labour
market is well documented with women more likely than men to be employed in
administrative and clerical, personal service and sales occupations. Men are ten
times more likely than women to be represented in skilled trades occupations, and
more likely to be found in plant and machine operative occupations, and managerial
occupations. Despite changes in the economy these distinctions still prevail. From
1991 to 2000 the proportion of both women and men in managerial, professional
and associate professional occupations increased slightly (from 9 per cent of female
employees to 12 per cent; and from 16 per cent of male employees to almost 20
per cent). However, as Table 7.5 demonstrates, the figures become more significant
when analysed across a wider time-frame. Since the 1970s the number of women in
management at various levels has increased substantially. The number of women in
clerical and secretarial occupations dropped slightly during this period (from 29 per
cent of female employees to 25 per cent) but is still the main occupational category
for women in the UK, followed by personal services and sales (Izuhara and Kennett
2003). A recent report by the Government Equalities Office (2010a) revealed that
only one in ten (7.3 per cent) directors of FTSE 250 companies were women, with
one in four FTSE 100 boards having no female directors, leading the report to state
that it is often the case 'that unconscious stereotyping leads to biased perceptions of
their competence and aspirations' (p1).

It is also the case that fewer women than ever before are without qualification
and the gap between men and women is narrowing. Between 1993 and 2000 the
number of women with degree-level or equivalent qualifications more than doubled
from 8 per cent to 17 per cent (13 per cent and 17 per cent for men respectively). In
addition, the proportion of women with no qualifications declined from 26 per cent
in 1993 to 18 per cent in 2000 (19 per cent and 24 per cent respectively for men).
However, age and ethnicity stand out as key variables in this data. Women aged
50–64 are most likely to have no qualifications (30 per cent) (Dench *et al.* 2002).
Ethnic minority women are more likely to have a degree or equivalent than the
overall British women (22.5 per cent vs 20.0 per cent). However, ethnic minority
women are also more likely to have no qualifications than the overall British women

Table 7.5 Women as a proportion of executives (%): UK, 1974–2001 (selected years)

	1974	1990	1995	2000	2001
Director	0.6	1.6	3.0	9.6	9.9
Function head	0.4	4.2	5.8	15.0	15.8
Department head	2.1	7.2	9.7	19.0	25.5
Section leader	2.4	11.8	14.2	26.5	28.9
All executives	1.8	7.8	10.7	22.1	24.1

Source: Equal Opportunities Commission (EOC), 2002 from Izuhara and Kennett (2003).

(17.1 per cent vs 12.7 per cent). Among women, it is the Pakistani/Bangladeshi group that is the least likely to have a degree or equivalent, 12.1 per cent compared to 19.3 per cent for British women in 2007 (Government Equalities Office 2009). Economically active women are more likely than a man to hold a tertiary degree thus indicating a stronger tendency for a more educated women to remain economically active than a less educated one. Whilst this might indicate that for more educated women the higher opportunity cost in becoming inactive is a serious consideration (ILO 2010) it might also be related to issues of class, ethnicity, household type, and the nature, conditions and context of labour market participation as women with different resources and at different stages of the lifecycle seek to accommodate the triple dynamics of labour market inclusion, household and caring responsibilities which ultimately impacts on their housing strategies.

Whilst the differences between men's and women's pay narrowed greatly during the 1970s – from 63 per cent in 1970 to 72 per cent in 1980 – following the introduction of the Equal Pay Act, in 2000, women in the UK earned 82 per cent of men's earnings levels, and 84 per cent in 2009 (based on mean hourly earnings). The earnings ratio decreases as age increases. In 2000, for those aged between 16 and 24 the earnings gap is low with a ratio of 97.1. For those aged 25–34 years the earnings ratio is 89.9, with a decrease to 79.5 for those aged 35–49, and 77.8 for those aged 50–64 (ONS 2001). As in other areas explored in this chapter ethnic origin influences the distribution of earnings. The earnings ratio is highest between black men and women at 92.3 per cent, with the greatest difference in earnings occurring between Indian women and Indian men with an earnings ratio of 73.4 per cent. Earnings for Pakistani Bangladeshi women and Indian women are substantially lower than all other groups (Izuhara and Kennett 2003).

An obvious factor impacting on the differences in earnings between men and women is that of part-time work. In 2008, 1.4 million men were in part-time employment, a 41 per cent increase on 1998, with 5.1 million women, an increase of 4 per cent on 1998. One of the most important factors influencing the incidence of part-time working amongst women appears to be the age of the youngest child. The proportion of women working part-time decreases as the age of the youngest child increases. Women with dependent children over 10 years old are no less likely to be in work than women who have no dependent children (ONS 2010). Comparing the part-time earnings of men and women indicates only a small difference with an earnings ratio of 97 per cent. In fact, women aged between 25 and 34 are likely to earn around 13 per cent more than men in this age group. However, if one compares women's part-time earnings with men's full-time earnings then the gap is much wider; the earnings ratio is 62 per cent. Again the ratio reduces with age ranging from 71.9 per cent for those aged between 16 and 24, falling to 57 per cent for those aged 50–64. In 2007 the adult minimum wage was £5.52, rising to £5.80 in 2009. Women are more likely to work in lower paid and often part-time jobs than men, therefore more women are likely to benefit from the minimum wage. However, Lissenburgh (2000) argues that female part-timers experience a greater degree of discrimination than female full-timers: their pay would increase by about 15 per cent if their human capital attributes were remunerated in the same way as men's. As a recent ILO (2010) study found 'The unfortunate fact remains that engaging in the labour market brings women less gains than the typical, working male (monetarily, socially and structurally)' (p. 6). In spite of the relative advances made by women in acquiring qualifications, participating in the labour market for the majority of women, either by maintaining continuity of full-time work or as flexible, part-time employees, has occurred in the context of continuing wage inequality and discrimination. According to Lissenburgh (2000) the benefits of labour market participation have been distributed unevenly and it is principally the younger cohort of women, and those at the higher levels of the occupational hierarchy who have benefitted the most. However, even here, the pay gap between men and women, although not as substantial as that between female and male part-time workers, can largely be attributed to gender discrimination.

Women's overall work burden in both the reproductive and productive economies has increased in recent decades. The care economy is a complex concept but there can be little doubt that the value of unpaid care work (unpaid household work) performed by women is underestimated and one of the biggest barriers to equality (ILO 2009), as female household work continues to be classified as non-economically active, and is considered to be outside the labour market in the private sphere, and therefore lacking in status and financial reward. There has been a growing trend for both men and particularly women towards non-standard forms of work, and part-time and temporary employment, which can be precarious and less well-remunerated, strengthening the link between these less standard forms of work and income inequality. As 'new risks in the labour and housing markets have to be met with individual solutions' (Christie 2000, p. 901) women clearly have varying capacities and scope to overcome these risks whilst at the same time reconciling work and family responsibilities. Whether the predominance of women in the part-time paid labour market can be attributed to choice, constraint, necessity or coercion must be considered in the context of class, ethnicity and household type and in relation to the promotion of the 'home-owning society' since the 1980s and the dual-worker model by the Labour governments since 1997.

Towards a dual-earning, home owning society?

Though owner-occupation had risen from 4.4 million to 12 million between 1951 and 1980, heavily subsidized by mortgage tax relief, the public rented sector had grown from 2.5 million properties to 7 million during the same period (ONS 1982). Thus, at the beginning of the 1980s still one third of all British households were in the public sector, a situation that was to change following the introduction of the 1980 Housing Act offering individual households 'a route out of their proletarian impasse into the free market' (Hay 1992, p. 57). However, as Hay (1992) points out, this process has been achieved not just by relying on the appeal of home ownership, but by 'penalizing' those who chose to 'deviate' from market participation, and increasing the material rewards of those sections who entered into the project. Substantial reductions on market value were offered by tenants purchasing their home, whilst the withdrawal of government rent subsidies was an average rent increase of 169 per cent between 1979 and 1987 (Clapham *et al.* 1990).

Those households most likely to be in a position to take advantage of the right-to-buy (RTB) were long-standing tenants, couples and older residents (a vast proportion of whom were women). For the increasing number of women (with children) entering local authority housing, more recent access to the tenure, low-incomes and their location often in less desirable parts of the stock (generally flats rather than houses) would have inhibited their ability to exercise their right to buy. Instead, their experience would have been of higher rents in an increasingly residualized and stigmatized tenure, as the loss of the better part of the stock in more favourable areas (Dunn *et al,* 1987; Kerr 1988), a lack of capital expenditure on the remaining stock, mainly lower quality, inner-city housing and the pervasiveness of the universal appeal of home ownership began to erode the reputation of council housing as a 'desirable' tenure (Malpass and Murie 1987). This tendency was accentuated by the 1988 Housing Act which broke the post-war consensus in which local authorities were seen as the main providers of social housing for rent. The emphasis was placed on alternative social landlords as the future providers of low-cost housing with local authorities confined to the role of strategic planners and enablers. In the 1980s, the housing boom enhanced opportunities for developers and housing financiers and home ownership spread to include a broader cross-section of society, thus fulfilling the belief in the 'moving column of progressive recruitment' (Forrest and Kennett 1994).

In Britain the 1997 Labour Government promoted the new politics of the 'third way', a central feature of which has been active citizenship, individual responsibility, asset-based welfare and the 'rebalancing' of the relationship between the state and the individual, between rights and responsibilities. For Prime Minister Tony Blair:

> The demand for rights from the State was separated from the duties of citizenship and the imperative for mutual responsibility on the part of individuals and institutions. Unemployment benefits were often paid without strong reciprocal obligations; children went unsupported by absent parents … The rights we enjoy reflect the duties we owe: rights and opportunities without responsibility are engines of selfishness and greed.
>
> (Blair 1997, p. 4)

The promotion of home ownership as the 'ideal' tenure for the majority of the population, and a source of identity, citizenship and asset accumulation has been a key element of this endeavour. This rebalancing of the relationship between the state and the individual has also been premised on a transition from a male-breadwinner model, to an adult-worker model (Crompton 1999; Lewis 2001), on which the growth of home ownership has increasingly depended, and a general shift in responsibility away from the institutional domain of the state towards the family, the individual and the market as providers of housing and care. This renegotiation of the meaning and content of citizenship and the increased focus on the active, individualized, commodified, responsible citizen has also contributed to shift in gender norms. In Great Britain, as in many other countries, this has been supported by the growing emphasis on in-work benefits, as well as the introduction of tax credits. In addition there has been an increase in childcare provision, maternity pay and parental leave, and the promotion of 'flexible working' options. The Work and Families Act 2006 came into force in 2007, with the intention of extending the scope of flexible working law to give carers of adults the right to request flexible working. Statutory maternity pay, maternity allowance and statutory adoption pay from 26 weeks to 39 weeks for babies born on or after 1 April 2007 has been introduced, the duration of benefits increased to 52 weeks, and fathers given the right to take up to 26 weeks Additional Paternity Leave. Since 1997 the number of registered childcare places in England has doubled to over 1.3 million. All 3- and 4-year-olds are now guaranteed 12.5 hours of free early education for 38 weeks per year for up to two years before reaching compulsory school age (the term following their fifth birthday in England), rising to 15 hours by 2010, with a longer term goal of 20 hours (Government Equalities Office, 2010b). Along with the development of Sure Start children centres in communities, financial assistance of up to 80 per cent with childcare costs for working families earning up to £58,000, Griggs (2010) also points out that grandparents provide £3.9 billion of childcare, yet only one in 10 receive any payment. It is working-class grandmothers on low incomes who are most likely to be providing childcare than other groups. They are also more likely to have to give up work or reduce their paid hours to care for grandchildren.

These developments have considerable housing implications, particularly where children are being looked after full-time. The most commonly recorded problems have related to overcrowding and problems meeting housing expenses.

For the lone parent, the Welfare Reform Act 2009 sets out new work-related requirements for those in receipt of out of work benefits (Job Seekers Allowance and Employment and Support Allowance ESA) which replaces income support for those unable to work. Changes mean that single parents will be required to be 'work ready' (to undertake training and other preparatory activities) when their youngest child is three years old (Griggs 2010). Enforcement of condition is dependent on the availability of childcare. 57 per cent of single parents are now in work. This is still significantly less than the Labour government's 2010 target of 70 per cent employment.

According to Smith (2005) 'Housing provision enjoyed by women has become increasingly to rely on resources she can access rather than resources of a domestic partner' (p. 143). Thus, in a society where home ownership has become the 'ideal tenure' a better understanding of the tensions between the increasing importance of formal employment as the key to inclusion, the continuing and increasing primary responsibility of women in caring activities, and access to affordable and appropriate housing it becomes essential to explore the gender dimensions in the allocation and control of resources, the 'power relations through which inequalities between women and men are socially constructed' (Christie 2000, p. 87) and the home and caring responsibilities which continue to be 'a defining characteristic of women's life experience' (Daly and Lewis 2000, p. 282).

In 1971 half of all households in England owned their own homes compared with 71 per cent at the peak in 2003 (see Table 7.1). Levels of home ownership remained at a similar level, fluctuating between 70 and 71 per cent up until 2008. However, in 2008 the level dropped to 68.3 per cent, and in 2009 stood at 67.9 per cent (EHS 2010). In Scotland similar trends have been evident with less than 40 per cent of the dwelling stock owner-occupied in 1981 compared to 60 per cent in 2008. Although the vast majority of households seeking a mortgage still comprise one male and one female the proportion is falling (59.4 per cent in 1999). An increasing number of cohabiting couples are buying a property together. In addition, the proportion of mortgages taken out in Britain by a woman in her own name alone more than doubled between 1983 and 1994, from 8.2 per cent in 1983 to 17.2 per cent in 1994 (CML 2000). This trend is clearly continuing with 29 per cent of single women owning their own house with a mortgage in 2006. Single male purchasers (22.7 per cent) continue to outnumber single female purchasers (17.2 per cent) but the gap is narrowing. However, it is still the case that men are more likely to own their own home either outright or with the help of a mortgage. More than three-quarters of men owned their home compared with three-fifths of women. In 2007 only 35 per cent of lone parents with children were owner occupiers, whilst 48 per cent of them were social renters (ONS 2010). In the private rented sector assured shorthold terancies have increased from 38 per cent of all private tenancies in 1993–1994 to 67 per cent in 2007–2008, with an average rent of £136 per week.

Affordability and owner occupation

Issues of affordability have always been pertinent in considering the relationship between women and owner occupation (Gilroy and Woods 1994). House prices have increased by around 240 per cent between 1992 and 2002 and in 2007 the average dwelling price in England was more than seven times the average salary. The average first-time buyer deposit in 2000 was over £15,000 for the UK as a whole, compared to less than £5,000 in 1996. In 2001, Wilcox (2001) stated that 'Average deposits, at just under 20 per cent of house prices, are now at their highest level for two decades (p. 49). More recently the UK economy has experienced a real slowdown, 'bottoming out' for two quarters after almost 16 years of unbroken rising gross domestic product (GDP). UK house prices, already very high and unstable for many years before the credit crunch, have fallen and although interest rates are currently at an all time low, for new borrowers, accessing home ownership may have become even more difficult. In March 2009, Abbey was offering its cheapest mortgage at a rate of 2.99 per cent fixed for two years but with a 60 per cent loan to value ratio, thus requiring a 40 per cent deposit. The bigger the deposit the better the mortgage rate you will receive.

In 2007 mortgage advances formed over 80 per cent of dwelling prices for first-time buyers. The gap between the UK average household income which is a measure of affordability, gradually widened over the 2000s and in 2004 saw a ratio of advance to income exceed 3:1 for first-time buyers, a picture that continued in 2007, indicating major affordability problems (Wong *et al.* 2009). A recent study by NHPAU (2009) highlights poor housing affordability in almost every area of the UK and highlights a number of examples including the following (p. 10):

- In St Albans, Hertfordshire, a key worker in their late-20s earning £19,000 to £25,000 a year would need a partner earning £30,000 to £36,000 to afford to buy a home;
- In Surrey, pay rates for nurses, teachers and police officers are below the average income in the county and key workers require income multiples of over six to afford a home of their own .

The study also highlights the increasing importance of parental help for first-time buyers and its impact on accentuating class inequality and a more polarized housing market. Average assisted deposits ranged from £12,900 in northern England to £57,000 in London, compared with £5,350 and £12,500 in the same two locations from unassisted first-timers. Unassisted buyers typically had lower incomes than assisted buyers – £22,500 against £29,000 in Scotland and £40,350 against £54,500 in London (NHPAU 2009)

Affordability concerns are associated not only with the ability to access owner occupation but also the ability to maintain and sustain the ensuing housing costs. In 2008, for example, lone parents with dependent children were recorded as spending almost one-quarter (24 per cent) of their monthly income on mortgage payments (ONS 2009a). During 2009, the total number of possessions was 46,000, compared to 40,000 in 2008 (CML 2010). Some 188,300 mortgages were in arrears equivalent to at least 2.5 per cent of the outstanding mortgage balance, a figure 3 per cent higher than at the end of 2008. These figures are significantly below initial estimates from financial institutions, a factor that can be attributed to historically low interest rates, lender forbearance, lower than expected unemployment rates and government measures that have combined to limit the adverse affects of the recession so far. However, evidence from the English Housing Survey (EHS) (2010) from 2006–2007 and 2001–2008 indicates that these experiences are not distributed equally across the population. Whilst in England as a whole 13 per cent of households buying with a mortgage reported either some difficulty in paying the mortgage or that they were in arrears, over 30 per cent of unemployed households, with at least one sick or disabled member, and those who had previously been repossessed reported some difficulties or being in arrears. Almost a quarter of lone parents (24 per cent) and ethnic minority households (23 per cent) were experiencing difficulties. (EHS 2010).

Accessing affordable housing?

Access to affordable housing has become increasingly difficult in the context of the growing inequality, the rising cost of owner occupation and as the availability of social rented housing has diminished as a result of transfer to home ownership and reduced construction. Turning to income distribution, the Gini coefficient of the UK at 32, was above the European Union (EU) average of 30 in 2008, indicating that the UK has higher than average growth at the top of the income distribution with those in the top 10 per cent having experienced faster growth in disposable incomes than those at the bottom. The top 1 per cent experienced still faster growth and the top 0.1 per cent the fastest growth of all (ONS 2010). In contrast, there is now a greater risk of in-work poverty and a greater concentration of people at the lower levels of weekly income, with nearly two-thirds of individuals living in households with below average, mean income. Groups with greater than average risks of being in the bottom 20 per cent of the income distribution were people in lone parent families and people in households from most ethnic minority groups, particularly Pakistani/Bangladeshi groups (ONS 2010). Single parents in hardship are 1.7 times more likely to experience worsened hardship if they belong to a minority ethnic group (Griggs 2010). For elderly people, retirement income for women is 40 per cent less than men's, and two-thirds of the poorest pensioners are women. Recent government measures introduced by Gordon Brown are seeking to ensure that by 2025, nearly half a million extra women will be entitled to a full basic state pension (which currently stands at £97.65 per week for a single person and £156.15 per week for a married couple). Time will tell if the current coalition Government will continue to support these measures.

So in the context of increasing inequality the notion of home ownership as the 'natural' tenure of choice has been promoted by governments and is a widely accepted ideology, whilst at the same time the social rented sector has become increasingly stigmatized and residualized (Forrest and Murie 1986). In contrast to the increasing presence of women-headed households entering owner occupation, it is also the case that a high proportion of households headed by women rent their house from social landlords, with lone parents with dependent children much more likely to rent their property than to own it. In 2009 around one-third (34 per cent) of these households in the UK were owner-occupiers whilst the remainder rented their homes, mostly from registered social landlords. In contrast, three-quarters (75 per cent) of households comprising a couple with dependent children were owner-occupiers, and a quarter rented (ONS 2009a). Whilst single men were more likely to rent from the private sector than single women, 25 per cent compared to 19 per cent, the pattern was reversed for renting from the social sector. In the social sector two-fifths (41 per cent) of single women were social renters compared with around a quarter of single men (24 per cent) (ONS 2009a).

In the UK currently over 1.7 million households are waiting for social housing. Total lettings for 2008/9 were 262,907. In Greater London total new lettings for 2008/9 by housing associations and local authorities to new tenants was 35,026. Households on the waiting list numbered 354,389. Research by NHPAU in 2008 showed that the annual housing need for social housing rose from 93,000 in 2002 to 155,000 by 2006 while the number of new social lets in the same period fell significantly (NHPAU 2008). These figures clearly highlight a high demand for social housing across Great Britain that simply isn't being met. In 2007, for the first time since 1983, more social housing was built than was lost through the right-to-buy. The Labour governments strategy was to be the delivery of high-quality, affordable housing within mixed sustainable communities. The 2007 Green Paper committed the government to providing at least 45,000 new social houses a year by 2010–2011, and over 25,000 shared ownership and shared equity houses a year (DCLG 2007). In contrast, the current Prime Minister, David Cameron, has introduced the idea of a more flexible approach to council housing, the end of 'council housing for life', and housing benefit removal for working-age claimants occupying a larger property than their household size warrents. In Scotland, the Scottish Executive committed to an increased annual budget for the supply of affordable housing in Scotland, resulting in the supply over the three-year period of 21,500 new affordable homes.

Nearly a third (34 per cent) of social renting households in 2009, who had been resident for less than five years, reported that they had been accepted as homeless before they were allocated their current home. This increases to nearly a half (47 per cent) among lone parents with dependent children. (ONS 2009a). The Housing Act 1996, places a statutory duty on local authorities in England and Wales to provide assistance to people who are, or are threatened with, unintentional homelessness, and fall into a priory category. The categories include pregnant women, women experiencing domestic violence, people with dependent children, those considered 'vulnerable' because of age or mental health. In 2001 the categories were expanded to include young people between 16 and 17 years old, those under 21 who are 'looked after', leaving a custodial sentence, or threatened with violence. Of the 15,000 households in England accepted as homeless in the first quarter of 2008, half were lone-parent households. Of these, 49 per cent were headed by a female and 4 per cent by a male. One-person households made up a quarter of the total number of households with 14 per cent sole males and 11 per cent sole females. During the same period, 45 per cent of households in temporary accommodation were female lone-parent households with dependent children and 3 per cent were male lone-parent households with dependent children. Overall, one-person households accounted for one in five households in temporary accommodation (ONS 2009b)

Conclusion

This chapter has explored the demographic, cultural and policy shift which has occurred during the last 30 years in Great Britain, and the implications for the housing opportunities of different groups of women. Women's access to housing, always differentiated, has become more polarized than in the past, sharpening the link between income, class, ethnicity and household structure. Just as housing policy was a critical ideological and material element of the post-war mode of development, so it has proved a lynchpin in the promotion of neo-liberal and 'Third Way' rhetoric in terms of the promotion of a 'property-owning democracy'. A raft of policies have sought to erode state responsibility, and increase reliance on individuals, families and the market during the last 30 years, an ideological shift which has had a powerful and differentiated impact on women and housing. The increasing emphasis on home ownership, the introduction of the right-to-buy in the 1980s, combined with the reduction in new construction, has been accompanied by substantial change in family arrangements, the world of work, and in the meaning and content of citizenship and inclusion.

The reconfiguration of citizenship has been accompanied by a growing emphasis on individualization, commodification and active citizenship, with paid work as the key to inclusion. Housing has become a commodity, a tradable asset, and a source of wealth accumulation. As increasing incomes and employment opportunities have enhanced the status of some women, particularly younger and better-educated cohorts, this has given them the financial means to secure housing independently, and in turn has facilitated access to this major source of asset accumulation and wealth. For some women then, opportunity and autonomy in housing choices are more accessible than ever before. It also seems to be the case, however, that the opportunities available to, and experiences of women have now become more polarized than ever before. As 'the citizen' has become increasingly equated with 'the consumer' and risks in the labour and housing markets have to be met with individual solutions (Christie 2000) the housing opportunities and experiences of women increasingly cannot be understood without reference to the gendered division of domestic and caring responsibility (Ungerson 1983) and the integration of different but overlapping spheres of activity – production, reproduction and consumption. Women's housing opportunities are linked with gendered patterns of inequality associated with the economic resource position of women, care strategies and the social and cultural conventions that structure women's housing choices. This in turn can be linked to discrimination, inadequate resources and cultural norms and expectations. Institutions and culture do matter, defining opportunities and constraints but also structuring preferences. Current housing policies, the promotion of the dual-worker model and a model of citizenship that places labour market insertion at its centre are in tension with the realities of the day-to-day lives of many women. Little consideration is given to the potential impact of greater work-related conditionality on the wider family and the welfare of children, or to the implications of raised employment rates among one group (lone parents) on another (older women) (Griggs 2010). As Innes and Scott (2003, p. 4) argue

> care is marginalized within that model, both through its absence from policy and also conceptually: adult-worker premises depend on conceptual and moral boundaries that position adulthood and individuality as attained through refusing or denying dependence and care.

Throughout the life-course women must negotiate and renegotiate different spheres of responsibility which impact upon and shape women's housing choices and strategies. Thus, whilst an increasing number of women are gaining access to the cultural capital, economic citizenship and asset accumulation associated with owner occupation in British society, for others low income, residualized social housing, exclusion and exposure to the increasingly punitive state would appear to offer few opportunities for empowerment, participation and asset accumulation.

8 Moving beyond the standard family model

The emerging housing situations of women in Japan

Richard Ronald and Mieko Hinokidani

Introduction

Among advanced industrialised nations, Japan has demonstrated considerable resilience in terms of gender divisions in rights over and access to housing. In the pre-war period, women's housing situations were determined by their relationship to the male head-of-household who held legal authority over the family. The post-war Civil Code sought to promote democratisation. Nonetheless the housing position of women was not significantly advanced as Japan moved towards a homeownership orientated society and male breadwinner family model. Most women still had few legal rights over family property and inheritance continued to pass along male lines. The state and company welfare system was also synchronised with a standard family model, with those outside family households receiving little assistance. In recent decades, Japan has suffered a prolonged economic downturn with increasing pressure placed on women as both labour market participants and domestic carers. Also characteristic has been a steep decline in marriage and fertility rates in context of intensive societal aging and growing economic divisions. Increasingly, households and life-courses have become fragmented. Although realignments in employment, marriage and family formation have begun to reshape women's housing conditions, institutional practices and social policies have failed to keep pace with change.

Women's housing conditions will be implicated in this chapter as both features and drivers of socio-demographic shifts and emerging patterns of inequality. Historical constraints on women's housing opportunities are addressed as well as the emerging transition away from the standard family system. Recent social changes have undermined the male breadwinner model and while providing opportunities for greater independence, have also enhanced inequalities and the vulnerability of many women. The first section of the chapter considers the social and cultural origins of Japanese family and housing practices. The focus is the interaction between the socio-legal institutionalisation of pre-modern modes of patriarchal authority and the modernisation of the family around a division of labour based on a heterosexual complimentarity of gender roles. The second section considers the institutional framework surrounding contemporary shifts in social, economic and household relations. While the socioeconomic basis of post-war social solidarity and economic growth had been male breadwinner, nuclear families and corporate paternalism, in recent decades this system has unravelled along with the undermining of employment stability, standard family formation and welfare security. The final section thus addresses the outcomes of this unravelling and how it is restructuring relationships between women and housing. New patterns of inequality are emerging among different categories of married women and in particular between married and single women.

The socio-cultural origin of women's housing conditions

The basis of 'modern' housing and social practices has been a distinctive institutional organisation of the family around the concept of *'ie'*, denoting in Japanese, the house, family and ancestral lineage (see Koyano, 1996). Late nineteenth-century Japanese authorities intensively advanced industrial, economic and military expansion, which required social interventions. *The Family Registry System* (1871) and marriage and inheritance laws established by the *Meiji Civil Code* (1898) set in place a single national model of the *'ie'* or 'family system'. This effectively enshrined a model of patriarchal authority in law. Under the new administrative regime the registered paternal head of household held any family property rights and exercised authority over the rest of the family, and was legally succeeded by the eldest son (Morishima, 1988). The *ie* system and concept of *ie* society reflect ideological interpretations of Confucian values concerning filial piety and hierarchical relations of obligation considered to be underlying pillars of Japanese society.

Under the *ie* system, the male head of household was afforded pater familias powers considered necessary to fulfil obligations to the state as well as maintain the status of the family for future generations. Decisions over the marriage and domicile of household members, regarded as important to family lineage, were determined by the father, often discounting individual wishes (Vogel, 1979; Yamanaka, 1988). The bride of the eldest son was commonly referred to, or considered as, *uchi no yome* (bride of the house/family). She was subject to the will of her in-laws and husband, and had responsibility for domestic work and care of the children and elderly. Once her husband became head of household she acquired considerable power within the household, especially over areas of household management and finance.

Along with rapid urbanisation and modernisation, however, nineteenth-century social reformers also sought to re-centre Japanese family life. There was some interaction between the indigenous notion of *ie* and imported western ideals of domestic life, which provided a dialectical axis in the formulation of the modern conception of the family. Whereas *ie* was central to legal, heredity and temporal conceptions of families, western notions of 'home' posited a more bounded space associated with 'modern' values concerning child rearing and family intimacy. For Sand (2003), new gender roles and moral meanings became embedded in daily material practices to provide substance to an emerging middle-class ideal of domestic life focused on the nuclear family.

In the modern period, gender identities were distilled from an interaction between quasi-traditional *ie* norms and an emerging urban middleclass mainstream. Male identities were influenced by both the social ideal of the head-of-household as well as their economic status in socioeconomic order, determined by their association with their company. Women alternatively were constituted as housewives and homemakers and bound to society and the new world of salaried labour through their spouse. The neologism *katei* ('household' or literally house and garden) entered the Japanese vernacular to denote the realm of the modern housewife and the role of the woman within it. From the 1890s, modern housewifery became a concern of social modernisers and expressed in a growing popular literature on *katei*, focused on domestic management.

In the early twentieth century, the conjugal family and its physical locale, the home, thus became the focus of identities, structuring a differentiation of gender roles and responsibilities. As in Anglo-Saxon societies (see Watson, 1986), the idealisation of a female domestic role and privatised home life helped maintain the powerlessness of women, dependant of their husbands or fathers as the legal owners or providers of housing. In Japan, the maintenance of a more traditional concept of family in *ie* practices, such as family registries, reinforced inequalities. Essentially, single women rarely had any rights to, or control over, their housing situation. Young married women were subordinate to their husbands and often in-laws, but gained symbolic power as they became mothers and mother-in-laws themselves, especially if they were the wives of first-born sons. Industrialisation also enhanced women's dependency on male-dominated family relations by limiting access to education and professional employment.

There was, nonetheless, public concern with women's conditions in the home. Early twentieth-century reformers promoted domestic modernisation, specifically in the kitchen. Exposure to Western lifestyles also inspired reformative ideas. Suzuko Misumi (1872–1921) was exemplary among progressive educators. She demonstrated, in house designs containing Western-style dining rooms and kitchens, how modern housing could reduce domestic work. However, her ideas did not achieve general acceptance during her own lifetime (Kitagawa, 2002). After the transfer of productive activities away from the home, it was supposed that the most important function of a house was the reception of its (male) master's guests, with kitchens considered an exclusively female work place. This perception oriented developments in spatial living arrangements and it was only after World War II that the claims of Japanese female architects (most notably Miho Hamaguchi), concerning the elimination of feudalistic characteristics of Japanese houses became widely recognised by Japanese modernist architects.

Post-war housing and standard families

The speed and scale of urbanisation and industrialisation in Japan was well ahead of other Asian nations, stimulating rapid urban migration and new household formation. By the 1930s, nuclear families were the norm, and by 1950 the majority were urban. However, women's and citizen's rights lagged considerably behind those of other industrialised nations. After World War II rapid economic growth became the state imperative and the advancement of public welfare and citizenship rights considered subordinate to this goal. The housing and socio-economic system which emerged was based around a complementary system of household formation determined by 'standard' male breadwinner nuclear families, 'enterprise society', in which workers and their families were supported by employers, and government policy orientated towards the promotion of construction along with minimal public welfare spending.

The policy logic was that a rapidly growing economy would strengthen the umbrella of Japanese company practices such as lifelong employment, seniority based pay and company benefits that protected employee's families, while government resources could target the stimulation of overall economic growth. As the vast majority of regular employees were men, women would be protected by the corporate benefits enjoyed by their husbands. These benefits included housing subsidies, such as company rental housing and housing loans, that supplemented savings and borrowing necessary for families to get onto an owner-occupied housing ladder (Sato, 2007). Government housing policies focused, on the supply side, on the expansion of modern compact family housing units near industry, while considerable resources went, on the demand side, into the Government Housing Loan Corporation (GHLC) (after 1951), which provided working family households long-term fixed-rate mortgages. The development of the owner-occupied sector not only drove economic output, but also constituted a means for households to accumulate assets in the form of residential property. In combination with company welfare, this was considered to offset underdeveloped state welfare provision.

The formation of standard families with male breadwinners thus became a state priority and a feature of the Japanese welfare state. In some respects, the acceptance of this model in housing policy improved material domestic conditions for women. The introduction of a dining kitchen in newly built public rental housing is a good example. The Western style dining-kitchen (DK) equipped with modern domestic facilities and specialised dining area won great popularity and became a symbol of modern living. In particular, kitchen modernisation improved women's conditions during the 1960s as the 'life improvement movement' expanded into rural areas, where women suffered the demands of both agricultural work and domestic duties. However, such improvement did not alter normative views on women's domestic roles nor male behaviour. Reformers had supposed the elimination 'feudalistic characteristics of Japanese houses' and introduction of western style modern living would reduce divisions between husbands and wives in domestic work responsibilities.

The post-war housing model combined with the modern family norm to effectively strengthen women's attachments to the domestic sphere, transforming the home from a realm for men to one of women, or from a 'house for men' to a 'house for women' (Nishikawa, 2004). This notion became embedded with the newly emerged category of 'full-time housewife', which sustained gender norms in different ways (Shinada, 2007). The 'full-time housewife' is a special concept in Japan, reflecting women's views vis-à-vis domestic work. An assumption has been that domestic work, although unpaid, has an equivocal value with paid employment. It also signified deliverance from the dual duties that women had born. Even progressive female commentators have promoted housekeeping and caring as estimable work that should be compensated by free time for work in the community (Ueno, 1982). In 1980, the number of households composed of a single male breadwinner with a full-time housewife and children reached its peak, 64 per cent of family households.

The symbolic building of the housewife role in the home, along with the standard family model, were appropriated by the housing industries as cultural icons in stimulating desires to buy new homes. Policy assumed that establishing a housing ladder and expanding homeownership would enhance the formation and middle-class orientation of families more capable of meeting their own welfare needs (Hirayama, 2007). In comparison with other developed nations, Japan has demonstrated a close link between cultural and institutional 'familialism' and the welfare system. The government has encouraged middle-class nuclear families to obtain 'husband earned' housing as 'family places' by helping 'standard families' through state assisted housing loans and a unique occupational welfare system (Hirayama and Izuhara, 2008, p 643). In the early post-war period, a flow of standard families along with a more or less standard life-course was established around the security of male company employment and movement up a housing ladder involving, at first, renting an apartment and then buying a condominium, and finally a detached family house on its own land (Hirayama, 2007). Intensified housing construction and commodification saw urban homeownership rates swell from around 25 per cent before 1940 to a more stable rate of 64 per cent by the mid-1960s. This was accompanied by overwhelming increases in standard families and, according to public surveys, identification with middleclass living standards (from 72 per cent in 1958 to 87 per cent by 1965 (Cabinet Office, 2004)). Despite economic prosperity, however, many households have been excluded from Japan's 'homeowner mainstream society' and suffered housing poverty (Honma, 1980).

Another key post-war development was democratisation, which involved the legal abolition of the *ie* system under the new Civil Code (1947), establishing greater equality between men and women. Nonetheless, the institutionalisation of 'familialism' in housing and welfare systems continued to structure legal rights, social and economic policies and labour market practices that strongly disadvantage women. Specifically, married women's dependency on their husbands was reinforced by labour market practices favouring male breadwinner families over dual income families. Moreover, social policies targeted family households, disadvantaging unmarried women with singles often not qualifying for subsidies or benefits. Also significant has been the gendered accumulation of housing assets. Unlike societies where joint ownership became normalised (Finch *et al.,* 1996) in Japan housing assets have been persistently and overwhelmingly held by men. Women's housing conditions are thus characterised by large numbers of women living in properties owned by their husbands or fathers, even where they have contributed considerably to the mortgage, over which they have few legal rights. Moreover, gendered inheritance practices also continue with the vast majority of family housing and financial wealth flowing to male heirs (Izuhara, 2002). Essentially, while the legal form of *ie* was abolished, it has continued to influence household practices and ideologies concerning the Japanese family.

Social transformations

In recent decades Japan has endured prolonged recession and undergone socioeconomic reorientation involving a radical restructuring of post-war social practices and policies. Institutional changes have strongly impacted labour markets, public policy and the housing system. This has shaped, and been shaped by, significant socio-demographic developments including a rapid social ageing, declining marriage and fertility rates, increases in divorce rates and a proliferation of more atomised or fragmented household types. A significant outcome is that the pillar of the standard, male breadwinner household has been undermined, marked by the decline in the ratio of such households, restructuring family conditions and housing opportunities for Japanese women. The next section considers these changes before going onto consider female housing conditions that are emerging along with the decline in standard family formation.

Work, policy and family

One of the most significant shifts has been the restructuring of the employment system. This has impacted standard families in two ways: by undermining the stability of male breadwinner employment and by increasing labour market participation of women. This has often been compounded by social policies that are, characteristically, both conservative, in that they have focused on family policies

138

that lack relevance to emerging social conditions, and neo-liberal in that they have sought to deregulate or dissolve existing support mechanisms and subsidies.

During the economic recession of the 1990s, corporations began hollowing out the main features of Japan's employment paradigm: life employment, seniority pay and enterprise unions. Particular pressure was placed on the government to amend the Dispatched Labour Law (in 1999), which allowed for the proliferation of casual employment. Although older male employees largely had their seniority pay privileges protected, younger male workers were increasingly hired on 'irregular' contracts without benefits or employment security. Between 1982 and 2006 the ratio of workers in irregular employment grew from 15.8 to 30.6 per cent. Increases among those aged 20–24, from 11.4 to 41.2 per cent was particularly extreme. Even those hired on a permanent basis have suffered the rollback in company benefits packages and declining income security as performance-based rewards have superseded seniority-based pay (Genda, 2001).

With the declining ability of husbands to provide stable incomes to support their families has come a substantial growth in female employment. The Equal Opportunity Act of 1986 and its major amendments in 1997 and 2006 ostensibly sought to enhance women's position and there has been a considerable feminisation of the labour market in Japan with female participation rates increasing from 58 to 68 per cent between 1980 and 2005. Nonetheless, recruitment and employment practices continue to advantage male workers while embedded gender norms in the workplace continue to sustain inequalities and powerlessness among women workers (Kondo, 1990). The feminisation of work has thus been characterised by an increase in women workers plugging the gaps generated by the erosion of secure male employment. Table 8.1 illustrates that less than half of women are full-time regular employees compared to 84 per cent of men, while 38 per cent of women are part-time workers compared to 8.5 per cent of men. Indeed, even though female employment has increased, the ratio of women in regular work has decreased between 1980 and 2005 from 63 to 48 per cent for women compared to 91 to 84 per cent for men. Even for women in career track employment, the chances of resuming a promotion trajectory, or even returning to work at all, are low after taking maternity leave, with companies assuming that childrearing has become the women's priority over the company.

Although job opportunities have improved for women, a substantial gap remains between female and male earnings and positions in regular employment. A central reason for the formation of the dual labour market in Japan is the tax and pension system which encourages married women not to exceed a maximum earnings limit. By limiting their income to 1.3 million yen p.a. wives retain their dependant tax credit status and remain covered by their husband's social security premiums. Following the logic of a male breadwinner model, the Class Three public pension category was introduced in 1985 to help protect housewives, who are entitled to 75 per cent of their husband's pension in the event of his death. However, this

Table 8.1 Distribution of employment and wages by gender and job type

		Full-time		Part-time		Total (average)
		Regular	Non-regular	Regular	Non-regular	
Type of worker	Male	84.0%	7.5%	0.3%	8.2%	100%
	Female	47.4%	14.6%	0.9%	37.1%	100%
Hourly wage (yen)	Male	2,094	1,324	1,342	1,059	1,949
	Female	1,465	1,041	1,068	939	1,203
Relative female to male wage		0.698	0.786	0.796	0.887	0.617

Source: Adapted from Yamaguchi (2008) MHLW Wage Structure Survey (2005b).

means that women earning wages above the threshold lose the right to a large portion of their spouse's pension and have to pay their own premiums, and may thus end up with a smaller pension than a married woman who never worked. Although legislation has sought to reinforce the protection of women, it has more effectively encouraged types of irregular and part-time employment that maintain women's dependency on their husbands. Moreover, it is based on the assumption that all women will form standard families with breadwinning husbands, justifying institutional inequalities as means of protection.

With labour market restructuring, it was estimated that in 2001 more than 60 per cent of family households relied upon dual incomes (Hirao, 2001). As the need to work has intensified, however, pressures on women as domestic carers have also increased. By 2002, one-fifth of the population was already over 65. This figure is expected to be one-third by 2030. Moreover, older people are living longer (on average 79 years for men and 86 years for women). In light of the underdevelopment of public welfare in Japan, the social costs of ageing have been largely borne by women as family carers. As a welfare state, Japan has been considered close to corporatist states in relation to occupational and status differentiated groups, similar to Anglo-liberal welfare regimes in regard to residualisation and the commodification of welfare goods, and also like Mediterranean regimes in terms of reliance on the family as a welfare provider (Esping-Andersen, 1997; Uzuhashi, 2001). In the early 2000s the introduction of Long Term Care Insurance (LTCI) sought to shift the burden of elderly care onto the state. However, LTCI policies have increasingly sought to perpetuate informal family care practices and focused on home centred provision in which responsibility for care continues to fall on women (Morikawa et al., 2007).

Government housing interventions have targeted economic rather than social objectives. Limited public housing has been provided, but mostly for family households. There have been few rent subsidies, and only available for specific housing types or specified locations. A small public rental housing sector was developed after the war, constituting as much as 7.6 per cent of housing in 1983. However, it is being gradually residualised and production of units for low-income households stopped in 2005. Local authorities provide the vast majority of public housing and target special categories of poor, such as the elderly, with no qualification for younger single-person households (except in some cases of domestic violence). The main mechanism of housing subsidy has been GHLC loans, again primarily for family households. There was no qualification for one-person households for GHLC mortgages before 1981, and until 1988 loans were only available to those over 40 years old. More recently, neo-liberalisation has become more evident in policies. Withdrawal of GHLC loan provision in 2007 marked a key step in state privatisation and deregulation in housing, but also destabilised housing conditions even for family households with regular employment.

There have also been fundamental changes in housing conditions since 1980 contributing to the economic destabilisation. In the 1970s, private sector investment in land was driven by increases in housing prices. The government subsequently began to improve lending conditions to maintain access to owner-occupied housing for families. In the 1980s a speculative bubble began to form with peak year house price increases (1987–1988) in Tokyo of between 22 and 29 per cent (Ministry of Construction, 1995). Although home purchase promised considerable capital gains, mortgage demands on incomes escalated along with an increase in the scale of indebtedness. Outstanding housing loans swelled from 48,229 billion yen in 1980 to 191,203 billion yen in 2000 (an escalation in the ratio of outstanding housing loans to GDP from 19.4 to 37.3 per cent). The 1990s began with a collapse in share values followed by sustained decline in nominal house prices, which dropped 40 to 50 per cent by the 2000s. Essentially, the downturn in the housing market undermined the housing ladder as demonstrated by the rapid fall in homeownership rates among new households. Between 1978 and 1998 the proportion of homeowners aged 25–29 dropped from one in four to one in eight, while for those aged 30–34 it fell from over half to one in five.

Volatile economic conditions since the 1980s have undermined both company employment and state policy bases of standard family and male breadwinner society. On the one hand company benefits have been withdrawn and employment security undermined, while on the other, state policies have lagged behind socio-economic changes and emerging inequalities, and sought to complement a company and standard family system that increasingly appears dysfunctional. For women, getting married had been fundamental to chances of participating in the benefits of company society or receiving government welfare subsidies. Welfare policies orientated around the male breadwinner model have made it difficult for unmarried women to receive government support (Yokoyama, 2002). In the post-bubble era, however, the advantages of being married to a breadwinner have been undermined. Housing conditions had been largely determined by the working husband's ability to move up the housing ladder and purchase a detached family-house. This too was eroded by changing social conditions. Women have consequently been called upon to contribute more to the household, both as earners and family carers. However, their increasing contribution has not been matched by improvements in their standing in the labour market or as the legal owners of the housing they pay for and inhabit.

Marriage and fertility

Social and demographic changes in recent decades have been dramatic and reflect growing instability in, and deterioration of, the standard family, breadwinner model and fixed life-courses. Rising marriage ages, falling fertility rates and increasing longevity have begun to reshape Japanese society and the constitution of households. There has been a propensity for increasing numbers of single households and couple-only households without children. According to the population census, the proportion of nuclear households (married couple and children) dropped below 30 per cent in 2005, while the number of single and couple-only households has almost doubled since 1980 and now accounts for half of all households (Figure 8.1). There is an even greater intensity in household atomisation and fragmentations in metropolitan areas and in Tokyo 43 per cent of households are now estimated to contain just one person. The majority of such singles are under 40 years-old and unmarried (IPSSR, 2008).

A major feature of declines in standard family formation and fertility has been an increase in the age of getting married and higher rates of people not getting married at all (Figures 8.2 and 8.3). Average marriage ages increased between 1970 and 2005 from 26.9 to 29.6 year old for men and 24.2 to 27.9 year old for women (Figure 8.2). Meanwhile, 33 per cent of women aged 30–34, 18 per cent aged 35–39 and 12 per cent aged 40–44 were unmarried in 2005 (MIAC, 2008). The phenomenon of 'never married' singles is likely to become more extreme over time as current cohorts of unmarried people age. Even though the advance of families with non-married parents has been common to advanced societies, in Japan cohabitation of non-married couples is both rare and unlikely to produce children. While almost 10 per cent of women in their 30s acknowledge a period of 'living with a partner' (assumed to be a heterosexual couple) less than two per cent of unmarried women of reproductive age live at any one time as an unmarried couple (IPSSR, 2008). Furthermore, less than two per cent of children are born to unmarried parents in Japan each year. Female-headed, single-parent families, including divorcees and widows, are thus relatively uncommon. Fertility has become a public issue, and while rates once peaked in 1947 at 4.3 children born on average to every woman, in 2004 this figure had dropped to 1.29 (recovering marginally to 1.32 in 2006).

In spite of all of these drastic socio-economical changes, gender norms are still powerful. According to the international comparison by the Cabinet office, the rate of agreement with the norm that 'men should work while women remain at home' was 30.5 per cent in Japan. This is the highest among 19 economically advanced

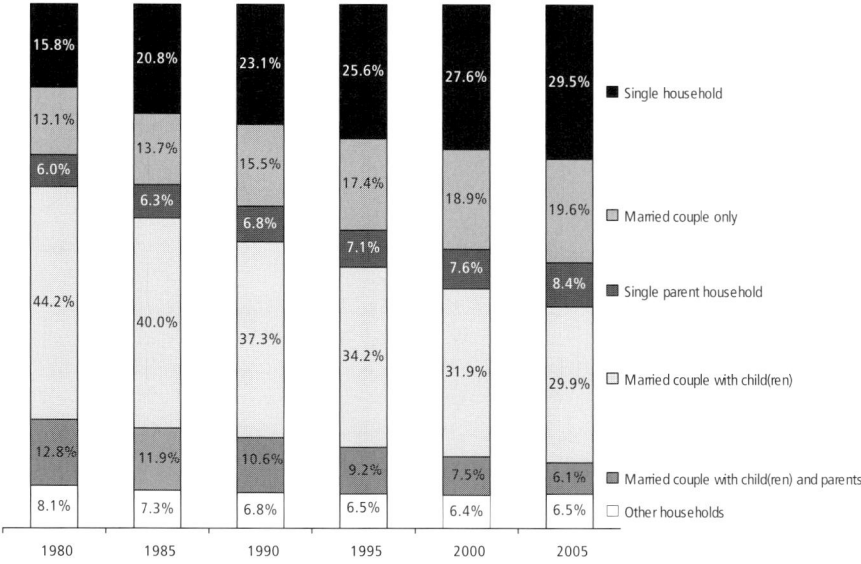

Single household

Married couple only

Single parent household

Married couple with child(ren)

Married couple with child(ren) and parents

Other households

8.1 Households by type. Source: Bureau of Statistics (2005).

countries, including Korea (Cabinet Office, 2005). It was only in the late 1990s that the number of dual-working family households exceeded that of single male breadwinner ones, although gaps in conditions for women continue to proceed (Iwama, 2008).

Housing situations

Women's social, economic and domestic conditions have arguably undergone a revolution in recent years. While the employment basis of the male breadwinner family model has been undermined, government policy mechanisms have responded poorly to changing household conditions. At the same time, traditional expectations of women have intensified. In the home there has been greater pressure on women as domestic managers and carers of children and elderly, and in the workplace gendered inequalities in pay and treatment continue even though women's legal rights, education levels and contribution in the labour market have increased. Stresses exerted upon the family are clearly evident in declines in nuclear family formation and the growth of single-households and lifestyles. These changes are having a fundamental impact on the housing system which was established on the basis of standard families following standard life-courses under the umbrella of regular male employment. The features of fragmenting housing and social systems are in turn shaping residential choices and the housing opportunities of women.

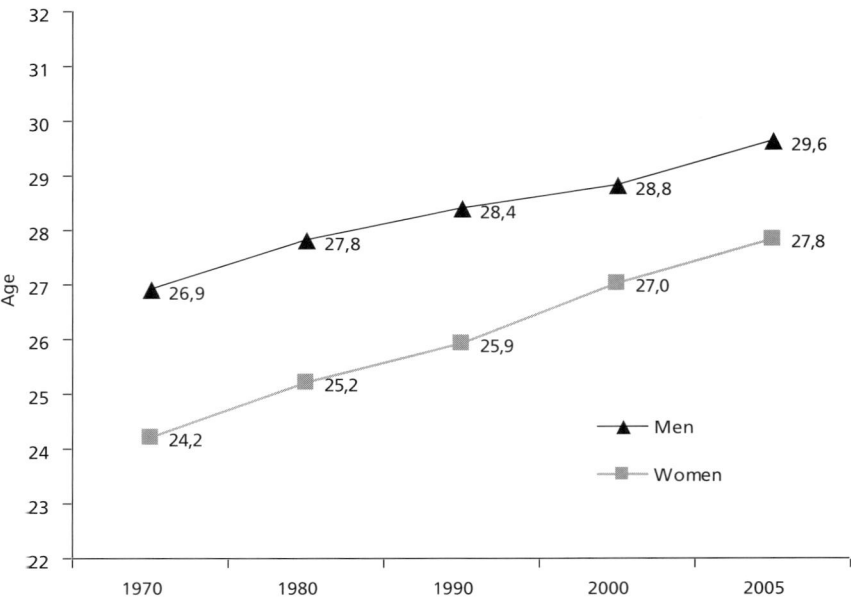

8.2 Average age of first marriage. Source: Bureau of Statistics (2005).

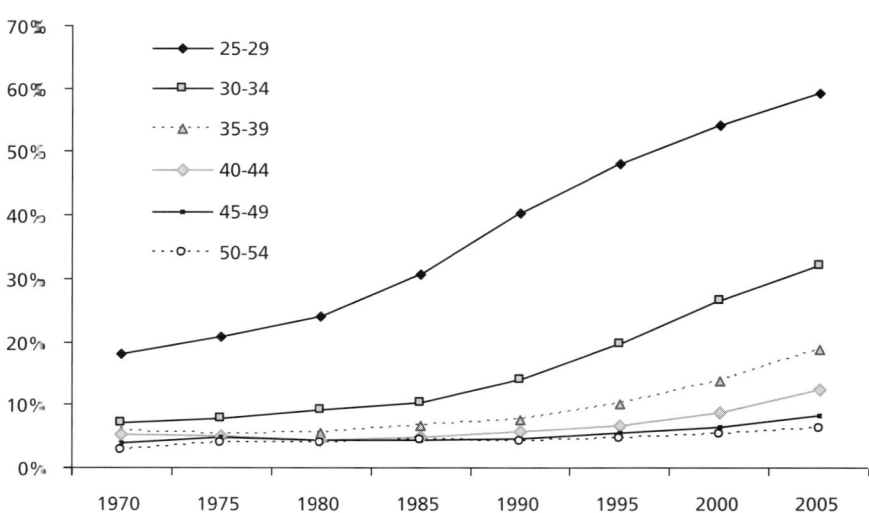

8.3 Proportion of never-married women by age-group. Source: Bureau of Statistics (2005).

Single women

In the 2000s, the notion of 'winners and losers' began to influence public perceptions of women and marriage. Following Sakai (2003), who sought to identify disadvantages faced by women who do not follow established paths into marriage and family life, the term 'loser dogs' was incorporated into discourses on the growing army of unmarried women, distinguishing them from the 'winner dogs' who marry and, it is assumed, enjoy the benefits of a system designed to support family units at the expense of individuals. The housing system has been fundamental to such a division as employment conditions, social policy and housing markets effectively erect barriers to stable, independent housing for single women. However, actual housing conditions for single women are quite diverse. While many remain in the natal home or have chosen to live independently in small, private rental units, there has been a growing market of single women in the condominium sector. Essentially, many women are negotiating life-courses and residential choices beyond the standard family model.

For a growing number of women, security and middle-class status is no longer assured by making a 'good marriage' to a man with a stable income in a regular salaried job. Ochiai (1994) suggests that as economic growth has slowed, young women have been increasingly unable to imitate their mother's marital choices. This has accompanied a growing frustration with women's role in the male breadwinner family model and a cultural shift in outlooks on marriage. Nakano and Wagatsuma (2004) contrast differences in expectations between young women and their mothers. They suggest that with improvements in occupational, educational and marital choices, women have gained greater control over their own lives with marriage becoming less important to life chances. The consensus over what constitutes a 'good life' has thus fragmented. Increasing numbers of women thus seek a companion rather than a wage earner, or choose to remain single. The idea that women should rightfully have choices has become embedded, among the younger female population at least.

There has been an evident shift in attitudes towards family formation, although there remains a desire to marry and have children. While the marriage market has been argued to be dysfunctional with considerable gaps emerging in men's expectations of potential wives and women's expectations of future husbands, rates of 'traditional' arranged marriages fell from 29.4 to 6.4 per cent between 1982 and 2005. A 2005 national Attitude Survey (IPSSR, 2008) found that for 90 per cent of women the most important factor for a potential marriage partner was the person's character, which was second to 'willingness and ability to help with housework and childcare' (59 per cent). Nakano (2010) found among older single women eager to marry, a desire to marry someone with whom they could develop an 'intimate and mutually supportive relationship'. However, many such women claimed that men failed to meet such expectations: personalities are poorly matched, men lack social skills, are domineering and unlikely to help around the house. The argument is thus that as the educational and employment standing of women has changed, so have their expectations of marriage, which are no longer focused on finding a husband who will provide household security and middle-class status.

Whatever the reasons may be, the decision not to marry reduces the housing options of the vast majority of single women who normally have few inheritance rights on their parent's property, do not qualify for housing assistance or mortgage subsidy and have an inadequate income to purchase their own home. While Japanese banks require a down payment of 20 per cent, the actual average down payment in 2005 was 32 per cent of purchase price, which was on average 36,360,000 yen. Even for family households, with growing costs the average age of entry into homeownership is now almost 40, about 10 years older than in the 1970s and much older than other homeowner societies (Moriizumi, 2003). Consequently, the decline in marriage rates has been accompanied by a considerable growth in the number of women staying on indefinitely in their parent's homes.

Adult children who remain indefinitely in their parent's home have become known as 'parasite singles' (Yamada, 1999). Between 1980 and 2005, the overall rate of 'parasite singles' increased from 23.9 to 42.6 per cent for those aged 25–29, and 7.6 to 24 per cent for those aged 30–34. One side of the explanation for the growth in this phenomenon emphasises a Japanese cultural tendency for parents to overprotect their children, delaying transition to independence (Miura, 2005). The fact that the post-war housing system drove a ladder of housing acquisition also means that most older Japanese people own their own, normally spacious detached home, in which to protect their adult children (homeownership rates are above 80 per cent for those over 60). In addition, the continued presence of male adult children at home has not been considered as significant, reflecting 'ie' traditions of intergenerational cohabitation, with the eldest son taking on obligations for care of the parents in old age and reciprocally inheriting the home.

The other side of the argument focuses on the growing 'selfishness' of young women, reluctant to take on the responsibilities of being a wife and mother. Yamada (1999) initially suggested the comfortable lives of women who live with their parents, with free meals, cleaning and laundry, affords them to spend their money on themselves (p. 11). Single children who continue to reside in the parental home as adults are not always expected to pay a formal rent or contribute to household expenses. While there has been higher overall male parasite 'singledom', recent increases have been most significant among younger women, increasing 18 to 41 per cent for ages 25–29, and from around 5 to 21 per cent for ages 30–34, between 1980 and 2000. However, while it may be true that many single women expect a decline in the quality of life should they marry and leave home, it has been argued that many unmarried women experience nothing of a free and selfish life of material consumption, but remain in the natal home because they have no choice, or because they choose to sacrifice their own interests for the needs of their families (Haruka,

2002). Nakano (2010) points out that as unmarried daughters get older, parents may begin to see them as a source for security, with the daughter taking care of their needs in old age.

Hirayama and Ronald (2008) argue that staying on in the family home is a rational economic choice for young people, especially in the case of young women who have poorer opportunities than men of regular employment, promotion and pay increases, irrespective of education. The main housing option for young singles on leaving home is the private rental sector. With declines in standard family formation, economic security and homeownership rates, between 1983 and 2003 the ratio of independent households aged 25–29 renting privately increased from 53 to 71 per cent, while for those aged 30–35 the increase was from 33.5 to 55 per cent. There are no subsidies for young single low-income renters, and stock is dominated by poorer quality small apartment units. Owner-occupied homes have an average floor-space of 124m^2 per whereas rental units have 46.3m^2. This compares to a respective ratio of 124 to 76m^2 in Germany, 114 to 76m^2 in France and 95 to 75m^2 in Britain (Oi *et al.*, 2007). For young singles, especially women, rent alone may take up more than a third of income and independent living may only be possible with continued support from parents.

For single women in non-regular work home purchase is usually not an option. Despite declines in price, the average price-to-income ratio in Tokyo, for example, is 5.2 for a condominium (MLIT, 2005). In Hirayama and Izuhara's (2008) survey of female housing assets, housing tenure strongly correlated with age, reflecting previous institutional conditions of the housing ladder, family formation and life-courses. Homeownership rates were 32 per cent for ages 30–34, 55 per cent for ages 40–44 and 70 per cent for ages 50–54. Many women appeared to have moved from a prolonged stay in the parental home into private renting and eventually homeownership, marital status being the key modifier of this transition. The average rate of owner-occupation is 54.6 per cent across all ages but is only 7.8 per cent for unmarried women. Hirayama and Izuhara conclude that the majority of women who climb up the housing ladder to homeownership do not do so as individuals but via marriage. 'As a result, the combination of the family orientated housing system and the increasing number of unmarried women has led to an inevitable increase in female households with limited housing choice' (p. 651).

Nonetheless, some single women have been able to take advantage of improved educational opportunities and labour market restructuring. There have been increases in single women in full-time, professional careers buying their own homes, especially apartments. A survey of condominium purchasers in 2004 found that 7.7 per cent of all purchasers were single women (Recruit, 2005). According to Matsumoto (1998) the geographic distribution of singles has certain features. Female homeowners are more concentrated in city centres with male owner-occupiers on the urban periphery. Yui's (2004) analysis identifies the growing market for single women who focus on convenience and short commutes in residential choices. A new market for young female singles has thus begun to emerge in metropolitan districts featuring 'compact condominiums' of 30–50m² with high specification, fashionable designs in trendy urban locations. It may also be suggested that housing investment may be particularly important to single professional women who are less likely to inherit property and face greater pressures to invest in order to provide for their own old age (Kawata, 2007).

Lone mothers

Housing conditions for single mothers in Japan have been particularly harsh, which is reflected in the exceptionally low rate of lone-mother-headed households. According to the 2005 population census, 7.1 per cent of family households are headed by single mothers. This compares to over 20 per cent in UK. Furthermore, most Japanese lone-mother households are divorcees and widows, and predominantly over 30 years old (Ezawa and Fujiwara, 2005). The number of single-mother households has, nonetheless, been in the ascendancy, increasing from 718,100 in 1984 to 1,225,400 in 2003. Government policy has supported single mothers by encouraging them to work rather than providing cash benefits. The rate of employment is exceptionally high at 85 per cent, although earning capacities are limited. The average income for a single-mother household in 2005 was 2.13 million yen compared to the average household, with at least one child, of 7.2 million yen (MHLW, 2006). Less than 7 per cent of single mother households receive Livelihood Protection (basic poverty assistance) while 60 per cent get Child Maintenance Allowance (MHLW, 2005a), which is means tested and unavailable for those earning more than 3.65 million yen.

Housing conditions for lone-mother households have been tight as a result of their inferior labour market position (and lower incomes), their exclusion from husband earned housing and cultural norms concerning mothering. Although single mothers are a priority group in the allocation of public rental units, such housing is limited and often located far from employment and day-care facilities, undermining access to work, which is central to government approaches to supporting such families. Figure 8.4 illustrates that most single mothers turn to the private rental sector or dwell with relatives or others (around 25 per cent have no independent housing). The 21 per cent rate of homeownership is also much lower than the 55 per cent female average. For Hinokidani (2007), lone-mother households thus have less living space than conventional households and have higher housing expenditure compared to income. Life Support Centers for Mothers and Children have been provided on a small scale in the post-war period, and since the late 1970s divorced women with children have constituted the majority of residents (many escaping domestic violence). As of the early 2000s, there were around 300 such centres accommodating around 2,000 families. Inevitably, institutional living is inadequate to the long term needs of many lone-mother families and ineffective in relaunching careers on the mainstream housing ladder.

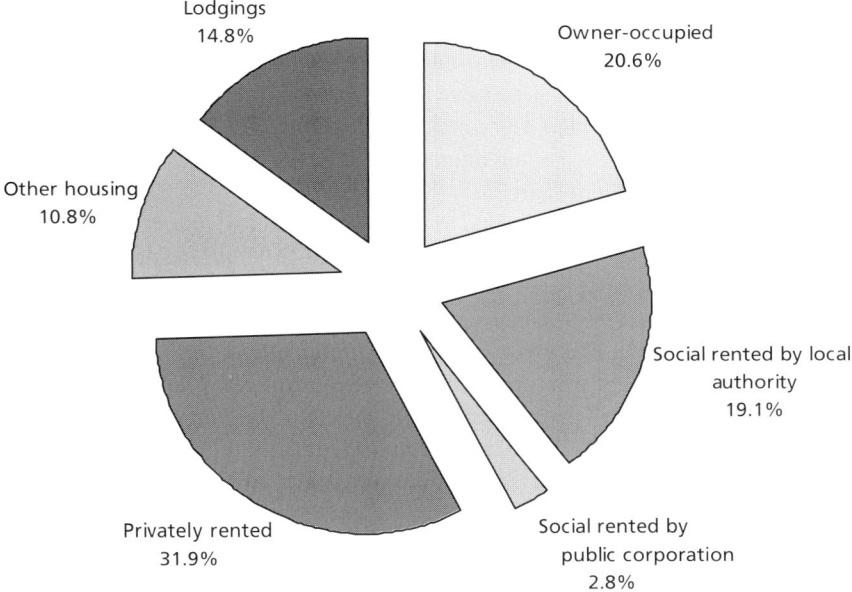

8.4 Distribution of housing tenure, lone-mother families. Source: Ministry of Health, Labour and Welfare (2003).

Married women

Notwithstanding differences with singles, housing conditions for married women are also inequitable and most continue to have few legal rights over the owner-occupied homes within which they dwell. Hirayama and Izuhara's (2008) survey found that 75 per cent of detached houses and 78 per cent of condominiums are owned by husbands as 'sole owners'. The proportion of wives having even some legal ownership over their own family property is as low as 20 per cent. Among women who do own a share, the rate of those who own 50 per cent or more is 16 per cent for detached houses and 23 per cent for condominiums. Of mortgaged households (96 per cent) the housing loan was held exclusively in the name of the husband in 90 per cent of cases. It appears that while women increasingly contribute to mortgage repayments, this tends not to be formally recognised.

In most economically advanced societies, wives hold rights over property held in husband's names that can be accessed in case of divorce. In Japan, however, women tend to be disadvantaged most by divorce and the separation of assets, and particularly in housing property negotiations and relocations. This is often because they have no legal share of the property, and in many cases the home is considered to belong to the husband's 'ie' with, often, in-laws owning a share of the property. While ownership can be contested, the cost of going to court normally outweighs the perceived advantages for many women. Around 91 per cent of Japanese divorces are uncontested (division of assets etc. by mutual agreement) (Sakata and Mackenzie, 2009). According to the Ministry of Health and Welfare 1997 survey, while the level of homeownership for men dropped from 43 to 41 per cent for men after divorce, for women the drop was from 29 to 11 per cent. The rate of those who moved home immediately after divorce was 71 per cent for women but only 28 per cent for men.

Clearly, there continues to be a fundamental female dependency on husbands in terms of access to and rights over housing. Furthermore, divorced women, especially those with children, tend to suffer in the longer term from employment instability and income inequality. This has not suppressed divorce rates, which increased from 0.73 per 1000 people in 1963 to 2.3 in 2003. The financial disadvantages faced by women who fall out of marriage, in light of the pressures of social ageing, has recently enjoyed some legislative recognition. Since 2007 divorcees may split the earnings related portion of the husband's pension that accrued during the marriage period, providing financial security of divorced women, many of whom served male breadwinner standard families, forfeiting the chance to earn their own pensions.

Housing situations in old age have historically been orientated around expectations of intergenerational cohabitation. In 1980, 60.6 per cent of those aged 65-plus lived with their children or their children's families. However, the incidence of such households had declined to 37.5 per cnet by 2005. Increasingly, elderly people are living longer as couples or, for women in particular, as singles (with women tending to outlive their husbands). Women also have a higher chance of living in an institution after the death of a partner (IPSSR, 2008). Nonetheless, numbers of care homes accommodating low-income old people are dwindling, meaning that care needs are expected to be met within the home. Recent reforms in elderly welfare, including the Long-Term Care Insurance system, that focuses on care in the home, have thus had a significant influence on older women's lives. Elderly singles who do not own their own home often face discrimination in the private rental market as landlords are reluctant to let to them, preferring younger occupants, who are less likely to become infirm or pass away during their tenancy. Considering the long term rise in never-married women, in future there are likely to be increasing numbers of single female elderly who do not own their own homes.

Conclusions

Housing conditions for Japanese women continue to largely depend upon men and marriage. Recent social and economic restructuring has, however, stimulated considerable changes in households and life-courses that have destabilised the post-war male breadwinner model and the 'husband-earned' owner-occupied housing ladder. Both new opportunities and inequalities have emerged for and among women that have been shaped by a housing and social policy system orientated toward familialism. The new lifestyles and life-courses of younger women are also reshaping the housing system with declining demand for suburban family housing and growing demand for compact urban apartments, driving the development of new types of city centre dwellings. While some women have taken advantage of improved education and employment opportunities, improving their capacity to buy their own homes, for many others economic restructuring has brought greater pressure to bear and housing choices have been limited. It appears that increasing numbers of women are not forming standard families, but instead remain in their parent's home or sustain a single-person household.

Masculinities and femininities have begun to respond to changing conditions. For men, the iconic male role within *'ie'* still resonates in hegemonic masculinities. However, with prolonged economic downturn and erosion of company society, the authority of the 'salaryman' has been diminished. The status of his female complement has also been transformed with the traditional housewife no longer the only ideal. Increasingly, female identities are responding to a greater diversity of aspirational types that include office ladies and professional career women. Attitude surveys have demonstrated strong desires to marry and have children among young women, although the assumption that this is an inevitable step in the life-course has diminished. Nonetheless, family homeownership remains the focus of the housing system and central to institutional welfare practices. Women's life chances are thus enhanced by a life-course that includes home purchase, although this appears strongly bound with marriage. However, owner-occupied properties are largely held in spouse's names with most women having little independent ownership, control or access to housing assets.

Considering the conservative and neo-liberal characteristics of Japanese governance, it seems unlikely that legislation and policy making will respond effectively to emerging social inequalities derived from housing and structured by gender. However, sharp drops in marriage and fertility combined with a large and expanding elderly population will put progressively more pressure on the government to act. Women in the meantime are negotiating their own routes through employment and housing and are increasingly forming new types of household beyond the standard family model.

9 Neo-liberalization and the invisibility of women's housing problems in Taiwan

Herng-Dar Bih and Yi-Ling Chen

Introduction

Feminism and women's studies have been making ground in Taiwan for two to three decades. However, research on the topic of women and housing policy remains limited. Feminist research in Europe and North America found that the social designation of women's roles in the areas of production and reproduction has affected their economic status, and in turn their housing condition. Consequently, the issue of women and housing should be approached from the perspective of the domestic obligations and economic marginalization of women (Saegert and Clark, 2006). In most cultures dominated by the heterosexual, patriarchal family, women are primarily responsible for the domestic sphere, a situation which contributes to their economic disadvantage. At the same time, in heterosexual societies, living space for gays and lesbians and the resources allocated to them by housing policies are limited. This chapter will examine the status of Taiwan's women in terms of changes in women's roles in the areas of production and reproduction, and the impact of housing policy on women.

The chapter is divided into three parts, starting with a review of housing studies in Taiwan and changes in housing policy. Since 1990, housing policies in Taiwan have been influenced by the processes of democratization and neo-liberalization, and this section of the chapter will discuss how the transformation has affected the allocation of resources in the context of changing housing policies, in particular the impact on low-income housing. The second section deals with shifts in the roles of women in the domestic sphere and the economy in Taiwan, and the third discusses the housing of women of different identities (e.g., single women, single mothers, foreign spouses, homeless women and lesbians).

Housing studies and housing policy in Taiwan

Women's housing problems remain invisible in Taiwan. Several reasons contribute to this invisibility. Women's studies have provided fruitful research in Taiwan, but as most researchers are trained in sociology, literary criticism and education, few have dealt with the issue of housing. Another important reason is how housing problems are defined. Research on housing draws mainly from three approaches: political economy, environmental psychology, and housing economics. The dominant approach is housing economics studying the production, sale and the related consumption behaviour of the housing market. This research has been influential on the housing policy in Taiwan. Housing economics advocates the importance of the market, with the state performing the task of establishing market rules and regulations, and then trusting the market mechanism to resolve housing issues without too much direct intervention. Because of the conviction in the power of the market, policies related to the disadvantaged also rely on the power of the housing market or non-government organizations, without prescribing forceful government intervention. Moreover, studies of housing economics rarely deal with gender as an important issue (Chen, 2000).

This chapter argues that the neo-liberal discourse in Taiwan encourages the state to enhance the commodification of housing, and every citizen to become consumers. This belief hinders the state in seeking alternative solutions other than the market. Any social welfare idea is treated as increasing the burden on the state. Many housing problems are not defined as 'problems' because the state does not want to provide solutions. Neo-liberal discourse also privatizes these problems and encourages people to believe that buying a home is the solution.

Changes in social policies

To analyse Taiwan's housing policy, it is helpful to begin by exploring social policies more generally, as both affect women's housing conditions. As a developing country, Taiwan's progress was directed by an authoritarian government from 1949 to the end of the 1980s, with the emphasis always on the economy. The concept of equity was non-existent, and in social discourse, it was believed that social welfare hinders economic development, and that the problems of social inequity could be resolved as the benefits of economic development filtered down to those at the bottom of society (Wong, 2004). Whether as a developing country with the goal of high economic growth, or as an authoritarian nation with the goal of political survival, Taiwan has had little time for social welfare with its goal of redistribution.

What limited social welfare initiated by the state was not the result of social pressure. Changes in social policies were primarily due to political crisis, and were therefore selective in their beneficiaries. Rather than targeting those most in need, benefits were distributed on the basis of national interest and were offered firstly to those who supported the authoritarian state and developmental regime.

Thus, social policies became a political tool (Wong, 2004, 55–58). For example, in the 1950s, it was for the purpose of maintaining the stability of the outsider regime (Kuomintang – KMT) that social policies were created to care for military personnel, government employees and educational workers (MGE) and employees of state-owned enterprises. By the 1970s, diplomatic crisis, slowing economic development and anti-KMT movements led to the extension of social welfare to cover other groups, such as child labour, the elderly, disabled persons, and the poor. Nevertheless, concrete social welfare benefited mainly the MGE, and while the Labor Insurance Act covered working persons, other policies for the disadvantaged were no more than proclamations (Wu, 2004).

By the end of the 1980s, the lifting of martial law and the ensuing social movements and pressure for democratization had forced the government into providing more social welfare to satisfy the public. Women's movements were also actively seeking to revise many patriarchal practices in law and requesting more support for families. Since the 1990s, social welfare spending has remained on the rise, although almost half of welfare spending is used in retirement pensions for the MGE (Wang, 2007). In contrast to MGE benefits, social security spending on low-income households has remained small: in 2004, only 2.2 per cent of the spending was on social assistance (DGBAS, 2006a). Because of the strict definition, low-income households make up only 1.23 per cent of the Taipei City population, a figure that is already higher than Taiwan's average of 0.87 per cent (DSAMI, 2008).

Although welfare spending in Taiwan reached the standard of over 4.4 per cent of GDP in the 1990s, it is not large compared to European and North American countries, and families have to perform most welfare functions (Lee and Ku, 2003). The principle of mutual support among family members and relatives is even manifested in the social welfare system. In the 1997 Social Assistance Act amendment related to low-income households, the calculation of household income was changed to include the income of immediate family members, regardless of whether they lived together. As a result, many single-mother families lost their low-income household status (Cheng, 2001). Cheng and Hsiung (1993) indicated that the state in Taiwan was patriarchal, capitalist and authoritarian. Welfare for women has been much increased in recent years, but it has far from socialized the domestic sphere. The lack of sufficient family support has two implications: the first one is that women continue to take the major responsibility for domestic work, a situation that hinders their economic status. The second implication is that the system leads every individual family to seek support from the market. Cheap, foreign domestic workers, mostly female, have become the solution for many well-to-do families in Taiwan.

Changes in housing policy

Like social policies, housing policy before the 1970s targeted only a small group of people, mainly the MGE, and a few illegal squatters and disaster-affected households. Social equality has hardly been a major concern of housing policies, let along gender equality. After the mid-1970s, the political and economic crises and the example of Singapore's public housing policy led to the government taking direct charge of public housing construction, with the creation of a large scale six-year public housing project in 1976. However, due to land acquisition problems, the price of the finished housing deviated from the range affordable to moderate- to low-income households, and the original goal of caring for these citizens was not accomplished. The project had aimed for the construction of 100,000 residences over six years, but in the end, only 67,794 were completed (CPA, 2006).

After the late 1980s, the state was forced by the pressure of democratization into providing significantly more housing, and from this period, the influence of neo-liberalism on housing policy could be seen, though the experience was different to that of the UK or the USA. As the process of Taiwan's neo-liberalization coincided with a phase of democratic transformation, the pressure from social movements and elections actually enhanced the state's intervention in housing, with the result of more housing projects being undertaken. However, an examination of the state's method of intervention reveals the gradual incorporation of market logic into housing policy, in that apart from directly undertaking public housing projects, the government also encouraged public housing constructions by the private sector. More importantly, the various low-interest home loan plans offered from 1990 were aimed at encouraging people to buy homes and enter the property market, on the one hand to invigorate the development of the home loan business of banks, on the other hand to facilitate the growth of the real estate industry. The free-market logic eventually turned into a principle guiding government intervention, and direct constructions of public housing gradually dwindled. By the end of the 1990s, the provision of subsidized loans had become the dominant housing policy, with the resolution of housing problems via the market mechanism the critical administrative logic (Chen and Li, forthcoming).

Although democratization in the 1990s had pressured the state into taking care of a wider variety of social groups, the MGE, especially the military, remained the biggest beneficiary. In 1996, an act governing the reconstruction of villages for military personnel and their dependents was passed, offering sizable subsidies for the reconstruction and privatization of these places, which demonstrated the significant political consideration in state interventions.

One of the key differences between housing policy and social welfare policies is that housing policy has always been a part of economic policy, and bears the function of promoting economic growth. The first large-scale six-year public housing project belonged to a six-year economic development programme, and the twelve development tasks promoted in 1979 included public housing. After the 1990s, as

Taiwan's economic development slowed and many industries relocated overseas, the government came to regard the real estate industry as a link in economic growth, hoping to revive the local economy through its stimulation. Therefore, whenever the economy came under pressure, the government would aid the real estate industry through low-interest loans and related tax reduction measures. In response to the global economic downturn of 2008, more low-interest loans were introduced and tax reduction measures implemented, as the government also looked into lifting restrictions on Mainland Chinese property investment in Taiwan.

On the surface, housing policy under the neo-liberal transformation of democratization appears to benefit more people, but major problems of fairness exist. First, the policy leans towards protecting the interests of the real estate industry, with the government immediately applying favourable interest loans and tax reduction measures when house prices fall and business slows. Although many studies have pointed out the unreasonableness of Taiwan's house prices, the government has not attempted to ensure affordability. Whilst the government has established the goal of assisting the real estate market to prosper, it could be argued that housing policy has not only failed to check the sharply rising house prices, but actually contributed to housing being overly expensive. At the same time, although the home-ownership rate is already extremely high (see Tables 9.1 and 9.2), the government has continued to encourage home buying, with the consequence that high levels of ownership are placing a substantial financial burden on home purchasers and, in turn, translating into a waste of social resources (Chen, 2005). One of the most incredible aspects of Taiwan's official housing statistics is that true transaction prices were not available until 2009. Real estate agencies concealed the actual price of transaction and were able to use the non-transparency to manipulate deals (Lu, 2008). Housing transaction disputes are the most serious form of consumer dispute in Taiwan, but the law offers only imperfect protection to home buyers.

Second, under the influence of neo-liberalism, housing policy targets mainly those who can afford to buy, and there has been little increase in housing for those of low income. With limited intervention, the government has created only about 5.4 per cent of all housing in Taiwan through its public housing schemes (including the encouragement of private constructions and provision of subsidized loans), and directly constructed just 2.4 per cent.

The neglect of low-income housing in housing policy means that the closest in Taiwan to the public housing of Europe and the USA is low-cost housing, residences built by the government and offered to eligible low-income persons for free. The scheme created only about 2,000 residences in Taipei City in the 1960s, and none since, taking care of only 2,048 households. As mentioned above, the criteria for low-income persons are relatively strict, so the number of eligible low-income is not many. The low-cost housing is dilapidated because Taipei City Government hardly provides enough funding to maintain it. There are 3,846 public

Table 9.1 Homeownership rate and ratio of housing price to disposable income, 1980–2000

	1980	1990	2000
Homeownership rate	76.58%	82.71%	86.52%
Ratio of housing price to disposable income	4.59	5.15	3.23

Source: (Peng & Wang, 2005:11).

Table 9.2 Homeownership rate and housing price to income ratio in Taiwan and Taipei City, 2006 and 2007

Taiwan	2006	2007	Taipei	2006	2007
Homeownership Rate	87.83%	88.14%	Homeownership Rate	81.02%	82.58%
Housing price-income ratio	6.6	7.1	Housing price-income ratio	8.8	8.6

Source: CPA, 2009; http://housing.cpami.gov.tw/house/default.aspx.

housing residences for rent in Taipei City, available at lower than market prices to low-income households and disadvantaged families for terms of 11 and 12 years, respectively. Eligible are single-parent families, persons over the age of 65 without spouse, low-income households, persons with disability, households affected by public construction (because of removal or demolition), indigenous families and three-generation families or grandparent-grandchild families (immediate family members registered at the same household for one year or above). Taipei City also has two homeless shelters, with 84 and 29 beds to accommodate 113 persons in total. The two emergency shelters for women, set up by the government and run privately, can accommodate 86 persons, and the Home of Wisdom rented to single-mother families is a residence for 92 persons in 45 apartment units (DSATPC, 2008). The amount of low-income housing is simply insufficient. Eligible low-income families in Taipei City without their own residence and not placed by the government can receive a monthly rental subsidy of NTD1,500. In 2007, the government began to integrate housing subsidization in the hope of discontinuing the old identity-based scheme, particularly the special subsidies offered to the MGE, and redefined eligibility by a looser term of lower-income. For people unable to afford housing, a monthly rental subsidy of NTD3,000 was offered for the term of one year. A total of 12,000 households benefited from the new scheme. In 2008, the number of households subsidized increased to 24,000. Because of the limited availability, the scheme included a review mechanism to facilitate the application of persons with disability, single-parent families, indigenous persons and victims of major disasters.

The influence of neo-liberalism can be seen again in the state's method of intervention in low-income housing. On account of the limited availability of public housing for low-income families, the government is eager for the involvement of non-government organizations. For Fu De Public Housing, one of the five low-cost housing projects, the government is hoping that its location by the new city centre will attract private developers on board, to solve the lack of funds of the much-needed reconstruction project. In addition, with respect to the difficulty with rental housing often encountered by low-income persons, the government is relying on the assistance offered by private, non-profit rental service organizations.

The goal of solving problems with low-income housing through non-government organizations or the private rental market is most clearly manifested in the draft for a housing act. Because of the state's neglect of housing policy, although the Ministry of the Interior had started to work on a housing act in 1999, it has not moved beyond the draft stage, as no consensus could be reached. In 2007, a comprehensive housing policy implementation scheme was finally approved (Lu, 2008), but it was dominated by the neo-liberal spirit of privatization. The scheme has three objectives: to perfect the housing market; to establish a fair and efficient housing subsidy system; and to improve the quality of the residential environment. It is clear that the top priority of the government's housing policy is to establish a market and encourage the involvement of the private sector, with low-income housing handled mainly through subsidization. The state plays the role primarily of facilitating market operations, and makes minimal direct intervention in the issue of housing for the disadvantaged, offering a small amount of rental subsidy, but otherwise passing the problem onto the rental housing market, non-profit organizations and individual landlords and communities. On the one hand, the regulation stipulates non-discrimination, but on the other hand, the government is not directly providing housing or solving housing problems. Although the policy is intended to convert public housing that is hard to sell into rental public housing, with the target of assisting 180 households of disadvantaged families each year, but since selling public housing isn't difficult, it has not been possible to provide more public rental housing.

The home-ownership rate among low-income families is relatively low at 32.5 per cent, and much lower than the 85.6 per cent among average families. It is obvious that low-income families require more help from the government (DGBAS, 2003), but the long-term neglect of low-income housing in government policy means that there are few low-income residences available for rent, and only limited and insubstantial rental subsidization. The problem of housing for low-income persons cannot be solved by relying on the housing market or non-government organizations.

How does the neo-liberal transformation of housing policies impact on women? Taiwan's housing policies have never taken gender into account. The most obvious example is that gender has been a missing category in government's housing reports until recently. After more than two decades' efforts by women's movements, official statistics have begun to add a gender variable. However, the housing survey questions are not intended to reveal women's housing problems. Although data collection has been extended to include gender, as well as some disadvantaged groups, the information is unable to provide a comprehensive picture of their real situation. One example is the lack of information about the home-ownership status of women.

Since the neo-liberalist logic of recent housing policies encourages individuals to act as consumers in the housing market, some women have been able to benefit from various low-interest home loan plans. In fact, the improvement of women's economic status has enhanced their opportunities of home ownership. In a survey on new homebuyers in five major metropolitan areas of Taiwan in 2008, 41.7 per cent were women (Institute for Physical Planning and Information, 2009, p. 91). The increasing number of female consumers also influences the production of housing commodities. More houses are designed according to women's taste and needs. For example, the kitchen becomes the centre of the house rather than being located at the corner. However, the real beneficiary of the neo-liberal reforms is the housing industry. Housing policies have strengthened the commodification of housing and continued to push housing prices to an unaffordable level (See Table 9.2). From this perspective, women's housing consumption is part of the neo-liberal system to help facilitate the housing market. However, the reality for many is the 'burden' of heavy and prolonged mortgage payments. The most serious problem is the class issue. Those on lower incomes suffer from little housing support from the state, especially poor women. Housing policies are not targeted at improving women's status in the domains of reproduction and production, nor in relation to the distribution of housing subsidies or the design of public housing.

Transformation of women's roles in the domestic sphere and the economy in Taiwan

The emergence of the women's movement in Taiwan was heavily influenced by the women's movement in the West. In the 1970s, Annette Lu Hsiu-lien initiated the advocacy of feminism, the awareness of which would guide those who later took up the mantle. In the 1980s, Li Yuan-chen gathered a group of feminists and founded the magazine, *Awakening*, which became the Awakening Foundation after the lifting of martial law and an important promoter of the women's movement. In the 1990s, Taiwan entered a period of democratization, and women not only participated directly in government, whether as permanent or politically appointed civil servants or legislators, but also actively pushed for political and law reforms through the joint force of women's groups and legislative and administrative departments. Such action was influential in the drafting of the Sexual Assault Prevention Act and the Gender Equity Education Act. In addition, through continued pressure on the state through social movements (Peng, 2007), women's participation in politics gradually progressed from the 'reserved-seats for women' system to 'gender mainstreaming'. From 2000, women's status in education, work and politics improved markedly. In 2004, 22.1 per cent of Taiwan's legislators were women, a proportion lower than that of Sweden but higher than those of China, Singapore, the USA, South Korea and Japan (DGBAS, 2007).

In 2008, women's work force participation rate was 49.7 per cent, an increase of 10.4 per cent from 1980, but still lower than men's participation rate of 67.1 per cent (Table 9.3). In 2007, the average salary of female employees (in the industrial sector and service sector) was 79.5 per cent of that of male employees, an increase from ten years ago by 7.4 percentage points (DGBAS, 2008b). However, a gap remains between the salaries of men and women, particularly in the industrial sector, where women's average salary was 69.2 per cent of men's. In the service sector, the gap was smaller, at 83.1 per cent. Women's labour market participation rate is higher for women aged between 25–44, single, and with higher education (Table 9.4).

Changes in family structure

Taiwan's family structure is also undergoing rapid change. Before the 1960s, the most common type was the extended family, which was replaced by the nuclear family in the 1980s (Chang and Chi, 1991). However, from the 1990s, family types became more diverse. From 1988 to 2004, the proportion of nuclear families (parents with at least one single child) declined year by year, from 59.1 per cent to 46.7 per cent, and that of three-generation families also dropped from 16.7 per cent to 15.2 per cent. Conversely, the proportion of married couples without children and single-person households grew rapidly, by 6.5 per cent and about 4 per cent, respectively (Table 9.5) (DGBAS, 2006b). Family structure is closely related to changes in the socio-economic environment. Because of the lengthening of the Taiwanese life span, up to the end of August 2006, the elderly population already made up as much as 9.86 per cent of the entire population, giving Taiwan an aging index of 53.9 per cent and contributing to the sharp rise in single-person and two-person households. Late childbearing and a falling birthrate further increased the number of two-person households, while the lack of a younger generation reduced the proportion of nuclear families. The decrease in the marriage rate and the increase in the age of marriage raised the proportion of single-person households (DGBAS, 2006b), whilst the rising divorce rate was the main reason behind the growth of single-parent families (Hsueh, 2002). The serious inadequacy of the childcare system has meant that young parents who have needed to work during the day have had to leave their children in the care of their own parents, which has elevated the number of grandparent-grandchild families (Y. S. Chen, 2006). Although the rate of population growth has slowed year by year, the contraction of the family structure and reduction in household size from 4.1 persons in 1988 to 3.2 persons

Table 9.3 Labour participation rate in Taiwan, 1980–2008

	1980	1990	2000	2008
Women	39.3	44.5	46.0	49.7
Men	77.1	74.0	69.4	67.1

Source: Chou, 2005; DGBAS, 2009.

Table 9.4 Women's labour participation rate by age, marital status and Education, 2008

	%
Age	
15–24	32.47
25–44	74.83
45–64	45.08
Marital status	
Single	58.38
Married	49.11
Divorced or widowed	30.88
Education	
Junior high school and under	29.46
Senior high school	55.40
College and above	65.35

Source: Statistics Bureau, 2009.

in 2004, and the resulting rapid expansion in the number of households has led to increasing housing demand.

Women and division of domestic labour

Although Taiwan's social welfare expanded considerably after the 1990s, its support to families was limited, and the responsibility of caring for the young and the elderly remained largely with the family. The existing dominance of patriarchy was weakened with the elevation of women's status in Taiwan, though its influence persisted (Lee, 2004). This could be seen in the division of housework, with women continuing to shoulder most of the unpaid labour at home. With regard to how married women cared for their children under the age of 3, in 2006, 65.8 per cent chose to take the responsibility themselves, a decrease of 6.5 per cent from 2000,

Table 9.5 The proportion of family types in 1988 and 2004 (%)

Family type	1988	2004
Nuclear family	59.1	46.7
Three-generation family	16.7	15.2
Couple	7.7	14.2
Single person	6.0	9.9
Single parent	5.8	7.7
Grandparent(s) with grandchild(ren)	0.8	1.2
Total	100	100

Source: (DGBAS, 2006b).

although still a high proportion. 22.4 per cent left their children in the care of their parents or relatives (DGBAS, 2008a).

The trend of 'men work, women stay at home' endured in the gender-based division of labour. In 2004, 75 per cent of women over the age of 15 regularly handled housework, took care of family members and managed their children, clearly higher than men's 31.3 per cent. Women continued to be the main person in charge of domestic activities (DGBAS, 2007). In 2006, the reason given by 51.7 per cent of women for not participating in the work force was to take care of housework, though that constituted a drop of 8.1 per cent from a decade ago (DGBAS, 2008a). Lin (2007) compares the role of women in Taiwan in the 1970s and the 1990s, and finds that the division of housework was similarly dominated by the market economy and patriarchal logic, with women in families depended upon as the state did not offer an obvious public childcare service. While industrial development loosened the patriarchal family, housework was transferred to economically disadvantaged older (or migrant) women by middle-class women, and the patriarchal division of labour continued to exist.

Could the gender-based division of housework ever change with the promotion of the women's movement and the elevation of gender awareness? Bih (1996) investigated the situation among married couples with a questionnaire and deliberately uses members of radical women's groups in Taipei for comparison. The female members of women's groups spent 2 hours and 15 minutes on housework each day, about one hour less than women in general, though there was almost no difference in the time spent by the husbands (just over 50 minutes). It can be surmised that the reduction of women's housework hours is due to a lowering of housework standard and frequency, the (paid) outsourcing of housework and the trained participation of children, rather than to any change in men's participation.

Gender implications of three-generation family households

A characteristic in the family structure of Chinese societies is three generations living together or to reside with elderly parents (Yi, 2008). According to a DGBAS (2006b) survey, in 2004, there were about one million three-generational family households in Taiwan, though the proportion of 15.2 per cent out of the total number of households had declined slightly from the 16.7 per cent in 1998. Of the elderly population, around 60 per cent lived with their offspring, and only 2 per cent were settled in care institutions. The living arrangement of three generations under one roof not only represents an image of the ideal family prized by traditional Chinese patriarchal society, but is a model that is encouraged by state policies. However, the romanticized myth of the heart-warming big happy family is often achieved on the back of the unpaid labour of the daughter-in-law: although it is the man's parents that are cared for and supported, the actual tasks of care belong to the daughter-in-law (Lan and Wu, 2005). Hu (1995) explicitly criticizes the state's advocacy of this type of living arrangement as operating to confine the public policy for senior welfare to the 'private' sphere.

Foreign/Mainland Chinese spouses and labourers

The long-term apportionment of care work to women and the private sphere in Taiwan's society has resulted in a low participation rates for women in the workforce which are currently at around 49 per cent. This is far lower than the 60 per cent participation rates of the USA and the 80 per cent participation rates of many northern European countries. According to statistics from DGBAS in 2000, 34 per cent of women left employment because of household commitments, marriage or pregnancy. At the same time, more women were choosing not to have children in order to avoid damaging their career, though some of them have outsourced the tasks to even more disadvantaged women. In 1992, Taiwan's government allowed the introduction of immigrant domestic helpers (for the double-earner family with children under twelve or elderly people above 70 years old) and care-givers (for Taiwanese households with members in a vegetative, paralysed or heavily disabled condition who need full-time care) in response to the increasing demand for workers to handle domestic tasks, such as childcare and nursing of the elderly and infirm. According to figures from the Council of Labor Affairs (CLA) (Lan and Wu, 2005) from 2002, there were over 120,000 government-approved immigrant domestic workers in Taiwan. Almost all were women, of whom 68 per cent were from Indonesia, 18 per cent from the Philippines, and the rest from Vietnam (Lan and Wu, 2005). By the end of 2005, that number had increased to 143,000, which accounted for 43 per cent of all immigrant labourers in Taiwan (Huang, 2006). Although at present the CLA has only allowed the introduction of care-givers in the category of 'social welfare immigrant labourers', many families hire immigrant labourers to assist with childcare and housework using false medical certificates or in the name of elderly relatives. Moreover, the work of caring for the elderly and infirm is low paid and round-the-clock. The recruitment of foreign women as domestic labourers reflects the fact that Taiwan's society still defines housework and childcare as the natural vocation of women, and does not challenge the prevailing gender-based division of domestic labour.

In the era of globalization, the sons of farmers, fishermen and labourers on the periphery of Taiwanese society lack competitiveness in the domestic marriage market, and have been marrying women from southeast Asia and Mainland China. This resolves their difficulty with marrying as well as obtaining unpaid labour for their families. According to figures from the Ministry of the Interior, in 1998, about 15.7 per cent of marriages involved a partner from Mainland China or southeast Asian countries, and in 2003, the proportion had risen to 31.9 per cent. Because of tightening policy on cross-border marriage, the figure dropped to 20.1 per cent in 2005 (28,427 couples). However, under the double restriction of the regulations and language barrier, most of these women are only able to engage in activities such as caring, nursing and domestic labour, silently shouldering a considerable share of Taiwan's home care burdens.

As yet, domestic labour and care work are not included in protections offered by Taiwan's Labor Standards Law, so there is no guarantee for the labour condition of household workers or the proper handling of conflict between labourer and employer. To counter the long-standing idea that domestic labour and care work are the job of low-skilled women requires the establishment of professional training and certification systems and workers' unions. The Council of Labor Affairs has recently stipulated that a child carer should be categorized as a type of technician requiring certification, and local governments have set up the Community Child Care Support Network, which is allied with non-government associations of child carers. In addition, the Peng Wan-Ru Foundation has been promoting a welfare mutual aid system of professional community care to achieve the goal of 'women helping out each other'. The Foundation offers professional training to child carers, housework managers and home care providers and helps to match labourer and employer while ensuring the regulation of service content and labour condition by standard form contracts. However, Taiwan still has much to learn from the welfare system in countries like Sweden and Norway, where care work is outsourced to professionals through a redistribution of tax revenues.

Housing problems faced by women of different identities

Taiwan's social welfare and housing policies expanded in the 1990s, but care provided to people of low income remains limited. The improvement of women's status has not elevated their economic status to that of men, and women continue to perform the role of domestic labourer, shouldering the responsibility of caring for other family members. This disadvantage in both the public and the private sphere affects the housing condition of women of different identities, especially poor women. Due to the lack of quantitative data, we use qualitative research to discuss the problems faced by single women, low-income single mothers, homeless women and lesbians.

Inheritance is an important route into home ownership in Taiwan. According to a 2006 Housing Survey, 12.7 per cent of households are living in the houses that were either inherited or were a gift (the survey did not disaggregate by gender) When the Civil Code was first established in 1929, women were already entitled to inheritance rights. However, even at the end of the 1980s, 83.5 per cent of daughters stated that they did not get anything from the division of familial property (Ministry of the Interior, 1989: 142). In the division of property, 98.1 per cent of the family estate went to their brothers. In terms of gifts from parents, daughters received more stock and cash than sons did, and they received approximately one-quarter of the total estate in the form of gifts (Chen, 1990). This is the most recent data available to show the intergenerational transfer of housing assets was primarily based on the patrilineal principle. However, there is no recent information about inheritance. Even in the early 1990s, although the law ensures daughters' inheritance rights, the share for daughters was relatively limited.

Single women

The increase in the number of single person households is significantly due to delaying the age of marriage. The high rural-urban migration of single women has also caused the increase of single-person households. Single women have been rewriting the history of gendered society and constructing non-patriarchal and alternative family deliberately, such as living alone, cooperative housing for women, living together with male partner without marriage and lesbian families, etc. They adopt non-traditional relations with their family and raise the autonomy of women. However, single women are facing an unfriendly housing market while they are pursuing a place to live. Under the package of the advertisement of 'live before marriage, rent after marriage' by the marketing company, being single becomes a temporary status in the life cycle. The layout of living space is thus not designed for single women. Moreover, the propaganda of 'low deposit and low total price' have concealed the fact of 'high unit price and high ratio of public facility' (J. Y Chen, 2006). Housing affordability is a problem for the single woman.

Single-parent families and their housing problem

One of the most obvious problems arising from changes in family structure is the rapid increase in the divorce rate and single-mother families. In 1970, the crude divorce rate of Taiwan was 0.36 (per 1000), which rose to 2.37 in 2000. In 2004, there were 548,000 single-parent families in Taiwan, a two-fold increase from 1988, and a proportional growth from 5.8 per cent to 7.7 per cent, due mainly to the rising divorce rate. Of the 548,000 single-parent families, 167,000 included children under the age of 18. The rapid increase in single-mother families can be seen by the fact that in 75 per cent of the families, the mother was the primary earner, an increase of 53,000 families from 1988. In contrast, the increase in the number of families in which the father was the primary earner was slight, by 2,000 only (DGBAS, 2006b).

In Taipei City, the proportion of families headed by a female primary earner keeps increasing, from 20.3 per cent in 1999 to 25.2 per cent in 2006. However, in terms of family income, poorer families are more likely to be supported by a female primary earner. By splitting families evenly into five groups by income, it is shown that the proportion of families headed by a female primary earner is as high as 38.4 per cent in the group with the lowest income. Among high-income families, the proportion of those headed by a female primary earner decreases to 13.3 per cent (DBASTCP, 2006).

Another indicator of women's economic disadvantage is the condition of elderly women. In 2005, most elderly women above the age of 65 in Taiwan were supported financially by their children or spouse, and the 65.5 per cent was far higher than the 34.5 per cent among men. Next were those able to support themselves, though the 17.3 per cent was far below the 49.2 per cent among men. This demonstrates the comparatively poor financial independence of Taiwan's elderly women (DGBAS, 2007).

'Poverty feminization' refers to the predominance of women in a nation's population in poverty, especially of female-headed families. From the changes outlined above, it is clear that Taiwan's society is facing the trend of an increase in impoverished female householders along with the increase in female-headed families largely as a result of the rising divorce rate. Therefore, in handling the issue of low-income housing, single-mother families must not be overlooked. Cheng (2006) examines the social condition of low-income single mothers from the perspective of social exclusion. Many single-mother householders are unable to join the employment market because of the necessity of caring for the children. Should they join the labour market, they are likely to be limited to work which requires low levels of skill, is low paid, provides poor benefits and requires flexible hours within a labour system which is permeated with discrimination and occupational sex segregation, and which can ultimately deprive women of their social insurance status. The force of exclusion faced by indigenous and elderly women is particularly evident. It goes without saying that these mothers in poverty are excluded from the financial market transaction system because of their lack of 'credit'. The difficulty of finding and securing a place to live is also unavoidable for single-mother families. In the culture of patriarchy, single-mother householders are almost uniformly without 'family', excluded from both their parents family and their ex-husband's family. At present, Taiwan's policy of disadvantaged public housing leans towards providing for moderate-income families/households, which makes the housing unaffordable to low-income families. Single mothers feel unsafe in the low-cost housing built for low-income households because the space is crowded and their neighbors have very complicated backgrounds. Some neighbors have mental illness. Some have drug problems. The concentration of poor people further turns it into an easy target of social exclusion from nearby communities.

Compared to low-cost housing, public housing offers a better living environment to single mothers but for a fixed period only and relatively higher rent. While the eligibility requirements of public rental housing are less strict than that of low-cost housing, the quota for single mothers is limited, and not many units are available. To pay the higher rent and maintain a quality of life, single mothers living in public housing projects need to take on extra jobs, hoping to free themselves from poverty through hard work before the end of the tenancy and, ultimately, own a home of their own. But for single mothers, the down payment of 15 per cent of the purchase price for a public housing unit is a very tall order. To benefit from the quota of public rental housing for single-parent families involves a wait of several years, and in any case, the rent is usually higher than NTD10,000 a month and there is little choice of area.

Homeless women

The government and academics have always had trouble defining homelessness. So far, Taiwan's academics have reached the following consensus over a definition of homeless persons as those who, for a certain period of time (above two weeks), have no fixed residence and whose personal income is lower than the minimum wage (Lin, 1995). There are about 2,300 officially registered homeless persons in Taiwan (Cheng and Chang, 2004). Joblessness, poverty, mental illness and failure of state housing policy are all causes of homelessness. Compared to joblessness and personal adjustment issues, family factors (domestic violence, discord at home) are more critical causes of homelessness for women (Lin, 1995). However, the danger of the streets (the threat of sexual assault) has forced some women to remain in the family and suffer an abusive relationship, unable to leave home but, nevertheless, falling under the condition of hidden homelessness. Homeless women living on the streets often need to attach themselves to men in order to avoid sexual assault. For the same reason, staff at shelters and similar institutions tend to segregate homeless women or restrict their activities, depriving them of their freedom and sexual needs. Whether they live on the streets or in an institution, homeless women have no privacy, or resting and storage space (Wu, 1999). Wu (1999) further points out that the patriarchal family ideology constructed through education and the media encourages women, already repressed by the family, to still seek to achieve a 'home sweet home'.

Lesbians and the home

Studies on women and housing rarely mention lesbians. As Wolfe (1992: 139) asserts:

> Lesbians and gay men, and aspects of our culture, have existed for thousands of years in every known society and nation, yet our … culture has been trivialized as a 'life-style' and our places, spaces and geography are unknown and invisible to most people. This invisibility reflects and is reflected in the heterosexist biases in our literature, including the literature on 'women and environments,' in which lesbians are rarely, if ever, mentioned and then only in passing.

It is difficult to establish the exact number of lesbians in Taiwan and the proportions of whom enter into heterosexual marriage, have a cohabiting partner or are single. Because of the stigma still associated with homosexuality in Taiwanese society, most gay and lesbian studies adopt the research method of using a small sample for in-depth interviews.

Marriage, as defined by Taiwanese law, is restricted to a monogamous heterosexual relationship. Under these circumstances, can lesbians make a family? Based on several interviews with lesbians, Li (2007) points out that lesbians tend to disregard the legal system of marriage in their definition of 'home', and are more concerned with whether their relationship is stable and long-lasting, since heterosexual marriage in any case offers little guarantee, and sometimes even more constraints. According to Chao (2005), '"old tomboys" often spend their lives constantly moving' (p. 68), and in their case, moving not only involves the hassle and stress of relocation, but is actually close to a 'diasporic' state of physical and mental migration. She explains the three reciprocal causal factors behind the frequent house moving of these lesbians: (1) because of their sexual/gender identity, older lesbians often have a ruptured or detached relationship with their family of origin; (2) although older lesbians also dream of everlasting love, the reality is simply different; (3) in the financial system of lending, the 'certification by household registration' and the requirement to add a relative as a guarantor presuppose that an individual's credit is necessarily guaranteed and defined by 'specific relatives' (i.e. immediate family members and male spouse), as a result, the older lesbians who are detached from their family of origin become persons of poor credit, and have difficulty obtaining home loans, which in turn injures their chance of maintaining the stability of their intimate relationships.

Lesbians not 'out of the closet' with their family of origin must lead a double life. At home, they become 'a person without story', because they have to conceal a most important experience of their life (Li, 2007). One lesbian came out to her family for this reason, but found no appropriate terms of address when her partner visited her home. Cohabiting, same-sex partners cannot present themselves as 'family-to-be', as can heterosexual couples (Tsai, 2006). One interviewee revealed that she has to hide her belongings on the eve of visits by the parents of her partner (who owns their residence), and so has no sense of belonging to the physical space of living.

To conclude, not only can lesbians make a family, they are making families with new formations (Li, 2007), with potential members including more than just her partner. Recently, some lesbians have taken up the strategy of living communally or with different couples as the remedy for not having children to care for them in their old age. They carefully maintain long-term friendships and promise to look after each for life.

Conclusion

Although the women's movement has been in Taiwan for more than three decades, and women's status is gradually improving, the topic of women and housing is rarely discussed in women's studies and housing studies. The contribution of this chapter lies in offering a feminist analysis of housing to promote an understanding of the housing issues facing women in Taiwan. Compared to the experience of the West, women and housing in Taiwan differs mainly in two aspects. First, patriarchal culture still exists in Taiwan, and patrilocal residence remains the predominant living arrangement, in which women take on most of the housework and responsibility for the domestic sphere. Second, social welfare cuts in the USA and the UK have led to the 'selling-off' of much public rental housing, but in Taiwan, the influence of democratization in the 1990s generated a significant expansion of social policies and state intervention in housing, though this has not improved low-income welfare or social support in domestic labour and childcare. This expansion is still based on the neo-liberal principle that the market is the best supplier of social services and housing.

The relative neglect of social welfare for low-income persons and their housing problems puts Taiwanese women in a patriarchal, heterosexual society at a serious disadvantage. Married women shoulder most of the burden of housework but occupy the least space in the family. Low-income single mothers have to deal with the instability of residence but the housing resources they receive from the government are not only extremely limited, but are also of poor quality. For some women, repression at home has forced them into homelessness, only to become victims of the threats of sexual assault and patriarchal culture on the streets and at temporary shelters. Lesbians have changed the definition of home with their family formation, but the heterosexual assumptions of society, the law and policies continue to affect their living space and their chance of obtaining housing resources from the state.

The neglect of social equity and gender issues in Taiwan's housing policy is most clearly manifested in the government's housing statistics. The various housing conditions of different groups in society are not analyzed in the official data, and with the housing market allowed a state of abandon, no actual transaction data has been made available. Consequently, without sufficient statistical information, this chapter is based on qualitative research and second-hand data, using interviews and related research to outline the housing conditions of women of different identities. It is hoped that by raising the issue of women and housing, the first step in demanding change in state housing policy has been taken.

10 A gender study on housing rights of women in urban China

Case study of a single-parent female domestic workers' group

Guo Hui-min

From British feminist writer Virginia Woolf to single-parent female domestic workers in this study, 'a room of one's own' has always been a woman's dream for independent space. However, women in different countries are faced with different sets of difficulties when they struggle to realize this dream. In China, the housing rights of women are included in rather general and vague laws and policies on property rights, and marriage and family rights that are enjoyed by both men and women. In reality, women's housing rights are closely related with marriage, work and income. The experience of single parent female domestic workers' groups in Xian in this study demonstrates how these complex relationships work. Focus group interview is the main method used for this study. Materials include records of interviews, focus group sharing, and homework done by group members. A small number of samples and data have been extracted from these materials for analysis. What is described in this study might not, therefore, represent conditions of the housing rights of all women in China. The study also has limitations in terms of sampling and material collection. However, as a pilot exploratory study, it captures the housing rights of single-parent female domestic workers by adopting a dynamic approach from a gender perspective. This helps to unearth gender discrimination in housing which is often rendered invisible by various systems and structures. By revealing the gender politics behind laws, policies, culture and market that affect the housing rights of women, this study aims to reveal the emptiness of mainstream rhetoric on women's rights and to search for paths for women's independence.

Few scholars in mainland China have shown concern for issues of gender and housing policy. Most studies on housing policy focus on the political impact of residential space and new communities on class formation (Wang, 2007; Zhao and Wang, 2008). Some are concerned with gender difference in architecture and space (Du, 2005; Tang, 2006; Wang and Zhou, 2007). Chan Kam Wah, a Hong

Kong scholar, has considered the relationship between feminist theories, cities and housing:

> Housing and cities are not 'neutral' and value free systems. Instead, housing and cities are developed on the basis of mainstream consciousness and social relationship of a society. The current society still places men above women and the society is dominated by male power, systems of housing and cities are therefore reflections of this consciousness and in turn reinforce gender inequality.
>
> (Chan 1997: 73)

He describes three approaches that have been adopted for change, and suggests that they could also provide the basis for future study: environmental determinism, add-on approach and deconstructionist approach (Chan, 1997). Actions that adopt an environmental-determinist approach attempt to foster gender equality by improving on housing and city design that reinforce inequality. This is the sphere of practice of feminist architects. The add-on approach is a practice in social policy. It does not aim at undermining the structure, but advocates incorporating social disadvantaged groups into beneficiaries of specific housing policies. Measures to rectify social exclusion that result in spatial resource redistribution could, therefore, sometimes be undertaken in the name of meeting special needs. In an incisive critique of housing policies in another article, Chan cites the experience of Hong Kong women victims of violence who apply for public housing. He points out that exclusion in the name of integration is a more profound kind of exclusion, and the result is aggravation of gender inequality (Chan and Chan 2003). This perspective not only deconstructs the political and cultural relations between women and housing, it also deconstructs the former two approaches.

This study attempts to deconstruct the complicity between public and private patriarchy in spatial resource distribution and the androcentrism of patrilocal residence which results in the housing right of women being hollowed out in laws and policies. At the same time, women who are single parents are incorporated as beneficiaries of low-rent housing policies in an add-on approach.

The housing right of women in China is yet to be constructed

In international human rights concepts, housing is not a commodity with four walls and a ceiling. It is instead a place where one can live in security, peace and dignity. Housing rights are therefore rights which every person is entitled to, and which are enshrined in international conventions such as the Universal Declaration of Human Rights of the United Nations.[1] In 1991, United Nations Committee on Economic,

Social and Cultural Rights issued General Comment 4 on the Right to Adequate Housing, the first paragraph of which stated:

> The human right to adequate housing, which is thus derived from the right to an adequate standard of living, is of central importance for the enjoyment of all economic, social and cultural rights.

In China, housing right is not a legal concept. It is a right yet to be constructed. Theoretically, housing rights cover the right to own and the right to inhabit a house. These rights are given expression in the Constitution, in civil laws and in property laws, albeit incomplete. In practice, the housing rights of Chinese citizens have been undergoing changes from the right to rent public housing to the right to own private housing. This takes place in a context of economic reform and housing system reform both of which have an effect on citizens' housing rights. The effect of the gender power relationship on housing right is indirect and complex. 'Women' as a term has often been used to represent the radical force that sabotages concepts, assumptions and structures of male discourse, but 'Women' itself has also been deconstructed, and not all women could be ascribed the same characteristics or the same marginal positions. 'Women' is not a single entity. In contemporary China, elite women who are exceptionally gifted or particularly resourceful might be able to prevail over the constraints of gender relationship and own housing units independently. On the other hand, women in general, marginalized women in particular, are faced with a different set of housing problems. Women's housing right is also not a homogeneous set of rights. It is closely related with social and economic changes and with a woman's work, socio-politico-economic status, marital status and mode of habitation after marriage. Few women own houses before they get married. The issue of the independent housing right of women often only becomes apparent when a woman divorces.

First, as a consequence of recent housing system reforms, women might face more problems than men in terms of the right to housing. Since the housing system reform, many factory plant, and agricultural land have been redeveloped into commercial residential buildings (*shangpin fang*). This has contributed to increasing class differentiation developed on the basis of the ownership of private housing. As McDowell points out:

> In all societies, home cannot remain simply as a physical structure. A house is a relationship of daily life and an erotic relationship as well. It is also the link between material culture and social interaction. A house is the embodiment of social position and status.
>
> (McDowell 2006: 125)

Because of socialist housing reform in the 1950s, most people had been living in publicly provided rental housing with small living space. Since the economic reform, demand for housing suddenly expanded. Anticipating an unstable economy, many people thought that buying a house was a more secure way to invest their savings. Government policies also helped to encourage the extraordinary boom of China's real estate industry. Since the 1980s, the core content of housing reform has been the commodification of housing. Various kinds of housing were made available in the market: housing units sold at cost price (Comfortable Project Housing), housing units sold at discount price (public housing provided by work units) and housing units sold at market price (commodity housing). There were also housing units made available as Economical and Comfortable Commodity Housing (*Jinji Shiyong Shangpin Fang*). The head of the family inhabiting a housing unit owns the unit. Even though it meant ownership of a housing unit only, people were still drawn to buying these housing units and in a short period of 20 years, the percentage of private ownership of housing surged to 80 per cent.[2] Housing reform not only resulted in public housing turning into private housing, it also led to the redistribution of housing resources which in turn created new forms of gender inequality. In China, housing and households are connected. In 2005, the gender distribution of heads of households in the cities and in the rural areas of China was as follows: national level, male 86.22 per cent, female 13.78 per cent; cities, male 79.78 per cent, female 20.22 per cent; rural villages, male 92.2 per cent female 7.8 per cent (ACWF News, 2008).

Household heads are usually also owners of the housing units. Most certificates of house ownership and certificates for the use of the house site in the rural areas are held by men (sometimes representing the family). Collusion between traditional customs and policies of housing reform has rendered women's right to house ownership less than that of men.

Second, the housing right of an urban woman, her work status and economic status are positively correlated. For a married woman, her housing right and the social and economic status of her spouse is also positively correlated. Housing has been and still is a benefit provided by work units. In spite of the housing reforms, many work units, especially units with a prospering business and those that enjoy a monopoly in their respective industry, still allocate housing units to their employees as a major employment benefit. Their employees can buy commodity housing at a discount price or cost price which is one-third or half of the market price. These housing units are usually built with funds collected from buyers. This practice has resulted in a double-track price system in the housing market. Article 23(2) of the Law on the Protection of Women's Rights and Interests enacted in 1992 states that gender equality should be guaranteed in the allocation of housing units and other benefits. When the law was revised in 2005, equal rights in housing was no longer emphasized. In reality, most work units do not have an overt housing policy that discriminates against women. More often, the housing benefit one enjoys is dependent on age, seniority, academic qualification and position at work. Whether a husband or a wife gets the housing benefit depends on the welfare system of a work unit and the status of the individual. Generally speaking, when both husband and wife work in the same work unit, the man usually claims the housing benefit because he usually occupies a higher post and is in a better position to claim the housing benefit.

In a survey undertaken by this researcher, it was found that a scientific research institution allocates housing according to the importance of the post occupied by the employees. The types and size of the housing units each post is entitled to are different but the prices of all the housing units are nearly the same. Housing units are allocated according to the scores gained by each employee depending on age, seniority, title/position, etc. No distinction is made between men and women. Unmarried workers over 35 years old and single parents may also apply for housing benefits. In the most recent allocation, the housing units were divided into five classes according to their size and design: Class 1 to Class 5. Among households who were allocated a housing unit, 839 households were allocated in the name of the man while only 296 households were allocated in the name of the woman. Women who were allocated a housing unit independently represented only 26 per cent of all beneficiaries. There was vertical segregation as well. There were 122 housing units in Class 1. Housing units in Class 1 were the biggest in size and they had also the best design. 113 men and 9 women were allocated Class 1 housing. Women represented only 8 per cent of the beneficiaries. Class 2 housing units were the second best. 275 men and 57 women got Class 2 housing. Women represented only 22 per cent of the beneficiaries. 96 men and 29 women were allocated Class 3 housing, and women represented 30 per cent of the beneficiaries. Women represented 32 per cent and 31 per cent respectively of the beneficiaries for Class 4 and Class 5 housing. The latter two figures were consistent with the percentage of women in the staff. It should be noted that in 326 households, both the husband and the wife worked for the institution, representing 33 per cent of all beneficiaries. Among these households, only 50 (15 per cent) had applied for housing allocation in the name of the woman. The other 276 households had applied in the name of the man. In other words, even though the number of women employees who moved into the new housing units was not very small, many got the housing units in the name of their husbands. Moreover, the percentage of women among owners of the housing units was lowest in the group who owned Class 1 housing.

Third, housing and marriage are closely related, especially in rural areas. Marriage customs and patrilocal residence often result in women's absolute subordination. The Rural House Site Usage Certificate is a legal document for the right to use the lot of land on which a house is built. In practice, the measure of 'the lot attached to the house' is implemented. Presently most building sites are attained by men before they get married. In rural areas, having a house for marriage is an important condition for taking a wife/daughter-in-law. Therefore, a man or his father is often the applicant for permission to build a house. Since the house is built before the wedding, the man is considered owner of the house, and by custom the house is considered the property of the man. While the bridegroom builds the house, the bride brings household durables to the new family. In rural customs, household consumables brought by the bride are considered dowry that she brings with her when she gets married. However, as the price of the house goes up, the value of the dowry depreciates. For women who lack the ability to earn a living independently, marriage is a means of survival, and there are women who marry for a house.

Fourth, in China a housing unit is usually considered the common property of a married couple. Some people learn of the existence and the implication of the matrimonial property ownership system only when they divorce and have to divide up the property (Xue and Hao, 2006). Laws governing the matrimonial property ownership system have, to some extent, established the principle of and the methods for dividing up a couple's property when they divorce. The matrimonial property ownership system consists of a system that is established by law and another which is contracted between a husband and a wife. Common property ownership takes the form of the equal right to handle the property during the course of a marriage, and the division of the property equally between a man and a woman subsequent to a divorce. However, since a house is often owned in the name of the man, and it is difficult to divide a house which is a real estate, housing becomes a big problem for divorced women. Many women have therefore chosen to remain in a broken marriage. In rural areas, women are faced with the difficulty of realizing their right to own houses, in particular the right to use the lot on which the house is built. When a woman belongs to another clan or comes from another village, her right to use the house site is rarely guaranteed when she is divorced or widowed.

Repressed desire for space and the rights of single-parent female domestic workers

Our concern for women's housing rights originated from the single-parent groups in our domestic workers' empowerment program. At first we looked at the issue as an issue of labour welfare. Later we realized that it was related with marriage and property rights. In 2001, with the support of Hong Kong Oxfam, the Women's Development and Rights Research Center at the Northwestern Industrial University launched the project, 'Marginal Workers Rights Self-Help Network' to enhance the capacity of the marginal women workers and to build the organization. The project has been targeting domestic workers. After three years, the first domestic workers' union that aimed at defending workers' rights was established in mainland China. The age of most union members is between 40 and 50 years' old, and most of them are laid-off workers of large enterprises.

At the beginning, rights training workshops were provided to over a 1,000 domestic workers. Core members were identified to form a union. At the same time, problems were being unearthed and suggestions were proposed to resolve the problems at the legal and policy level. One of the problems discovered at the time was the housing problem of single parents. Nearly half of the domestic workers taking part in the project were faced with the dual problems of unemployment and divorce. (This figure is an estimation based on disclosure by the workers in group meetings.) However, most of them did not want to talk about their divorce, neither did they admit that they were divorced when filling out the membership form because they were afraid of being looked down upon and worried that it might prevent them from being employed.[3] This became a problem in recruiting members for the single-parent groups. Fortunately, the problem was overcome and nine single-parent groups were established to discuss different issues, such as relationship with their former spouses after divorce, children's education and housing problems, etc. Sometimes, the groups met together to discuss various problems. Since they usually do not enjoy a day off, attendance at weekend meetings fluctuated. A total of 154 people have taken part in the group activities. Among them, 125 do not own their housing units and have been living in rented housing units or living with their relatives temporarily. We have summarized the housing problems of 14 of them based on the conversation during these group meetings (Table 10.1).

Among the 14 women, except for a former statistician and an unemployed woman, all were workers of state enterprises and large collectively-owned enterprises. Before they were married, they had been living with their parents, and that was before the urban housing reform. Except for two persons, all of them lived in housing units built by work units of their parents. Data from the table shows that the biggest housing unit was 70–80 square metres (for families of cadres or senior intellectuals). The smallest unit was only 12 square metres, and the size per person was only 2 square metres (for workers, in particular workers of large collective enterprises).

> I lived with my parents and siblings. There were seven of us. Since I was small, I had been living in the same place. The place we lived was 9 square metres. My parents' place was small. When I was a kid we lived in a public housing unit owned by the work unit. There were six of us. We moved into a condominium in 1977 and it was 33 square metres.
>
> (Lao Zhao)

> There were 11 of us and we all lived in a small housing unit of 36 square metres.
> (DQ Da Li)

In contemporary China, housing is symbolic of one's social status. These domestic workers have never been rich. Even before the economic reform,

Table 10.1 Housing conditions of selected members of single parent groups and their demands

	Before marriage		After getting married		After being divorced			Dream house		Policy Demands		
	Household members	Size of housing unit (m²)	Household members	Size of housing unit (m²)	Matrimonial house	Children and elderly	Size of rented housing unit (m²)	No. of rooms	Size (m²)	Low rental housing (m²)	Affordable rent (¥)	Monthly income (¥)
1	6	12	3	14	Nil	1 child	19	1		40m²	50	800
2			3	15	Nil	1 child	9	1		1 room	10	400
3	6	40	3	18	Nil	1 child	13	1		1 room	50	700
4	5	47	3	55	Nil	1 child	10	1		20 m²	60	300
5	6	18	4	42	The housing unit was divided up and she got 15 m²	1 child		2		60 m²	50	325
6	4	24	5	45	Nil	1 child	Changes all the time	2		40–50 m²	Below 100	1000
7	6	20	8	40	Nil	1 child + 1 elderly	20	2	60	60	Below 100	1300
8	10	80	4	34	Nil	2 child	Changes all the time	3	80	2 rooms	Below 80	600
9	9	60	4	20	Nil	2 child	15	1		30	50	450
10	11	36	5	18	Nil	2 child	14	1	20–30	30	40–50	800
11	5	70	3	18	Nil		7	1		20–30	1/3 of income	400
12	5	30	3	19	Nil		15	1		1 room	50–60m²	900
13	4	30	3	37	Nil		15	1		1 room		950
14	9	65	3	20	Nil	2 child + 1 elderly	20	2	60	30–50	Unable to rent a housing unit	700

ideological rhetoric such as 'working-class people are the leading class and the master of the country' had not made any difference to the hard life of workers in reality. It got worse when workers were laid-off, became unemployed, or divorced. A house has its practical use. It is a place for rest both spiritually and physically. It is a place where one goes about one's daily chores and a place that shields one from wind and rain. It is also where a person finds his/her last scrap of dignity. We asked in a group meeting:

> What sort of housing unit do you want? Please draw your dream house on the paper, and write down your demands in terms of housing policy.
> 'Dream house'? Everyone was excited, but that lasted only for a while and everyone expressed hopelessness:

> I am uncertain I will ever be able to have my dream house. There is no hope. This is just a game to fill one's stomach by drawing a cake, though I do hope the dream comes true.
>
> (DQ Da Zhong)

The women finally drew the kind of housing units they wanted. Many drew a housing unit with only one room plus a kitchen and a bathroom and its size was only a dozen square metres. The biggest housing unit that was drawn had only two rooms and the size was only just over 30 square metres. They did not know that the government had proposed that for a middle-income family, the living space should be 27 square metres per person. And, according to Shaanxi Information Centre, in 2005, the average size of the floor area for each person in Xian was 20.6 square metres.[4]

The domestic workers' desire for space has obviously been repressed. Such a limited desire for space and minimal policy demands was influenced by their marginalized status and low level of income. In spite of this, they expressed a desire for their own place. As factories are being torn down and farm land is being expropriated, these domestic workers see high-rise residential and commercial buildings mushrooming around them and hear stories of the rich spending millions on housing. But they could only draw on paper their dream house. A worker even placed hope in religion:

> I went to the church and asked God to help me find a man who loved me. I want to have a home. It does not have to be big. I need a home to go back to when I am scared.[5]

Work and housing: shift in space as a result of retrenchment, reemployment and exclusionary housing welfare

Globalization's effect on women is manifold. 'For women taking part in this process, the shift has to do with proletarianization.' (McDowell 2006: 2) Single-parent female domestic workers have lost housing benefits as a result of retrenchment. Whether from a historical perspective or from a comparative perspective, what the Chinese working class is experiencing today is unprecedented, according to Perry (2005). In her study on Filipino domestic workers, Taiwanese scholar Lan Pai-jia has studied in-depth the relationship between transnational migration of domestic workers and globalization, the segregation of and struggle between women, and the identity split of overseas domestic workers as madam at home and servant overseas (Lan, 2003, 2004, 2005). But the identity split of Chinese domestic workers is that of laid-off workers and housekeepers. New class differentiation is created by capital which makes use of the market to produce differentiation in space. Women constitute 85.1 per cent of the domestic workers in mainland China, and 56.1 per cent of the domestic workers are working population in urban areas (63.7 per cent are laid-off workers, and 36.3 per cent are retired workers)[6]. Among retrenched workers, change of laid-off workers' identity in the same geographical location is common. The reality is that workers enjoy welfare and benefits granted by their work units while housekeepers enjoy no social benefits at all.

The effect of economic reform and globalization on different regions varies. Regional difference results in differentiation among the population and change in space. Compared with the more developed regions in the eastern part of China, economic development of Xian has fallen short of people's expectation. Its ranking among big cities in terms of economic development once fell to as low as 23rd (*Economic Daily,* 2001). As a result of economic underdevelopment and economic pressure, many women workers laid-off from large state-owned enterprises have become domestic workers. Both gender repression and class differentiation between women could be observed in this process. When some elite women suggest that domestic chores should be eliminated, some women workers are being forced to leave their posts in large industrialized production and work as domestic workers. From being masters of their factories and working in the public arena to becoming servants and working in a private space, the psychological imbalance that is created with n these workers is so immense that it is difficult for others to comprehend. Most of them work by the hour. They have to take care of their own families at the same time. When a female domestic worker meets a female employer, they often realize that while their difference might be a result of the different cultural and skill capital that they own, it might also be a result of the difference in the resources that their work units own, or simply because the latter married a man who became rich. Workers who have been through Mao's era when they felt proud to be a member of the working class find that their social status has deteriorated. They mock themselves by saying that they are 'masters who have become servants' and 'generals who have become slaves'. This has created an identity split within these workers: working class as the leading class in the society (theoretically they are still connected with their original work units), and the urban lower class who work as housekeepers. A domestic workers' job as carer is a kind of emotional labour. For single-parent female domestic workers, as they try to overcome the pain of divorce, they have also to take care of the elderly and the children of their employers, a job which sometimes involves emotion. The difference between the beautiful big houses of their employers and their own small rented housing unit also reminds them of their social status. For the workers, the spatial shift in work is in fact a result of social exclusion in space. From being a laid-off factory worker to becoming a domestic worker, the change does not only involve a change from a labour relationship (*laodong guanxi*) to a service relationship (*laowu guanxi*), it also implies exclusion by their original work units and loss of welfare and benefits, since they are also no longer entitled to cheap housing units provided by their original work units.

Marriage and housing: shrinking of space as a result of divorce

Most members of the single-parent female domestic workers groups lived in low-rent housing units provided by the work units of their husbands after they got married and before the housing reform (the two were closely connected). The biggest size of a housing unit for a family of three was 55 square metres. This was considered quite good in those days. The smallest size was 14 square metres, and it was mid-level in terms of housing standards. After divorce, only one person from the group lived in a housing unit of 15 square metres, and she only has the right to live there, but not to own the property. All the other women lost their housing units after they divorced. Some left their husbands because of domestic violence, with the only options available to them being to return to their own families or rent peasant houses which were far away from the city centre. A woman worker said:

> I divorced in 1995 and returned to my parents' home. I went back to live in my work unit in 1997. In 2005, I returned to my parents' home again because of demolition and relocation. My ex-husband took over the housing unit and got the right for relocation. The man owns the house after a divorce because the couple is usually living in the family residential compound of the work unit of the man.
>
> (DQ Wang Jie)

Because of divorce, the issue of women's independent housing right emerges. Women's dependency in terms of housing right has been covered by so-called common property in marriage. US scholar Lenore J. Weitzman discusses the relationship between gender and welfare in her book, *The Divorce Revolution*, and points out that the average standard of living of women and children in US went down by 73 per cent after divorce while that of men went up by 42 per cent (quoted in Xu and Zhang, 2003). This sheds light on the fact that women's property right might perhaps be built only on the basis of marriage.

Some women felt hurt by their divorces. In group meetings, members wrote about the injuries caused by their divorces and what they have been feeling:

> I was beaten up; things were smashed; I was scolded; kids were pathetic; parents and siblings were anxious; depressed; worried that I would lose contact with my children.
>
> (DQ Wang Jie)

> I had nowhere to go; no means to earn a living; running about all the time; pathetic; sleeping in different places; children complained; my family complained; *Hun de bei.*[7]

> I feel shame; want to revenge; want to kill him – to cut his throat with a knife. Self-empowerment and independence? One becomes helpless after divorce and no matter where she goes, she is bullied.

A house is often where we have our home. All members of the domestic workers' groups are living with their children, but they do not have housing units of their own. In group discussions they said that the first need of single-parent domestic workers was housing.

> I hope I have my own housing unit, even if it was only 10 square metres – a small place as a shelter after a day's hard work.
>
> (DQ1, Wang Jie)

> I hope to have self-confidence in my life. If you have your own place after you finish working, you feel more stable.
>
> (DQ4, Zhang Jie)

> Without a housing unit, my child could not concentrate when studying. Both my child and I feel inconvenience in everyday life. It's painful not to have your own place. Economically tight, insecure. The environment of the rural area where I rent my place is bad. It's not good for the child's health. It's going to be inconvenient when my child grows up.
>
> (DQ5, Du Jie)

Housing is a big issue in my life. It is related with household registration. If you don't have a housing unit, you have no where to register your household. The housing unit where one registers one's household affects which school the child attends and the schools one can choose from. (Without our own place,) we had to register my parents' place, and when the child goes to school, we will have to pay high school fee. Only when one has a secure home will he/she be able to build a career. If a person does not have a home, everything is just fantasies.

(DQ8, Da Li)

Housing is a most distressing issue in my life. First, without a housing unit, you've got no shelter, no place to rest, no space of your own. It is a problem which exhausts me and which I want to resolve very much. Living in my parents' place means that I'll have to deal with problems between my relatives. It's very tiring. Housing is a big problem.

(DQ10, Lao Zhang)

When you've got a housing unit, you've got a home. When I've got my own home, I will feel more secure inside me. Even if there might be many worries in life, you feel safe at home and you could relax. One has to have one's own place during one's lifetime. The second problem is children's school fee. There's simply no way to resolve it.

(DQ20, Dong Jie)

So how could they get a housing unit?

Private housing: a right which single-parent female domestic workers could not afford

A common experience of members of the single-parents groups was losing two 'homes' at the same time. The big home was the factory; the small home was the real home. This is how people interpret the earlier era today. For a while, 'love your factory as your home' was the virtue of the working class. 'Five Virtues Family' (outstanding in such five aspects as law-abiding, diligent study, family planning, domestic harmony and industrious and thrifty management of the household) was an applause for the small home. Even though income was low and housing conditions were poor, the factory was big. The politics of space in Mao's era were: The small home and the big home (factory) and even the state were all one. There was the saying that 'small streams are full when the water level of the big river rises'. Adding to this is the ideological pride since the working class was considered the leading class. The desire for space as the master of the country surged continuously – 'liberate two-thirds of the down-trodden people in the world', 'post the red flag on Wall Street'. To liberate the whole world was the dream of a few generations. 'As public servants, living in public houses, scrimping and saving to pay the party fee' was not uncommon in those days. However, as terms such as globalization, opening up and economic reform are becoming clichés which people use to tease each other, public housing units are fast turning into private housing units. Property rights involving housing which is considered private space is now protected by law. A woman worker often discovers that there has been a shift for her in terms of space only after her emotional turmoil. As she moves from the factory to 'home', there is no more a 'home' she could return to. The housing unit which the work unit of her husband granted to them was there no more. The other side of 'patrilocal residence' is: 'you have no residence when you don't have a husband', 'leave your husband and you leave you house'. A woman can only go to live in someone else's house.

The women workers said that buying a private housing unit was largely a fantasy:

> It is too difficult for this dream to come true, and I don't know how to plan for it. My wish is that the larger society shows concern for single mothers and provides housing units for single mothers and their children. For this to happen, we have to save some money from our food. With some savings, there is a 40 per cent chance to realize this wish.
>
> (DQ Lao Dong)

> I want to buy a small housing unit but it's economically impossible for me. It is a far off dream. I am already over 50, and I cannot make big money. It's very difficult to realize this wish.
>
> (DQ Da Zhang)

Some think that this generation will never be able to own a housing unit, so they place their hopes in their children. However, they were also worried that even if they worked hard to pay for the schooling of their children, the children might not be able to find a job after they graduated from universities. If the children could not find a job, they would have no stable income, and housing would still be a problem:

> I'll work hard and my child will study hard so as to enter a good university. We'll save up money after the child goes to work, and then we may get a loan to buy a housing unit. (The dream) is small and very far off.

> I will persist and struggle to raise my son. When he finishes university, he will get a loan to buy a housing unit. There is a 60 per cent certainty. (The state has to) resolve the problem of employment difficulty of university graduates.

In the large and middle sized cities of China, the housing price to income ratio and the burden of mortgages are known to be the highest and heaviest in the world.[8]

A right which one cannot afford cannot be considered a right. For the marginalized and disadvantaged, such as female domestic workers, private housing is a right they cannot afford. They demand only for the right to live in low-rent housing units provided by the state.

Conclusion: hollowing out of women's housing right and the limitation of program intervention

'Patrilocal residence' is a common form of matrimonial residence and housing system. Whether in the form of *fen fang*, a form of low rent housing provided by work units as part of employees' welfare and benefits, or in the form of 'commodity house' the market price of which is decided by the cash income of the population, or economical housing units (*Jinji Shiyong Fang*) that are built for the middle- and lower-income groups and cheap rental housing system built in the name of benefiting the disadvantaged groups, they have not truly been able to resolve the problem of the housing right of poor women. In this country, the social system, customs, culture and the market all collude to a certain extent. It is a collusion between public patriarchy and private patriarchy. Not only does it appear as gender blindness prevalent in laws and measures on housing, it might also result in the violation of the housing rights of marginalized and poor women who are faced with many forms of shrinking space and exclusion. As McDowell (2006: 3) argues

> For some of these women, their voyage might not involve geographical movement far and wide; it might only be a local voyage; there might not even be any physical movement. Instead, as women enter factories, or work as domestic workers in elite families, and when they gain connections with other times and places by means of western information technology or due to the permeation and cultural domination of popular culture, the connections they experience and their displacement are the results of economic, social and cultural changes. Whether the movement involves the physical body, it is nearly always related with the renegotiation of gender difference.

Loss of housing rights by some single parent female domestic workers has occurred hand in hand with their social marginalization subsequent to retrenchment and unemployment, divorce, low income and urban housing reform. The dual repression of work and marriage has led to their near complete loss of social space and private space. They are experiencing the shift from the public space (industrial production and big factory workshops) to the private space of their employers. In this process they have lost the right to housing benefits provided by their original work units. At the same time, due to divorce, they are excluded from the housing units which are considered common property in the matrimonial family. Even though legal interpretations with regard to the division of property as a result of divorce emphasize again and again equal rights in housing, and express concern for the rights of women and children, it has little influence in real practice.

There is only one last choice, and that is cheap rental housing in cities. This may be a way to deal with the problem of the housing rights of these workers. Cheap rental housing is housing provided by the government for urban people whose low standard of living makes them eligible and for families who face housing problems. Presently, cheap rental housing is mainly provided in the form of subsidized rent, and complemented with the allocation of low rental housing or rent reduction. According to the regulations of Xian city, any family whose average size of residence is below 7 square metres per person is eligible to apply for cheap rental housing. Some time ago, the government of Xian raised RMB 19.02 million to build cheap rental housing. 6,186 families who did not have a roof over their heads were the first group to benefit from the plan. The Women's Development and Rights Research Center and the city's Women's Federation had called on the government of Xian to include single parents as beneficiaries for the cheap rental housing plan. After much negotiation, the government refused our demand on the basis that the need was much more than the supply. However, the government agreed to subsidize the housing expenses of families that were unable to rent a cheap rental housing unit by providing each single parent family with 10 yuan every month as a rent subsidy (it was subsequently raised to 40 yuan). The tentative highest rent subsidy for each family benefiting from the cheap rental housing is 150 yuan per month (but the rent of a housing unit in Xian is at least 300–500 yuan per month).

This small subsidy is inadequate to greatly improve the living conditions of the single-parent female domestic workers. It only provides some psychological comfort. For this group of women, housing rights are a far off dream and rights that they cannot afford, just like the right of gender equality stated on the Law on the Protection of Women's Rights and Interests. In order to realize one's rights, one has to have the ability, the resources and the capital, and these are what this group of women are lacking.

A small house is still a dream drawn on paper. Rights is also an empty word for many women in mainland China.

11 Women and housing inequalities in Hong Kong

Chan Kam Wah

Introduction

Hong Kong is a city full of interesting and paradoxical phenomena in terms of studies on women and housing. Hong Kong is a global city and yet it is still very much dominated by traditional Chinese culture; a *laissez-faire* capitalist economy and yet it has one of the largest public housing programme amongst world cities. This unusual mix of culture, politics, and social practice has resulted in a complex housing system. Although women in Hong Kong have largely broken through the social constraints of a traditional feudal society, they are still a disadvantaged group in the housing system. Taken-for-granted assumptions in patriarchal society coupled with liberalist economic values have restricted the housing opportunities of women, both in the private and public housing sector. Women of disadvantaged social background such as lone mothers, new immigrant women, and older women are discriminated in the private housing market. Their needs are also being neglected in the public housing system, which is mainly geared toward the needs of 'conventional families'. This chapter aims to show that structural constraints coupled with taken-for-granted ideology and social practice contributes to the reinforce Hong Kong women's disadvantaged position in the housing system.

This chapter starts by outlining the development of housing policy and the situation of gender equality in Hong Kong. These descriptions highlight the social changes and power dynamics that have significant impact on women's housing opportunities. It then goes on to elaborate the disadvantaged housing position of women from various social backgrounds including lone mothers, women suffering domestic violence, new arrival women, women living alone, older women, women as home owners. Evidence in Hong Kong has shown that these women face various difficulties in accessing adequate housing resources, or their housing needs are largely neglected. In the next section, I focus on how gender-blind housing design and urban planning in Hong Kong contributes to reinforcing women's marginal position, threatens women's safety, and confines women at home. This chapter concludes by recommending a fundamental review of housing policy, and mainstreaming a gender perspective in housing policy planning and housing practice.

The development of housing policy in Hong Kong

The development of Hong Kong is phenomenal. Hong Kong developed rapidly from small fishing and farming villages to a global city in about half a century. Today, Hong Kong has a population of about seven million crammed into an area of about 1,100 square kilometres. Space is so precious that most people can only afford to live in small flats in high-rise buildings. This creates great difficulties for women who have to take care of the family. Hong Kong was a British colony before 1997, at which time sovereignty was transferred back to China. Social policy in Hong Kong still has a hint of the British colonial legacy, and yet it is a Special Administrative Region (SAR) under the Chinese Communist government. Hong Kong is supposed to be a *laissez-faire* capitalist state; however, the proportion of social housing is one of the highest amongst the advanced capitalist economies in the world. In 2008, public rental housing represented 28.7 per cent of the total housing stock, while government subsidized sale flats represented 15.8 per cent (Census and Statistics Department 2009a: 177). Social housing has played an important part in the rapid urbanization and economic growth of Hong Kong. These rapid social changes have created paradoxical phenomena and a unique mix of cultural and social practice.

The history of public housing development can be traced to a huge fire in a squatter area, the Shek Kip Mei district, on the Christmas Eve of 1953, which left more than 50,000 victims homeless. The government started to provide public rental housing to accommodate the victims. This provided the dynamic for the huge public housing programme which took place during the following decades. However, studies have shown that public housing has not developed on humanitarian grounds. It has been a strategy utilized to pacify the poor and avoid social instability, and more importantly, to reclaim the land in the city centre and urban periphery occupied by squatters and old buildings in order to make way for industrial and commercial development (Castells *et al.* 1990).

This economic-oriented strategy has dominated the development of housing policy ever since. The situation has worsened over the last two decades, during which time a few large private housing developers have come to monopolize the housing market (Fung and Forrest 2002). A study by the Hong Kong Consumer Council showed that between 1991 and 1994 the top five developers produced 60.3 per cent of the new housing units (Hong Kong Consumer Council 1996: Annex 3). Hong Kong has developed the myth of being a 'housing market led economy' in which policy makers and the public believed that rising housing prices was equivalent to economic prosperity. Social inequalities and the negative impact of housing speculation have largely been sidelined (Chan 2000). Although house prices fell during the Asian financial crisis in 1997 and the global financial tsunami in 2008, they rose again rapidly without warning in 2010. For example, in March 2010 a second-hand, middle-class housing unit in the urban area of Tai Koo Shing cost HK$7,997[1] per square feet; a new unit in the Island Crest in the Western District cost HK$13,195 per square feet (Centadata 2010). According to official statistics, in 2008 the median monthly income of the working population in Hong Kong was only HK$10,500 per month (Census and Statistics Department 2009a: 47). That is, for a unit of about 1,000 square feet in the above example, it is equivalent to 762 months and 1,257 months respectively of an average worker's salary. It is not surprising to see that affordable housing for both the working-class and middle-income group has become a conspicuous issue in Hong Kong (Chiu 2007, Lee 1994). Rising house prices and rents creates great difficulties for women such as lone mothers and women living alone to secure decent accommodation in the private housing market.

Public housing also tends to neglect the needs of women with particular housing needs. In Hong Kong, public housing allocation is based on the ideology of 'family as a unit' (see Chapter 1 for more details). That is, those women who are not living in a conventional family such as lone mothers, women living alone, and older women not living with their children may find difficulties in accessing public housing. Moreover, the strategy of privatizing public housing which began in the 1990s has reduced the stock of public rental housing substantially (Yu 1997). On the one hand, the Hong Kong government encourages the public to buy private housing with various subsidies, or to buy government-subsidized flats through policies such as the Home Ownership Scheme and the sale of public rental housing. On the other hand, the public rental housing programme has been cut substantially to encourage home purchase (Chan 2000). It is becoming more difficult for lower-income women to access public rental housing.

The disadvantaged position of women in the public housing system is partly due to the lack of gender sensitivity in public housing policy planning and implementation. As in many other countries, policy making, urban planning, and the housing management professions are dominated by men (Chan, forthcoming). The Housing Authority is responsible for public housing policy planning and implementation in Hong Kong. In 2008/09, among the 26 appointed Housing Authority members, only five are women (Hong Kong Housing Authority 2009:100). Up to the present time, statistics on gender and housing in Hong Kong are scarce, making the study on gender inequality in housing very difficult. Women's housing problems are largely hidden, and gender as an issue is not on the agenda of the Housing Authority.

Social changes and gender inequality in Hong Kong

The domination of men in the Housing Authority reflects men's domination in society at large. Hong Kong is a global city and was a British colony for about 150 years; it has been heavily influenced by European and American cultures. Paradoxically however, Hong Kong is still very much dominated by Confucianism and traditional Chinese culture, especially in family and gender issues.

Hong Kong lacks a strong women's movement. An indigenous women's movement only started in the mid-1980s (Lee 2000, Leung 2004). There is no strong feminist voice in the Executive Council and Legislative Council of the Government. Ironically, neither the Women's Commission nor the Equal Opportunity Commission necessarily upholds a feminist perspective. Hong Kong is dominated by neo-liberalist and individualist ideology, coupled with traditional Chinese culture. The more progressive feminist organizations or grassroots-oriented women's groups tend to be marginalized and excluded in the political system.

In recent decades, rapid social changes have had a significant impact on women and the family. With industrialization in the 1960s and 1970s, and the economic restructuring in the 1980s and 1990s, there are more opportunities for women in the labour market. The labour force participation rate for women rose from 48.9 per cent in 1986 to 53.1 per cent in 2008, while that for men fell from 80.5 per cent to 69.7 per cent (Census and Statistics Department 2009b: 75). However, the income gap between women and men is still substantial. Overall, women were only earning 70.8 per cent of that of men in 2008 (Table 11.1). The gap is especially obvious in lower income occupations such as elementary occupations (50 per cent), plant and machine operators and assemblers (64.3 per cent), and service workers and shop sales workers (66.7 per cent). This gap has actually widened in the last two decades. In 1993, women were earning 75 per cent that of men (Census and Statistics Department 2009b: 113). One of the reasons is that with financial crisis and economic fluctuation starting from late 1990s, more and more women have been marginalized in the labour market and have had to take up low-paid and unstable jobs. In April–June 2005, there were 94,600 women and 56,300 men employed in part-time jobs (Census and Statistics Department 2009b: 102). The number of women in part-time jobs has increased more rapidly than that of men in the last decade.

The impact of labour market changes in recent decades is complex. On one hand, some women enjoy more opportunities in employment, which helps to liberate women from traditional roles. This is especially true for women in higher-income occupations such as managers and professionals. On the other hand, lower-income women may face more intensive exploitation and poverty; they have little choice other than working in low-paid and unstable jobs. The cost of living, especially housing expenses, is rising rapidly while their wage is not. For example, the median monthly income of employees in Hong Kong increased only marginally from

Table 11.1 Median monthly employment earnings (in HK$) of employed
persons by occupation and sex, 2008

Occupation	Female	Male	F/M %
Managers and administrator	30,000	30,000	100
Professionals	28,000	30,000	93.3
Associate professionals	15,500	15,000	103.3
Clerks	9,500	9,800	96.9
Service workers and shop sales workers	7,000	10,500	66.7
Craft and related workers	8,000	10,100	79.2
Plant and machine operators and assemblers	6,300	9,800	64.3
Elementary occupations	3,500	7,000	50.0
Overall	8,500	12,000	70.8

Source: Census and Statistics Department 2009b: 113 Table 5.3.

HK$10,000 in 1996 to HK$10,500 in 2008. For women in elementary occupations, the median monthly wage has actually fallen from HK$3,800 to HK$3,500 (Census and Statistics Department 2009b: 113). That is, it is becoming more difficult for low-income women to solve their housing problem. With the traditional gender division of labour still prevalent in Hong Kong, especially among working-class families, women may face intensive exploitation in the workplace, and then have to take up a second shift after work involving household chores (Hochschild 1990).

There are also significant changes in the family and marriage that affect women in Hong Kong. Both men and women tend to marry at a later age. The median age at first marriage for women rose from 22.9 in 1971 to 28.3 in 2007, and from 27.8 to 31.2 for men in the same period (Census and Statistics Department 2008a: 19). The total fertility rate in Hong Kong is falling rapidly, from 3,459 per 1,000 women in 1971 to 1,024 per 1,000 women in 2007 (Census and Statistics Department 2008a: 18). The average family size reduced from 4.5 in 1971 to 3.0 in 2007 (Census and Statistics Department 2008a: 19). The lower fertility rate and fewer children in the family do not imply less work for women. On the contrary, with rising demand on quality of care and increasing competition in the education system, the pressure on women is ever increasing. With smaller family sizes, it also implies that women have less accessible to support from relative than in the days when extended families were prevalent.

A lower birth rate also leads to an aging population. The number of people aged 65 and above increased from 147,000 in 1967 to 871,000 in 2007, representing an increase from 3.9 per cent to 12.6 per cent of the total population and the median age of the population rose from 20.3 to 39.9 (Census and Statistics Department 2008a:16). The aging population exacerbate the housing problems of older women.

This also increases the burden of caring for the older people in the family, which is still regarded as primarily women's responsibility.

In view of these social changes, the family is facing ever-increasing stress, and it is not surprising to see that divorce and family breakdown have been on the increase in recent decades. The number of divorces decreed rose sharply from 0.09 per 1,000 population in 1973 to 2.66 per 1,000 population in 2007 (Census and Statistics Department 2008a: 18), and the lone-parent family is becoming a more conspicuous issue in Hong Kong. As expected in a traditional patriarchal society, it is predominantly women who take up the childcare duties after divorce. However, housing policy and housing services are not providing adequate support for lone mothers.

Hong Kong is a migrant society in the sense that a high proportion of the population was not born in Hong Kong, but migrated from Mainland China. With increasing social exchange between Hong Kong and Mainland China, the number of cross-border marriages has risen sharply. The number of cases of Hong Kong men marrying women in Mainland China has increased from 15,776 in 1986 to 28,145 in 2006 (Census and Statistics Department 2009b:35). As a result, there are increasing numbers of new arrivals from Mainland China, who are predominantly women and children coming to Hong Kong on the grounds of family reunion. These women and new immigrant families face a lot of difficulties, of which housing is one of the most severe due to the restrictions on new arrival families accessing public rental housing.

Rapid economic growth and social change have not helped to solve the housing problems of women. In fact, the neo-liberalist, individualist ideology coupled with patriarchal culture has, in many ways, exacerbated the ability of many women to meet their housing needs.

Access to housing resources

To illustrate the problem, I am going to look at the experience of accessing housing resources of several groups of women, including lone mothers and women suffering domestic violence, new arrivals, women living alone, older women, and women as home owners.

Lone mothers and women experiencing domestic violence

It has been pointed out that rapid social change has led to a rising divorce rate and increasing numbers of lone-parent families. Official statistics showed that the number of lone parents increased from 34,538 in 1991 to 72,326 in 2006 (Table 11.2), more than double in 15 years. This is an underestimation to a large extent. Since divorce is still regarded as a disgrace in Chinese culture, many women are reluctant to initiate formal divorce proceedings even though their husband is no longer supporting the family or has disappeared completely. Most lone-parent families are female-headed; 80 per cent in 2006. Lone mothers have less chance to work than their male counterpart, 54.5 per cent as compared to 70.3 per cent in 2006; and their incomes are much lower, HK$9,345 as compared to HK$12,150 in 2006. From Table 11.2, we can also see that the median household monthly income of a lone-mother family has actually decreased in the past ten years, from HK$11,500 in 1996 to HK$9,345 in 2006. From these data, we can see that women are taking up more responsibility of looking after the children after the divorce. However, they have access to fewer resources to deal with the problem, and the situation is getting worse, not better.

Chan's (1997) study showed that low-income lone mothers faced many difficulties in solving their housing problems. With low income or depending on social security, they can only afford very cheap accommodation in slum areas, and will most likely be renting a room and sharing a flat with several other households. Very often, they and their young children have to face the threat of sexual harassment from men sharing the flat, and mal-treatment from other women in the flat, not to mention the difficulties of taking care of children in this overcrowded and unhygienic environment. Lone mothers with young children are not welcome in most private housing. Landlords worry that they are unable to pay their rent and landladies worry that lone mothers will seduce their husband. There are many

Table 11.2 Statistics on lone-parent families

		1991	1996	2001	2006
Number of lone parents	F	23,059	30,402	45,072	57,613
	M	11,479	11,907	13,388	14,713
	Total	34,538	42,309	58,460	72,326
Economic activity status-working (%)	F	64.1%	60.0%	52.8%	54.5%
	M	86.5%	83.6%	71.0%	70.3%
Median monthly household income (HK$)	F	7,750	11,500	10,371	9,345
	M	8,600	15,000	14,000	12,150
Living in public rented housing	F	52.2%	50.7%	44.4%	52.3%
	M	55.9%	49.6%	48.4%	46.4%
Owner-occupiers	F	32.4%	32.3%	30.3%	26.9%
	M	28.0%	31.9%	35.0%	36.8%

Source: Census and Statistics Department 2009b: p. 39 Table 2.10; p. 40 Table 2.11; p. 41 Table 2.12; p. 42 Table 2.13; p. 43 Table 2.14, p. 44.

barriers preventing low-income lone mothers from accessing decent accommodation in private housing.

Housing policy in Hong Kong stipulated that people seeking a divorce and taking care of the children could be granted 'conditional tenancy' of public rental housing with the recommendation of the Social Welfare Department. That is, they would be allocated a public housing flat temporarily until their divorce is decreed. If they have the right of custody of their children, they can remain in the flat; otherwise, they have to move out. Stable accommodation is particularly important to lone-mother families. However, the assessment of the Social Welfare Department is very stringent. In practice, many lone mothers and their children living in poor conditions in the private housing are regarded as not having genuine need (Chan 1997: 112–19). In recent years, with the cutting of social security, many welfare recipients such as lone mothers are portrayed as greedy, lazy, reluctant to work, and welfare dependent (Leung and Chan 1998). Being affected by the dominant negative perception of lone mother, very often, social workers in the Social Welfare Department tend to be very strict in the assessment of lone mother's need.

The situation is more difficult for women facing domestic violence. Many battered women and their children have to escape from the matrimonial home for safety while their husband stays put (Chan and Chan 2003). According to existing housing policy, lone mothers seeking divorce can stay in the matrimonial home if they are taking care of their children and their husband has to move out. Very often, the Housing Department refuses to take any action to re-house the husband. They regard these family conflicts as 'internal affairs' and ask the women to convince their husband to move out. Moreover, under existing housing policy, the one moving out of the public housing flat has to give up their rights of tenancy. That is, they are not entitled to another public housing unit, but have to apply again as a new applicant and join the long waiting list. This creates difficulties and conflict between husband and wife seeking divorce. Consequently, many women and children facing the threat of violence have to move out of the matrimonial home and look for accommodation in the private market. For home owners, the situation can be worse. Because those who own a flat are not entitled to public housing services, some women even have to relinquish their share of the property in order to be qualified for re-housing by the government.

Women and children suffering from domestic violence are able to move to shelters for battered women. However, shelter services are very restrictive in Hong Kong. They can only stay in the shelter for three months at most. Shelter services are not closely linked with the Housing Department. In most cases, the battered women and their children cannot secure a public housing unit before they leave the shelter.

In view of the difficulties of finding accommodation and other social services, many women have to remain with their husband, even though they live under the constant threat of violence. Sometimes this situation occurs even though they are seeking a divorce or have the divorce decreed. Since they are unable to afford alternative accommodation they and their husbands have to stay under the same roof. In recent years there have been shocking incidences where the violent husband has killed their wife and/or the children. It is extremely difficult for women to escape from a violent marital relationship due to the lack of social support. Whilst a woman might be abused by one man if they stay with their violent husband, it seems that if they become a lone mother they may be 'abused' by others, such as employers, landlords, housing officers, social workers, and policemen. In this sense, housing policy and other social policies are creating the problem and reinforcing domestic violence.

New-arrival women

New arrivals from Mainland China are also becoming an increasing cause for concern, especially after the transfer of sovereignty in 1997. Officially, 'new arrivals from Mainland China' only refers to those recent immigrants from Mainland China residing in Hong Kong for less than seven years. In reality, many new arrivals are being discriminated against and excluded in Hong Kong even though they have lived here for over 10 years. In recent years, most new arrivals from Mainland China are women and children. According to the Census, among the new arrivals coming to Hong Kong in 2006, 29.2 per cent are children age 15 or below and 27.3 per cent are women. In 2006, the numbers of new-arrival women living in Hong Kong is 150,437, this is more than double as compared with 66,666 new-arrival men (Census and Statistic Department 2009b: 22). Studies have shown that new arrivals in Hong Kong are being discriminated against and socially excluded in a variety of ways (Law and Lee 2006). The situation of new-arrival women, facing the double disadvantage of ethnic and gender discrimination, could be much worse (Lee 2004). Median monthly income of new arrivals is HK$6,000 as compared to HK$10,000 for the whole population in Hong Kong in 2006 (Census and Statistics Department 2007: 41, Table 6.6). There is no breakdown of official statistics on income of new-arrival women. However, academic studies have shown that most new-arrival women usually can only find low paid and unstable jobs in the labour market, putting the income and working conditions of new-arrival women far below that of Hong Kong people (Lee 2004).

New-arrival families are being discriminated against explicitly in public housing policy (Chui 2002). According to the eligibility criteria for public rental housing, one of the requirements is that: 'On allocation, at least half of the family members must have lived in Hong Kong for seven years and are still living in Hong Kong' (Hong Kong Housing Authority 2009: 119). That is, new-arrival families failing to fulfil this criterion will lose their rights to public housing services. Bearing in mind that in the 'new-arrival families', at least one of the spouses, husband or wife, is a full Hong Kong citizen, these citizens lose their housing right simply because their spouse and children join them for family reunion.

In 2003, the Hong Kong Government published a Population Policy (Task Force on Population Policy 2003), in which one of the major strategies is to restrict new arrival's access to welfare. New arrivals have to reside in Hong Kong for seven years or above before they are allowed to claim social security benefit. This put new-immigrant women in a very disadvantaged position. If they have any problem with their marriage and they want to divorce their husband, it would be very difficult for them to get any social support. They are not qualified to apply for public housing, and they are not eligible for social security. That is why new-arrival women are very vulnerable to domestic violence. Many new-arrival women are forced to depend on their husband even though they might not happy in the marriage. Again, housing and other social services are constructing and reinforcing new-arrival women's subordination to their husband.

Women living alone

One important social change in recent decades is that there is increasing number of women living alone. The number of women living alone increased from 58,088 in 1986 to 182,648 in 2006, more than triple in 20 years (Census and Statistics Department 2009b: 38, Table 2.9). With increasing economic opportunities and influence from Western culture, more women are reluctant to depend on a man or the family. However, they have to face various difficulties in solving their housing problem. As we have pointed out earlier, housing price and rent in Hong Kong is notoriously high, and so it is difficult for lower and middle income group to buy or rent a decent accommodation. This is especially true for women because the income of women is relatively lower than men (see Table 11.1). In addition, women living alone have a greater concern relating to security and safety. Ultimately, they have to pay more in order to secure decent and safe accommodation. Therefore, it is less likely that lower-income women could afford to live alone. Official statistics show that the median income of women living alone is higher than that of men (Table 11.3), and is much higher than median income of the female population in that year.

For those higher income women who can afford to buy a flat in the private housing market, they may face some disadvantages in securing a mortgage. Although housing mortgage financing business is competitive in Hong Kong and gender discrimination is not obvious, banks used to offer a lower mortgage interest rate for preferred customers such as civil servants, teachers, and men with a stable family. Women living alone are in a less favourable situation.

It is difficult for women living alone to access public rental housing. Public housing allocation is largely based on 'family as a unit', of which 'family' is regarded as 'at least two related persons living together' (Hong Kong Housing Authority 2009: 119). For one-person non-elderly (below age 60) applicants, they have to register on a separate waiting list of lower priority to the 'ordinary families'. In fact, it was not until 1984 that one-person and two-person families

Table 11.3 Median monthly income (in HK$) of those living alone by sex

	1991	1996	2001	2006
Female	4,750	12,000	15,000	13,000
Male	5,000	10,000	14,000	12,500

Source: Census and Statistics Department 2009b: 153, Table 10.4.

were allowed to apply for public housing. However, the provision of one-person flats is very limited, and most of these flats are reserved for older people. With all these difficulties, the housing system seems to discourage women from living alone and reinforce women's dependence on the family.

Older women

Hong Kong is facing the problem of aging population as in other economically developed countries. Among the elderly population, a high proportion is female, especially among the more elderly groups. For example, in 2008 for the 80–84 age group the male to female ratio is 679:1,000, for the 85 and above age group the ratio is 457:1,000 (Census and Statistics Department 2009b: 9, Table 1.2).

To a certain extent, Hong Kong still cherishes some aspects of traditional Chinese culture such as filial piety and respecting the elderly. Public housing applicants aged 60 and above and families applying with an elderly member are given higher priority. However, the provision of elderly housing and social service support for elderly people living alone in public housing still lags behind the ever-increasing demand. It is also the case that for both the elderly person and their family members the traditional extended family living arrangements might not be the most desirable (Chan and Lee 2003). More elderly people prefer to live alone or with their spouse only, instead of living with their children's family. In 2006, 14.5 per cent of the women and 11 per cent of men aged 65 and above were living alone (Table 11.4), and 21.2 per cent of the elderly were living with spouse only (Census and Statistics Department 2008b: 44). Due to the lack of income, many elderly living alone rely heavily on public housing, for example in 2006, 53.6 per cent of the elderly living alone lived in public rental housing, 38.4 per cent of the elderly living with spouse only (but not with their children) lived in public rental housing (Census and Statisitcs Department 2008b: 51, Table 7.8). However, housing policy is insensitive to these social changes and still assumes that it is customary for elderly people to live with their children. We can see from Table 11.4 that higher proportions of elderly women are living alone as compared with their male counterparts.

One of the important issues of developing public housing for the elderly in Hong Kong is the location. As expected, the elderly population tends to be concentrated in older districts. In the urban area such as the Kwun Tong District, Eastern District and Wong Tai Sin District, there are 11 per cent, 9.7 per cent and 8.8 per

Table 11.4 Persons aged 65 and above living alone in domestic households

	2001		2006	
	Female	Male	Female	Male
Living alone	48,749	36,018	58,931	39,898
% of population aged 65 and above	13.6%	11.2%	14.5%	11.0%
Total population aged 65 and above	358,213	320,884	405,240	361,985

Source: Census and Statistics Department 2009b: 151, Table 10.2.

cent respectively of the elderly population living in these three areas (Census and Statistics Department 2008b: 55). The land in the urban area is so valuable that the government is redeveloping areas of the inner city into commercial or high-end private housing residential areas. A substantial proportion of public housing for the elderly is developed in remote new towns or newly developed areas which are far from their children's home in the urban centre. Research findings have shown that although some elderly prefer to live alone, they also prefer to live near their children so that they can get some support when needed (Chan and Lee 2003). Conversely, they are also then available to offer help to take care of young grandchildren. Mutual support and exchange among family members are important activities in Chinese society, which is especially true among women in the family. Elderly housing developed in remote areas weakens elderly women's social networks. Moreover, public housing policy in Hong Kong is very inflexible; transfer from one housing estate to another is difficult, especially transferring from a rural area to an urban area. It is difficult for the elderly and their children living in different public housing estates to transfer to estates close to each other. This creates many problems with providing care and support both for the elderly and the children (mostly women) taking care of the elderly parent.

Women as home owners and housing wealth

Home ownership and housing wealth is another dynamic contributing to the disadvantage of women in Hong Kong. Hong Kong does not produce official statistics on housing wealth, not to mention the gender difference in the possession of housing wealth. However, it is still a common practice for men to inherit the housing properties of the family. Theoretically speaking, housing property is family wealth that is shared equally between all family members. This seems to be true as long as women are living in a conventional family. However, when the marriage breaks down as we have pointed out earlier regarding the situation of lone mothers and battered women, they may not be entitled to their share of the housing wealth.

Or, in the case of women living alone, it is more difficult for them to negotiate favourable mortgage terms.

Hong Kong is still dominated by patriarchal ideology, and men are generally regarded as the 'head' of the family. In Census enumeration, each household is asked to identify a 'household head', and they can report more than one household head. In 2006, about 70 per cent to 80 per cent of the households identify an adult man (aged 35 to 60) as the household head, which is much higher than that for women (Figure 11.1). This reflects the fact that men are still in an advantaged position compared to women, and in command of housing wealth and housing resources. This is particularly marked in rural villages in Hong Kong. Under the 'small house policy' in rural villages, only men, not women, are entitled to build a house and inherit land in the village (Hopkinson and Lao 2003: 24). The government is reluctant to change the legislation to protect women's housing rights, even though there are vigorous protests from women. In this sense, men are protected by law and traditional cultural practice to control housing resources, and women have to depend on men in order to enjoy these resources.

Another problem with home ownership is the pooling of resources among family members to purchase a 'family house', which is a common practice in Hong Kong among lower-middle-income families. Housing prices in Hong Kong are so expensive that for many families it requires several members to contribute to pay the mortgage. Very often, working daughters living with their parents have to contribute to pay the mortgage. However, it is customary in Chinese culture for men to inherit the family properties. When the daughters get married they have to move out to live with their husband. When the sons get married, they are expected

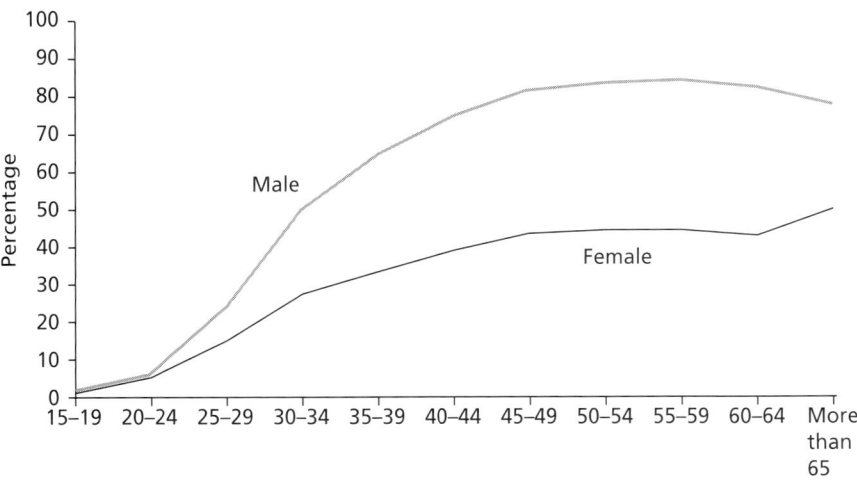

11.1 Household headship rate by age group and sex, 2006. Source: Census and Statistics Department 2009b: 157,Chart 10.1.

to stay in the family house and inherit the property. In this way, the daughter's contribution to the family house is transferred to the son. Although this practice is unfair, most women do not question the arrangement with their parents as this is regarded as filial piety in Chinese culture.

In some cases, when the elderly father dies, the family house is not passed to his wife, but the son. Women are expected to depend on a man, their husband. If their husband dies, they depend on their son. As revealed in Chan and Lee's (2003) study on elderly people living alone in Hong Kong, some older women with traditional beliefs transfer the family house to their son after they become widowed. However, their son may not take up the responsibility of caring for the elderly women, and they are required to move out of the house, or the property might even be sold. In this way, some elderly women home owners end up homeless, or have to apply for public housing services.

Discrimination by design

With a population of about seven million in an area of around 1,100 square kilometres, Hong Kong is extremely overcrowded especially in the urban area. Under the 'housing developer-led economy', most of the land in the city centre is reserved for commercial and business usage, or for high-end middle-class private housing development. Low-income families have to move to remote new towns in rural areas or the New Territories. This has been accomplished by the massive development of social housing in the New Territories, which started from the 1970s. In 2008, 51.7 per cent of housing stock was in the New Territories. On Hong Kong Island, where most of the expensive upper- and middle-class housing is concentrated, only 10 per cent of public rental housing and 11.5 per cent of subsidized sale flats are located. In contrast, 54.4 per cent of the public rental housing and 65 per cent of subsidized sale flats (including various types of government subsidized home ownership schemes) are built in the New Territories (Table 11.5).

The higher income groups and the commercial and industrial sectors are reluctant to move to remote new towns. It is extremely difficult to find a job there, and travelling to the city centre is time consuming and costly. Most women have to stay at home while men travel long distances to work in the city centre. Women are isolated from their supportive network, and there is a lack of support from the husband due to the long working hours and travelling time (Chan 1997). On the other hand, underpinned with the ideology of the 'domestic ideal' (See chapter 1 for more details), mainstream urban planning has assumed that women will take care of the home, and the government has neglected the development of social service support such as child caring and family services. Under these circumstances, women's burden of homemaking is increased, and it is not surprising that there are many family problems, domestic violence, juvenile delinquency, and high crime rates in the remote new towns such as Tin Sui Wai and Tuen Mun.

Table 11.5 Stock of permanent quarters by type and area, 2008

	Public rental housing		Subsidized sale flats		Private housing		All housing	
	No. (000s)	%	No. (000s)	%	No. (000s)	%	No. (000s)	%
Hong Kong Island	72.1	10.0	45.6	11.5	352.6	25.2	470.3	18.7
Kowloon	256.8	35.6	93.3	23.5	395.1	28.2	745.2	29.6
New Territories	392.7	54.4	258.1	65.0	650.9	46.5	1,301.8	51.7
Total	721.6	100	397.1	100	1,398.7	100	2,517.3	100

Source: Census and Statistics Department 2009a: 116–17, Table 8.1.

High crime rates are common in many housing estates both in new towns and urban areas, due to the poor design and low quality of housing management services. This threatens the safety of women, who are more vulnerable to crime and sexual attack. Many women have to stay away from certain public areas or avoid going out at high-risk hours. Some would ask a man, husband, father, brother or boyfriend, to accompany them if they need to go out. This restricts women's mobility, use of public space, and choice of employment; and reinforces their dependency on a man.

Interior housing design can also play an active role in discriminating against women. Space is precious in Hong Kong, most housing units in both private and public housing estates are very small. Dominant housing design in Hong Kong seems to assume that the kitchen is only used by women. In order to make the flat look more spacious, the kitchen is as small as possible. This does not only make women's work more difficult, but also discourages other family members from participating in cooking and other household chores. This also creates difficulties for women taking care of young children, or may even threaten the safety of children.

Another typical problem with the gender-blind housing design in Hong Kong is the clothes drying racks in public housing. Due to the lack of space, there is no place for drying clothes inside the public housing flats, except on a drying rack hanging outside the high rise building. The clothes drying racks are so poorly designed that some women have fallen to death from the high rise buildings whilst leaning out to hang the clothes. The Housing Department is reluctant to improve the design, and claimed that those women were not using the facilities properly.

Conclusion

Hong Kong is a global city, yet it is still dominated by traditional patriarchal culture. Economic growth in recent decades has provided opportunities for some women to liberate themselves from traditional culture. However, this has also led to family and social changes that have increased the burden on women. This is further exacerbated by gender-blind housing policy and housing practices, underpinned by reo-liberal and Confucian ideologies. From the housing experience of various groups of women such as lone mothers, battered women, women living alone, older women, and women home owners, as well as through the examination of how existing housing and urban design discriminates against women, we can see that women's housing problems are not a consequence of their individual inadequacy. These problems are socially constructed in the social structure and social practice of which the housing system plays a significant part. Women's contribution to the household is largely neglected, undervalued, and exploited. To solve the problem, we need a fundamental reflection on and reconstruction of existing housing policy and practice.

12 Conclusion

Patricia Kennett

In the context of contemporary economic, political, social and cultural transformation this collection draws together contributions from developed and less-developed societies in Europe, the USA and East Asia in order to highlight the nature, extent and impact of these changes on the housing opportunities of women. The chapters seek to contribute to comparative housing debates and analysis by highlighting the gendered nature of housing processes, locating these processes within wider structured and institutionalised relations of power, and to show how these socially constructed relationships are culturally contingent, and manifest and transform over time and space.

Gender divisions refer not only to the allocation of resources between men and women, but also embrace issues associated with the control of resources, and the power relations through which inequalities between women and men are socially constructed across different locations (Christie 2000: 87). Gender refers not only to the differences between men and women, it is also masculinity and femininity, or the socially constructed definition of what it means to be male and female. The housing system draws upon and reproduces widely and long held notions of femininity and masculinity (Dowling 1998), which in turn, influence and reinforce the ways in which the spheres of production, reproduction and consumption overlap to create disparity in access to and control over resources.

Whilst housing systems vary widely across societies in terms of tenure patterns, types of subsidy, levels of investment, governance, etc, strategies of deregulation, privatisation, marketisation, and the promotion of home ownership have become almost universal, although pursued with varying degrees of enthusiasm by governments in different societies. Great Britain (Chapter 7), the USA (Chapter 4) and Australia (Chapter 4) stand out as key examples of societies where the 'home-owning' ideal has been constructed and maintained in policy and everyday discourse. As a consequence, whilst demand for social housing has continued to grow and, in many societies, it remains a key source of housing security for women, it has become, or is in the process of becoming (Hong Kong for example, Chapter

203

11), increasingly residualised and exclusionary in terms of location, quality and reputation. As access to appropriate housing has come to rely more on individual resources and strategies it becomes increasingly important to move beyond a view of household as a neutral concept or as a 'joint utility', and to recognise the complexity and gendered nature of the interlocking arenas of production, reproduction and consumption.

As mentioned above, and highlighted in the previous chapters, the interaction between the spheres of production, reproduction and consumption is neither a static relationship nor a uni-dimensional relationship. The specific configurations are influenced by culture, institutional norms, ideology, and the influence of social movements, and are differentiated along the lines of class, ethnicity, age and household status. In many societies in recent years there has been substantial change in gender norm roles particularly amongst younger, well-educated cohorts, in the ways that men and women interact, and a renegotiation of the overall work burdens within both the reproductive and productive economies. A growing number of women are living independently, participating in the labour market, having fewer children, later in life or not at all. However, as Pascall and Sung (2007: 7) argue:

'Nowhere do welfare states' promises bring gender equality in practice. Even in Scandinavian countries women earn less, care more, and have less power then men.

In Sweden, generally regarded as a relatively wealthy society, with good-quality housing, gender equality and comprehensive family policy (Chapter 6, this volume), growing ethnic and socio-economic segregation, inequality and polarisation have impacted on women's access to good-quality housing, and have been accompanied by the emergence of persistent homelessness. Pareja-Eastaway and Sanchez-Martinez (Chapter 5, this volume) highlight the persistence of the male breadwinner model in southern European countries, with particular reference to Spain, as traditional social and religious norms and kinship relationships prevail, and formal equality between genders not attained until the mid 1970s. In East Asian societies Confucian gender and traditional family hierarchies prevail, and have been institutionalised within different political, institutional and policy contexts. Nevertheless, 'The Confucian influence on women's position in society can be best represented with the virtue of three obediences: "to the father, husband and the son"' (Lee 2005a, in Pascall and Sung 2007: 4), and 'the family's key role in the provision of welfare'. As the contributors to this collection argue, this has resulted in housing conditions for women continuing to largely depend upon men and marriage. Recent democratisation in Taiwan, and a prominent women's movement has done little to improve the housing opportunities of women given the emphasis on 'the neo-liberal principle that the market is the best supplier of social services and housing' (Bih and Chen, Chapter 9, this volume). In China, recent fundamental social, economic and housing reforms has seen the right to rent public housing transformed into the right to own private housing. However, women's housing opportunities are now mediated by class differentiation, marriage customs and patrilocal residence, insecurity and inequality, creating an increasingly problematic and polarised housing environment for women.

Women, representing half the world's population, continue to undertake most caring work in societies across the globe. Markets have come to dominate housing provision, and through the lens of the market … 'unpaid work – including the care which all humans need – is labelled burdensome because it costs women time or states money' (Smith 2005: 4). With reference to British housing there have been attempts to 'inject a dose of care-fullness' into the social sector', in terms of enhancing security of tenure, and improving quality and accessibility of homes. However, Smith argues that this has served only to reinforce 'an ethical and problematic divide between social renting and owner occupation' (Smith 2005: 4). In spite of the 'care-fullness' incorporated into the social rented sector in British housing the reality for many women in this tenure is of an increasingly residual and stigmatised tenure, combined with an increasingly coercive state promoting labour market inclusion and marginalising care responsibilities.

As the chapters in this collection highlight, the range of affordable housing options is diminishing in the context of the privatisation and individualisation of housing provision. As Tually points out in Chapter 3, there is clearly a need for more affordable housing options across tenures. This needs to be accompanied by the recognition of the value of caring and household activities and an approach that incorporates the values, contribution and constraints on women, and an understanding of how these contributions and constraints evolve throughout the lifecourse of many women as they negotiate their different spheres of activity. This would go some way to enabling women to make real choices in relation to housing and labour market paths, rather than to be required to fit into a housing and labour market construct that is inherently male. The societies covered in this collection face many common challenges which have serious implications for women in the housing arena, such as an aging population (the majority of whom are women), the changing nature of households, rising divorce rates and separation, increasing income inequality, and continuing gender inequality (in spite of regulatory measures to eliminate gender discrimination). The recognition of the increasing diversity of households types, the enhanced value and quantification of the value of unpaid care work, raising the quality and diminishing discrimination in the labour market, particularly in part-time work would rebalance the relationship between the economic resource position of women in the sphere of production, her responsibilities in the sphere of production and the conventions and sanctions that structure women's housing choices.

Notes

2 Women's housing rights

1 The Habitat I conference resulted in The Vancouver Declaration on Human Settlements, UN doc. A/CONF.70/15, June 1976, and Habitat II produced The Istanbul Declaration on Human Settlements, A/CONF.165/14, June 1996.

2 By Resolution 1991/26 the Sub-Commission, at the time still called the Sub-Commission on Prevention of Discrimination and Protection of Minorities, appointed one of its members, Justice Rajindar Sachar as the Special Rapporteur on the right to adequate housing. He subsequently produced four reports between 1992 and 1995.

3 The first Special Rapporteur, Miloon Kothari was appointed in 2000 by the then UN Commission on Human Rights. The mandate was continued under the newly created UN Human Rights Council. Kothari was succeeded by Raquel Rolnik in 2008

4 UN Habitat, the special UN agency for human settlements is mandated by the UN General Assembly to promote socially and environmentally sustainable towns and cities with the goal of providing adequate housing for all. The organization runs various housing programmes and is on the verge of launching a worldwide campaign with respect to the manifold problems of urbanization.

5 UN doc. A/res/55/2, 18-09-2000, para. 19.

6 Article 25(1) of the UDHR reads in part: 'Everyone has the right to a standard of living adequate for the health and well-being of himself and of his family, including … housing …. While the UDHR is not a legally binding treaty, it is regarded as reflecting international customary law.

7 Among other instruments, the right to housing is contained in art. 5 of the Convention on the Elimination of All Forms of Racial Discrimination; art. 27 of the Convention on the Rights of the Child; and art. 43 of the Convention on the Protection of the Rights of All Migrant Workers and Members of Their Families.

8 The most important CSOs that influenced the development of the right to housing are the Habitat International Coalition (HIC), a coalition of more than 400 housing NGOs, and the Centre On Housing Rights and Evictions (COHRE).

9 The CESCR is a body existing of 18 independent experts that monitors compliance with the ICESCR.

10 According to art. 21 of the ICESCR, the Committee is permitted to adopt General Recommendations as authoritative interpretations of (parts of) the Covenant. There General Recommendations or Comments are sent to all states parties and have to be taken into account when the states report to the Committee in accordance with art. 16.

11 The conditions mentioned are enumerated in para. 8 of CESCR General Comment 4, The right to adequate housing (Art. 11(1) of the Covenant), 13 December 1991.

12 This becomes, for instance, clear from art. 6 of General Comment 4 and art. 11 of General Comment 7.

13 According to feminist scholars like Catherine MacKinnon and Sandra Fredman there is no such thing as gender neutrality. If men and women are treated the same, this means that women are treated according to the male standard, since 'man has become the measure of all things'. Fredman, S., Discrimination Law, Clarendon Law Series, Oxford: Oxford University Press, 2002, p. 9.

14 Undoubtedly the fact that at the time when the CESCR adopted the two General Comments only one of the 18 Committee members was female has played a role. Since January 1997 the Committee has had four female members at the maximum. In June 2009 there are three female members.

15 I will come back to *de jure* and *de facto* equality and the importance of article 5 Women's Convention in section 3. Due to space constraints it is impossible to go into CEDAW's possibilities in detail here. For further reading see my doctoral thesis, Women and Housing: Gender Makes a Difference, Antwerpen, Oxford: Intersentia, 2007.

16 CESCR General Comment 3, The nature of states parties obligations (Art. 2, para. 1 of the Covenant), 14 December 1990.

17 In 1990 the CESCR organized a day of general discussion which was attended by experts from CSOs, UN Habitat and the ILO. As core elements of the right to housing were mentioned: security of tenure, affordability, accessibility, habitability, popular participation in decision-making, choice, equality of access and non-discrimination and availability of legal remedies. UN doc. E/C.12/1990/3, CESCR, Report on the 4th session, paras 281-285.

18 CESCR General Comment 3, para. 5.

19 This so-called typology of obligations was originally thought up by Henry Shue. See his book Basic Rights, Subsistence, Affluence and US Foreign Policy, Princeton, NJ, 1980.

20 Article 3 reads: 'The States Parties to the present Covenant undertake to ensure the equal right of men and women to the enjoyment of all civil and political [economic, social and cultural] rights set forth in the present Covenant. In June 2009, 164 states were party to the ICCPR and 160 to the ICESCR.

21 In June 2009, 186 states are party to the Women's Convention.

22 See CCPR General Comment 28, Equality of rights between men and women (article 3), 29 March 2000, especially para. 5 and CESCR General Comment 16, Article 3: the equal right of men and women to the enjoyment of all economic, social and cultural rights, 13-05-2005, paras 6-8. Para 2(f) of the Women's Convention reads: States Parties condemn discrimination against women in all its forms, agree to pursue by all appropriate means and without delay a policy of eliminating discrimination against women and, to this end, undertake: (f) To take all appropriate measures, including legislation, to modify or abolish existing laws, regulations, customs and practices which constitute discrimination against women.

23 Article 5(a) Women's Convention reads: States parties shall take all appropriate measures: (a) To modify the social and cultural patterns of conduct of men and women, with a view to achieving the elimination of prejudices and customary and all other practices which are based on the idea of the inferiority or the superiority of either of the sexes or on stereotyped roles for men and women.

24 Charlesworth and Chinkin describe gender as: '… the excess cultural baggage associated with biological sex. "Gender" draws attention to aspects of social relations that are culturally contingent and without foundation in biological necessity.' Charlesworth, H., and Chinkin, C., The Boundaries of International law; A Feminist Analysis, Manchester: Manchester University Press, 2000, p. 3

25 Beijing Platform for Action, UN doc. A/CONF.177/20, Annex II (17 October 1995). In paras 31, 47, 58(m) specific difficulties with regard to the right to housing are discussed. Also see Centre on Housing Rights and Evictions (COHRE), Women and Housing Rights, September 2000.

26 Special Rapporteur Sachar maintains that a large part of women is de jure homeless since: 'It is clear that in most countries of the world women have neither a right to the home in which they were born nor to the home they live in after marriage.' UN doc. E/CN.4/Sub.2/1995/12 (12 July 1995), paras 45–49.

27 For instance, Sub-commission resolution 1998/15 (21 August 1998), Women and the right to land, property and adequate housing and Commission on Human Rights resolution 2005/25 (15 April 2005), Women's equal ownership of, access to and control over land and the equal rights to own property and to adequate housing.

28 Commission on Human Rights resolution 2002/49 (23 April 2002), para. 13.

29 Abdullahi Ahmed An'Naim suggests internal discourse and cross-cultural dialogue as a method to achieve progress in cases where cultural habits clash with universal norms like non-discrimination and equality for women. See his chapter 'State Responsibility Under International Human Rights Law to Change Religious and Customary Laws', in: Cook, R. (ed.), Human Rights of Women, National and International Perspectives, Philadelphia, PA: University of Pennsylvania Press, 1994, pp. 167–88

30 According to figures published by the World Bank in 2008 1.4 billion people earn less than US$ 1.25 a day.

31 Division for the Advancement of Women, The Feminization of Poverty, Women 2000, Gender Equality, Development and Peace for the Twenty-first Century, New York, 5-9 June 2000. Also COHRE, 2003-2005 Activity Report, pp. 12–13.

32 This is for instance the case in Islamic countries that rely on the religious laws expressed in Chapter 4 of the Qur'an, that determine that a son gets twice the share of a daughter, a brother double the share of a sister, and a husband half of his wife's inheritance, while a wife is only entitled to a quarter of her late husband's estate.

33 This may for instance happen to Hindu women in India. Desai, S., 'Engendering Population Policy', in: Krishnaraj, M., Sudarshan, R., Shariff, A. (eds.), Gender Population and Development, Delhi: Oxford University Press, 1998, p. 53.

34 COHRE estimates that between 2003 and 2006 over 2 million people in Africa were evicted and almost 3.5 million people in Asia and the Pacific. In the same period nearly 175,000 people in the Americas and over 16,000 people in Europe were forcefully removed from their homes. COHRE, Global Survey on Forced Evictions; Violations of Human Rights 2003-2006, number 10, December 2006.

35 CESCR General Comment No. 7, para. 4.

36 Female exogamy entails that a woman marries outside her own community and leaves for the community of her husband.

37 E. Enarson, 'Gender issues in natural disasters: talking points on research needs', in: ILO Working Paper 7, Crises, Women and other Gender Concerns, Geneva: Recovery and Reconstruction Department 2002, p. 8.

38 An example is the North Indian temple city of Vrindavan where about 50,000 widows and children live supporting themselves by begging from tourists or by getting paid to pray for others during ceremonies.

39 This habit is still prevalent in Central Asia and Central and Southern Africa.

40 UN doc. E/CN.4/1995/42, Preliminary report by Radhika Coomaraswamy, Special Rapporteur on Violence Against women, para. 118.

41 International Helsinki Federation for Human Rights (IHF), Women 2000, An Investigation into the Status of Women's Rights in Central and South-Eastern Europe and the Newly Independent States, Vienna: Agens-Werk, 2000, particularly pp. 45, 96, 148, 206 and 334–335.

42 Economic dependence is often mentioned as the reason why women stay in spite of domestic violence. See e.g. the investigation conducted in Croatia, Lithuania and Turkmenistan, IHF, Women 2000, pp. 23, 130, 288 and 469.

43 For examples, see UN doc. E/CN.4/1998/54, report by the Special Rapporteur on Violence against women Ms Radhika Coomaraswamy, paras. 208-211 and UN doc. E/CN.4/1999/79/Add.2, Report of the Representative of the Secretary General on Internally Displaced Persons, Mr Francis Deng, para. 50.

44 UN doc. E/CN.4/1996/52, Report of the Representative of the Secretary General, Francis Deng, para. 47.

45 World Health Organization (WHO), Anthology on Women, Health and Environment, 1994, in particular pp. 92–105.

46 World Health Organization, Environmental Health Newsletter, December 1995 (No. 25), Chapter 'Water, sanitation and women's health', and Dankelman, I., Gender and Environment: Lessons to Learn, UN doc. EGM/NATDIS/2001/OP.2, para. 2.2.

47   General Comment 4 para. 8 (a), further clarified in CESCR General Comment 7, especially para. 8.

48   Zenabaworke, T., 'Women and Land Rights in the Third World: The Case of Ethiopia', in: Muthoni Wanyeki, L. (ed.), Women and Land in Africa; Culture Religion and Realizing Women's Rights, New York: Zed Books 2003, pp. 67–68. Also Agarwal, B., A Field of One's Own; Gender and Land Rights in South Asia, Cambridge: Cambridge University Press 1994, p. 3.

49   In China, where female exogamy and the severance of ties with the community after a woman's marriage is also a known practice, the authorities have developed legislation that guarantees women the right to return to their original community. A woman's right to access to land and housing is reserved for her in case anything goes wrong in her relationship with her husband or she is widowed. UN doc. CEDAW/C/CHN/5-6, Combined fifth and sixth report of China (10 June 2004), p. 53 (English version).

50   In certain states like Yemen, Bangladesh, Jordan and Cameroon, it has been laid down in the law that a married woman has to reside where her husband decides to settle down. In other states, where such legislation is lacking, women may *de facto* be unable to use their right to freedom of residence because of societal habits.

51   UNDP, Human Development Report 1995. Gender and human development. United Nations, New York, 1995, pp. 74–78.

52   The UNDP figures that worldwide about 30 per cent of all families is headed by women.

53   Numerous examples may be found in International Helsinki Federation for Human Rights , Women 2000, An Investigation into the Status of Women's Rights in Central and South-Eastern Europe and the Newly Independent States, Vienna: Agens-Werk, 2000.

54   The idea that because of the principle of due diligence a state can be held responsible for acts of private persons was decided for the first time by the Inter-American Court in the Velásquez-Rodriguez case. Since then several human rights bodies and organs have followed suit. Due diligence entails that in cases of grave and structural human rights violations by private parties, a state should do everything in its power to prevent these violations and if notwithstanding preventive measures a violation does take place, the case must be thoroughly investigated and the perpetrator(s) must be prosecuted and punished. Furthermore, the victim should receive a form of reparation. See e.g. CEDAW General Recommendation No. 19 Violence Against Women, UN doc. A/47/38/1992, para. 9 and Maastricht Guidelines, article 18: Acts by non-state entities.

55   The UNHCR has developed guidelines for refugee camps. See UN doc. EC/SCP/67, Guidelines on the Protection of Refugee Women, 1991.

3 Women and housing

1   It is also important to note here that Australian university students have had to contribute towards the cost of their education since 1989 under the Higher Education Contribution Scheme (HECS – now known as the Higher Education Loan Programme), with people earning over a certain income threshold paying a percentage of their weekly income towards their HECS debt. This cost has placed an impost on many women in particular, especially since 1996 when the then federal government increased the amount of HECS charged on all courses and differentiated rates depending on the course studied. It has also been noted as a factor in the financial pressures on some people when entering the housing market.

2   Australia's total fertility rate declined significantly during the period in discussion. That is, declining significantly from a peak of 3.55 babies per woman in 1961 to 2.9 babies per women in 1966 (post the introduction of the contraceptive pill and associated freedom in lifestyle choices for men and women), and again declining significantly in 1976 to 2.1 (below replacement level fertility) and then to 1.94 in 1981 to a low of 1.73 in 2001 (ABS 2008a; 2008b; 2008d). Fertility rates have remained relatively stable since 2001, with the recent small baby boom increasing the current rate to a 25 year high of 1.93 in 2007 (ABS 2008d).

3 Full-time adult ordinary time earnings at November 2008 were A$1,243.00 for males and A$1,032.20 for females (ABS 2009a: 4). The gender-based income disparity is even more pronounced when all employees total earnings for males and females are considered – here the gender pay gap is 35 percent (A$1,101.70 versus A$720.10).

4 Research by Clare (2001) further contextualises the difference in workforce participation rates between the genders, pointing out that in 2000 men averaged around 38 years of full-time equivalent labour force participation, while women averaged 18 years.

5 This group also includes a small proportion of middle-aged women caught in the 'caring sandwich'; simultaneously caring for their children and ageing parents (see Australian Women's Coalition 2005; HREOC 2007: 93–94). Given increasing longevity and the increasing age of mothers generally, more middle-aged women will likely find themselves in this position, or, caring simultaneously for their elderly parents and their grandchildren (ABS 2005a; 2005b).

6 The figures presented in Tables 3.4, 3.5 and 3.6 are not directly comparable. This is because the ABS data on the wealth of Australians in 2006 and of baby boomers in 2004 uses a different definition of net worth, i.e. extended to include other assets held by individuals/households such as the value of cars, home contents and collectibles (AMP.NATSEM 2007: 17).

7 Defined by NATSEM as people aged 45–64 in 2004 (i.e. born between approximately 1940 and 1960).

8 Generation Xers are defined in the report as people born between 1961 and 1976 (AMP.NATSEM 2003).

9 The Age Pension is the Australian Government's income support payment for people aged over 65 (women previously qualified for the pension at 60, but recent changes in eligibility criteria are progressively raising the age of qualification for women to 65 by 2014). It is designed to ensure all Australians have an adequate source of income in retirement; with the amount of support received by eligible people varying depending on their personal circumstances, assets and other income (Centrelink c2007).

10 Statistics on the prevalence of violence suggest that around one in six adult women (16.8 per cent) have experienced partner violence since the age of 15 (ABS 2007f). However, it is widely accepted that most incidences of such violence are not reported to authorities, and especially among certain groups of women (See Tually et al. 2008). Statistics on the extent of domestic violence then are likely to be underestimates.

11 With the level of unmet need for women presenting to domestic violence support and accommodation services now at 50 per cent (AIHW 2005).

12 Of course it should also be noted here that 2009 data indicates Australians lost an average of around A$24,000 in wealth since the start of the global financial crisis and since wealth peaked in early 2008 (Commonwealth Securities calculations from Federal Treasury data quoted in Brinsden 2009).

13 Australia's Indigenous population is much younger than the non-Indigenous population (21 years versus 37 years in 2006) (ABS & AIHW 2008:1–4), and has a much higher fertility rate: 2.4 babies per woman for Indigenous women in 2007 compared with 1.93 babies per women for all Australian women (ABS 2008a: 6–7).

14 In 2010 this payment was A$5,000, paid in 13 fortnightly instalments with eligibility dependent on an income means test (Family Assistance Office 2009: 5).

15 Statistics on household size (in private occupied dwellings) show a decline from 3.5 persons in 1966 (ABS data quoted in Hugo 1986) to 2.6 persons in 2001 and projected to fall to between 2.2 and 2.3 persons in 2026 (ABS 2004c: 21).

16 See the suite of publications at http://www.ahuri.edu.au/nrv/nrv3/nrv3_assoc_docs.html

17 Established by the federal government in May 2008 as an independent group operating at arms length from government and reporting annually to the Minister for Housing, and whose terms of reference include 'producing an annual State of Supply Report that assesses information on land supply and demand for housing from all levels of government and the private sector' (Commonwealth of Australia 2009b).

18 Households are considered in housing stress if they are in the lowest two income quintiles (the poorest 40 per cent of households) and paying more than 30 per cent of income in housing costs (see Yates and Gabriel (2006)).

19 Research released by AMP.NATSEM on the issue of housing affordability and housing stress in the decade to 2005–2006 points to the difficulty lower income renters are increasingly having entering home ownership (AMP.NATSEM 2008: 19–22). Their analysis shows that the poorest renters (those on less than half median income for renters) needed a staggering 27 times their income to purchase a median price house in Australia (A$350,000) in 2005–2006, compared with 16 times their income a decade earlier. Single-parent renters and lone-person renters were among those facing the worst affordability problems in terms of access to home ownership, with (median) house price to income ratios of 11.6 and 15.5 respectively, compared with a national average for renters of 9.0 and much worse affordability problems than a decade early (7.6, 11.0 and 5.9).

20 Data presented on the decline of the social housing sector in Australia to 2008 shows a decrease in properties from around 400,000 in 1996 to 390,000 in 2008, and that had the share of the housing stock in 1996 continued over the last decade this sector would now comprise some 480,000 dwellings (National Housing Supply Council 2009: 82).

21 This plan is a response to the global financial crisis, aimed at stimulating the construction industry, and increasing affordable housing options for Australians, especially the homeless.

22 For details of funding and programs to address homelessness see http://www.fahcsia.gov.au/sa/ housing/progserv/homelessness/Pages/place_to_call_home.aspx and the housing components of the Nation Building Economic Stimulus plan announced by the Federal Government in February 2009 – http://www.economicstimulusplan.gov.au/housing/pages/default.aspx.

23 In a shared equity arrangement 'a homebuyer applies for a loan to purchase a share in their home, entering into an arrangement with another party [i.e. a financial institution …] which owns the remaining share. Shared equity loans are designed to assist people who are unable to afford the repayments on a mortgage loan for the full purchase price of a property, but whose incomes do allow them to repay a smaller loan' (Qld DoH 2008).

24 Such as offered by the South Australian government's home lending agency HomeStart Finance.

5 Social change and housing systems

1 http://www.migualdad.es/ss/Satellite?pagename=MinisterioIgualdad/Page/MIGU_home&language=en_GB

2 Until very recently, companies and public bodies were not concerned with work–life balance.

3 Between 1991 and 2004, the number of separations increased by 107 per cent, while divorces went up by 93 per cent, according to Reports by the Consejo General del Poder Judicial.

4 In 2006, widows received an average of €483 per month.

5 Risk of poverty is defined as having an equivalised disposable income below 60% of the national median.

6 Using the information on the financial and housing markets in European countries during the 1990s, Maclennan et al. (1998) found that the yearly inter-regional mobility rates as a percentage of population were: 1.23 per cent and 1.07 per cent in Germany and France, 0.5 per cent and 0.56 per cent in Italy and Spain (1993 data). Thus, it seems that in the aggregate data, there is a negative relationship between ownership and inter-regional mobility rates in these countries.

7 The current pension system does not provide adequate solutions.

8 Ley Orgánica 1/28 December 2004 (BOE, 29), Medidas de Protección Integral contra la Violencia de Género.

9 Social housing or Vivienda de Protección Oficial (VPO) is divided into four types: the special system, the general system, regulated price and the special system for rent, with a limitation on the maximum size, public financing and limited selling prices. The renovation of houses is also eligible for public aid. Dwellings stand as VPO for a minimum period of 30 years.

10 Given the huge amount of supply that is unsold, which is estimated at around 1 million, some ACs are promoting a change in qualification from free dwellings, which are usually for sale, to regulated or protected dwellings, which are usually for rent.

6 Women's housing in Sweden

1 Artisans, masters and farmers were obliged to provide lodging or housing for their apprentices, servants and agricultural labour force from the sevententh and still in the nineteenth century and in some cases up to the mid-twentieth century. For patrons, as well as rural manufacturers and industrialists it was deemed a moral duty, as well as rational, to rent out dwellings to their employees, who lost their housing when they were dismissed from their jobs. This system was gradually abolished during the twentieth century.

2 These very influential researchers and politicians may be more known to an international audience through Gunnar Myrdal's book *An American Dilemma: The Negro Problem and Modern Democracy* (1944), and Alva Myrdal's work for UNESCO and later for nuclear weapon disarmament. They were both dedicated Social Democrats all their lives.

3 Other suggestions of theirs regarding architecture and collective households were also tried out but later partly or wholly abolished.

4 According to the brokers' statistics for 2009, the price per square metre was on average 18,717 SEK in the country, which means 1.12 million SEK for a two-room flat of 60 m^2. In Stockholm city, the corresponding prices were 54,175 SEK per m^2 and 3.25 million SEK for a two-room flat. Single-family houses, which are usually twice as large, were sold at an average price of 1.93 million SEK; in Stockholm 3.7 million SEK (www.maklarstatistik.se/aktuellt/pm-2010-01-14. aspx). (100 SEK≈9.76€ or 13.54 USD).

5 Ironically, this conviction has made the current Swedish housing policy the target of EU's attention in relation to the Service Directive which claims that state support to MHCs will distort the competition on the housing market to the disadvantage of private landlords, unless the MHCs take a special responsibility for vulnerable groups, that is, qualify as social housing (EU Commission 2005).

6 The number of flats with five rooms or more was reduced by 2,544 to 33,303 or 7 per cent 2003–2008 (Statistics Sweden's databases).

7 Women, housing and citizenship in Great Britain

1 Since devolution in 1999 Scotland has been able to establish its own parliament and to pass primary legislation. The National Assembly of Wales is a devolved administration which had, until 2007, only secondary legislative powers. Since 2007 the Welsh Assembly has been able to make its own laws on those devolved areas in which they have been given Legislative Competence Orders. Primary legislation passed in Westminster applies to Wales. Housing policy in Wales has followed a fairly similar pattern to England. Where appropriate and where data are available differences in polices and housing developments will be identified. The chapter draws on data from a range of surveys and sources, some of which cover England, or Scotland, or England and Wales, and others Scotland, England and Wales.

2 Unmarried, cohabiting couples are increasingly entering into formal joint property ownership arrangements (see Izuhara and Kennett 2003) since they do not enjoy the same legal rights and entitlements as married couples in areas such as property and inheritance rights, access to a partner's pension, and tax breaks. If an unmarried partner dies, their pension is not automatically transferable to the remaining cohabitee, nor is ownership of their home. The 'common-law marriage' does not exist in modern law, and women have no automatic call on their partner's property or estate.

10 A gender study of housing rights of women in urban China

1 Universal Declaration of Human Rights Article 25 states: 'Everyone has the right to a standard of living adequate for the health and well-being of himself and of his family, including food, clothing, housing and medical care and necessary social services…'. The International Covenant on Civil and Political Rights Article 1 also states: 'All peoples may, for their own ends, freely dispose of their natural wealth and resources … In no case may a people be deprived of its own means of subsistence.' The International Covenant on Economic, Social and Cultural Rights Article 11 states: 'The States Parties to the present Covenant recognize the right of everyone to an adequate standard of living for himself and his family, including adequate food, clothing and housing, and to the continuous improvement of living conditions. The States Parties will take appropriate steps to ensure the realization of this right…'

2 On 28 December 2007, the News Office of the Ministry of Housing and Urban–Rural Development published the following information: current total investment in housing in cities and towns all over the country has reached RMB67 billion yuan which is over RMB40 billion yuan more than the last five-year period. The average total size of housing units built each year is 60 billion square metres. Built-up area per head in cities and towns has increased from 22.8 square metres at the end of 2002 to about 28 square metres in the end of 2007. By the end of 2006, ownership of private housing in cities and towns reached 83 per cent. It is a breakthrough in the building of a housing security system. In 2007, RMB 770 billion yuan had been invested in the building of cheap rental housing, far exceeding the accumulated total of all the previous years. The living conditions of an accumulated total of 681 thousand low-income households improved as a result. The Economically Affordable Housing system has been improved gradually and normalized. The Housing Accumulated Fund system has helped the working class to resolve their housing problems. By the end of October, 2007, over 110 million working persons were contributing to the Housing Accumulated Fund, and a total of RMB1.54 trillion yuan was gathered. The fund has helped to improve the housing condition of over 4.2 million workers and provided over RMB1 trillion yuan as capital for the building of cheap rental housing. See 'National Work Meeting on Construction Held in the Capital: A Call for the Thorough Implementation of the Scientific Outlook of Development; Foster Urban-Rural Construction for a Sound and Fast Development' (in Chinese) This report was challenged and criticized by some web users: see: http://finance. people.com.cn/GB/8215/47801/59168/6858581.html. According to Chen Jie of the School of Management, Fudan University:

> The rate of home ownership usually means the percentage of residents living in housing units that they own in comparison with the percentage of residents living in rented housing units. To the knowledge of this writer who has been undertaking research in this field, there has not been any official and authoritative statistics on home-ownership rate in cities and towns that is based on the above definition. What we have is only data announced by the Ministry of Housing and Urban-Rural Development on private ownership of housing units … The so-called private home ownership means only that a property is owned privately and not publicly. The term 'private home ownership' is used vis-a-vis 'public ownership'. It does not mean that the housing units are occupied by the owners.
>
> Chen (2006)

3 In general, employers do not like to employ divorced women to work as domestic workers thinking that the latter may pose a threat to the stability of their marriage, especially if the age of a domestic worker is close to their own age. This is why most domestic workers do not talk about their divorces. Some keep it a secret even in the union.

4 http://news.hsw.cn/gb/news/2005-03/23/content_1732159.htm

5 Quotation taken from homework of single-parent groups in project files.

6 White Paper on Domestic Service Sector in China (in Chinese), China Employment Training Technical Instruction Center, Department of Training and Employment, Ministry of Labour and Social Security; Study on Legal Questions of Domestic Service Sector in China (in Chinese), The Center for Women's Law & Legal Services, Beijing University, http://www.womenwatch-china. org.

7 A local popular saying. Hun means "muddling along", bei means "against the tide", that is, not to be able to live like the others.

8 'Housing price to income ratio' is the ratio of the price paid by an average family for a housing unit to the total annual income of the family in a given place or city. The ratio is used to examine the ability of residents of a place to purchase a housing unit. This concept is much disputed in China and there has not been a consensus on how to calculate it. It has been calculated that the housing price to income ratio in the city of Beijing is as high as 27:1. That means a couple, even if they do not eat or drink, will need 27 years to buy a home. In international standard, it is considered fair for the housing price to income ratio to remain between 3–6:1. However in Beijing, even when the cost of mortgage is discounted, the ratio is as high as 17:1 which far exceeds the international standard. See: http://www.cssa-gre.org.uk/article/2009/0822/article_18130.html.

11 Women and housing inequalities in Hong Kong

1 Exchange rate in early 2010, roughly US$1=HK$7.8, £1=HK$12.

References

1 Introduction

Balchin, P. and Rhoden, M. (2002) *Housing Policy: An Introduction*, 4th edition, London and New York: Routledge.

Brion, M. and Tinker, A. (1980) *Women in Housing*, London: Housing Centre Trust.

Carter, J. (1998) 'Postmodernity and Welfare: When Worlds Collide', *Social Policy and Administration*, 32(2): 101–15.

Chan, K. W. (forthcoming), 'Women and Housing Organizations', in S. Smith, (ed.) *International Encyclopedia of Housing and Home*, London: Elsevier.

Chan, K. W. (1997) *Social Construction of Gender Inequality in the Housing System: Housing Experience of Women in Hong Kong*, Aldershot: Ashgate.

Chan, K. W. and Chan, Fung Yi (2003) 'Inclusion or exclusion? Housing battered Women in Hong Kong', *Critical Social Policy*, 23(4): 526–46.

Clapham, D. and Smith, S. J. (1990) 'Housing Policy and "Special Needs"', *Policy and Politics*, 18(3):193–205.

Coleman, A. (1990) *Utopia on Trial*, revised edition, London: Hilary Shipman.

Coleman, C. (2000) 'Women, Transport and Cities: an Overview and an Agenda for Research', in J. Drake, S. Ledwith, and R. Woods (eds) *Women and the City: Visibility and Voice in Urban Space*, Basingstoke and New York: Palgrave.

Dale, J. and Foster, P. (1986) *Feminists and State Welfare*, London: Routledge and Kegan Paul.

Darke, J.; Ledwith, S. and Woods, R. (eds) (2000) *Women and the City: Visibility and Voice in Urban Space*, Basingstoke and New York: Palgrave.

Davidoff, L. (2003) 'Gender and the "Great Divide": Public and Private in British Gender History', *Journal of Women's History*, 15(1): 11–27.

Davidoff, L.; L'Esperance, J. and Newby, H. (1976),'Landscape with Figures: Home and Community in English Society', in J. Mitchell and A. Oakley, (eds), *The Right and Wrong of Women*, London: Penguin.

Davis, C. (2001) 'Gender and Housing', in M. Harrison with C. Davis (eds), *Housing, Social Policy and Difference: Diability, Ethnicity, Gender and Housing*, Bristol: Polity Press.

Delphy, C. and Leonard, D. (1992) *Familiar Exploitation: A New Analysis of Marriage in Contemporary Western Societies*, Cambridge, MA: Polity Press.

Dewan, R. (1999) 'Gender Implications of the "New" Economic Policy: A Conceptual Overview', *Women's Studies International Forum* 22(4): 425–29.

References

Fairstein, S. S. and Servon, L. J. (eds) (2005) *Gender and Planning: A Reader*, New Brunswick, NJ and London: Rutgers University Press.

Ferguson, I. and Johnstone, C. (2001) 'Postmodernism and Social Welfare: A Critique', in M. Lavalette and A. Pratt (eds) *Social Policy: A Conceptual and Theoretical Introduction*, 2nd edition, London, Thousand Oaks, CA and New Delhi: Sage Publications.

Fincher, R. (2007) 'Space, Gender and Institutions in Processes Creating Difference', *Gender, Place and Culture*, 14(1): 5–27.

Fitzpatrick, T. (1996) 'Postmodernism, Welfare and Radical Politics', *Journal of Social Policy*, 25(3): 303–20.

Foucault, M. (1980) *Power/Knowledge: Selected Interviews and Other Writings 1972–1977*, translated and edited by C. Gordon, London: Harvester Press.

Gibson-Graham, J. K. (1996) *The End of Capitalism (As We Knew It): A Feminist Critique of Political Economy*, Malden, MA and Oxford: Blackwell.

Gibson-Graham, J. K. (2003) 'Feminising the Economy: Metaphors, Strategies, Politics', *Gender, Place and Culture*, 10(2): 145–57.

Gilroy, R. and Woods, R. (eds) (1994) *Housing Women*, London and New York: Routledge.

Hallett, C. (ed.) (1996) *Women and Social Policy: An Introduction*, London and New York: Harvester Wheatsheaf.

Harrison, M. (2001*) Housing, Social Policy and Difference: Disability, Ethnicity, Gender and Housing*, Bristol: Policy Press.

Harvey, D. (2000) *Spaces of Hope*, Berkeley, CA: University of California Press.

Hayden, D. (1980) 'What Would a NonSexist City be Like? Speculations on Housing, Urban Design, and Human Work', *Signs*, 5(3) supplement: S170S187.

Hayden, D. (2002) *Redesigning the American Dream: Gender, Housing, and Family Life*, revised and expanded edition, New York and London: W.W. Norton & Company.

Land, H. (1980) 'The Family Wage' *Feminist Review*, 6, pp. 55–77.

Lefebvre, H. (1991) *The Production of Space*, translated by Donald Nicholson-Smith, Malden, MA and Oxford: Blackwell Publishing.

Lewis, J. (ed.) (1983) *Women's Welfare, Women's Right*, London: Croom Helm.

Marcuse, P. (1989) The pitfalls of specialism: special groups and the general problem of housing, in S. Rosenberry and C. Hartman (ed.) *Housing issues of the 90s*, New York: Praeger.

Massey, D. (1994) *Space, Place and Gender*, Cambridge: Polity Press.

Matrix (1984), *Making Space: Women and the Man Made Environment*, London: Pluto Press Ltd.

McDowell, L. (1999) *Gender, Identity and Place: Understanding Feminist Geographies*, Cambridge: Polity Press.

McNay, L. (1992), *Foucault and Feminism*, London: Polity.

McNay, L. (2004) 'Agency and Experience: Gender as a Lived Relation', in Lisas Adkins and Beverley Skeggs (eds) *Feminism after Bourdieu*, Oxford: Blackwell Publishing.

Morris, J. and Winn, M. (1990) 'Housing and Gender Division', in *Housing and Social Inequality*, London: Hilary Shipman.

Pascall, G. (1997) *Social Policy: A New Feminist Analysis*, London: Routledge.

Pickup, L. (1988) 'Hard to Get Around: A Study of Women's Travel Mobility', in J. Little, L. Peake and P. Richardson, (eds) *Women in Cities: Gender and the Urban Environment*, London: Macmillan Education.

Pugh, C. (1997) 'The Household, Household Economics and Housing', *Housing Studies*, 12(3): 383–92.

Silbaugh, K. B. (2007) 'Women's Place: Urban Planning, Housing Design, and Work-Family Balance', *Fordham Law Review*, 76(3): 1797–852.

Smart, B. (1985) *Michael Foucault*, London: Routledge.

Smith, S. J. (1990) 'Income, Housing Wealth and Gender Inequality', *Urban Studies*, 27(1): 67–88.

Smith, S. J. (2005) 'Housing, Gender and Social Policy', in P. Somerville and N. Sprigings (eds) *Housing and Social Policy: Contemporary Themes and Critical Perspectives*, London: Routledge.

Taylor-Gooby, P. (1994) 'Postmodernism and Social Policy: A Great Leap Backward?' *Journal of Social Policy*, 23(3): 385–404.

Ungerson, C. and Kember, M. (eds) (1997) *Women and Social Policy: A Reader*, Basingstoke: Macmillan.

Watson, S. (1986a) 'Women and Housing or Feminist Housing Analysis?', *Housing Studies*, 1 (Jan.): 110.

Watson, S. (1986b) 'Housing and the Family: The Marginalization of Non-Family Households in Britain', *International Journal of Urban and Regional Research*, 10(1): 828.

Watson, S. (1988) *Accommodating Inequality: Gender and Housing*, Sydney: Allen and Unwin.

Watson, S. (1991) 'The Restructuring of Work and Home: Production Aand Reproduction Relations', in J. Allen and C. Hamnett (eds) *Housing and Labour Markets*, London: Unwin Hyman.

Watson, S. (1999a) 'City A/genders', in Sophie Watson and Lesley Doyal (eds) *Engendering Social Policy*, Buckingham and Philadelphia, PA: Open University Press.

Watson, S. (1999b) 'A Home is Where Heart is: Engendering Notions of Homelessness' in P. Kennet and A. Marsh (eds) *Homelessness: Exploring the New Terrain*, Bristol: Policy Press.

Watson, S. and Austerberry, H. (1986) *Housing and Homelessness: A Feminist Perspective*, London: Routledge & Kegan Paul.

Weisman, L. K. (1992) *Discrimination by Design: A Feminist Critique of the Man-made Environment*, Urbana, IL and Chicago, IL: University of Illinois Press.

Wekerle, G. R. (2005) 'Gender Planning in Public Transit: Institutionalizing Feminist Policies, Changing Discourse, and Practices', in S. S. Fainstein and L. J. Servon (eds) *Gender and Planning: A Reader*, New Brunswick, NJ and London: Rutgers University Press.

Woods, R. (1996) 'Women and Housing', in Christine Hallett (ed.) *Women and Social Policy: An Introduction*, London and New York: Harvester Wheatsheaf.

3 Women and housing

ABS (2010) 'Apparent retention rates', in 'Education and Training' Chapter 10 in *Year Book Australia 2009–2010*, Cat. no. 1301.0, ABS, Canberra, pp. 386–387.

AIHW: Marcolin (2005) 'Female SAAP clients and children escaping domestic and family violence 2003-04', *AIHW Bulletin no. 30*, AIHW cat. No. AUS 64, AIHW, Canberra, September.

AMP.NATSEM (2003) *Generation Xcluded, Income and Wealth of Generation X*, AMP.NATSEM Income and Wealth Report Issue 6, November 2003.

AMP.NATSEM (2005) *Love Can Hurt, Divorce Will Cost – Financial Impact of Divorce in Australia*, AMP.NATSEM Income and Wealth Report Issue 10, April 2005.

AMP.NATSEM (2006) *Who Cares? The Cost of Caring in Australia 2002 to 2005*, AMP. NATSEM Income and Wealth Report, Issue 13, May 2006.

AMP.NATSEM (2007) *Baby Boomers – Doing it for Themselves*, AMP.NATSEM Income and Wealth Report, Issue 16, March 2007.

AMP.NATSEM (2008) *Wherever I Lay My Debt, That's My Home*, AMP.NATSEM Income and Wealth Report, Issue 19, March 2008.

AMP.NATSEM (2009) *She Works Hard for the Money, Australian Women and the Gender Divide*, AMP.NATSEM Income and Wealth Report, Issue 22, April 2009.

Austen, S. and Redmond, G. (2008) 'Women's incomes', in *Australian Social Trends 2008*, Cat. no. 4102.0, Australian Bureau of Statistics, Canberra, 153–57.

Australian Broadcasting Corporation (2008) 'Housing affordability "sinks to record low"', ABC News Stories, 28 May 2008. Online. Available HTTP: <http://www.abc.net.au/news/stories/2008/05/28/2268260.htm> (accessed 29 May 2008).

Australian Bureau of Statistics (1994) 'People with degrees', *Australian Social Trends 1994*, Cat. no. 4102.0, ABS, Canberra.

Australian Bureau of Statistics (2001) 'Education and Training' Chapter 10 in *Year Book Australia 2001*, Cat. no. 1301.0, ABS, Canberra, 403–28.

Australian Bureau of Statistics (2002) 'Trends in childlessness', *Australian Social Trends 2002*, Cat. no. 4102.0, ABS, Canberra, 37–40.

Australian Bureau of Statistics (2004a) *Disability, Ageing and Carers, Australia: Summary of Findings 2003*, Cat. no. 4430.0, ABS, Canberra.

Australian Bureau of Statistics (2004b) *Experimental Estimates and Projections, Aboriginal and Torres Strait Islander Australians*, Cat. no. 3238.0, ABS, Canberra.

Australian Bureau of Statistics (2004c) *Household and Family Projections Australia 2001 to 2026*, Cat. no. 3236.0, ABS, Canberra.

Australian Bureau of Statistics (2005a) 'Grandparents raising grandchildren', *Australian Social Trends 2005*, Cat. no. 4102.0, ABS, Canberra, 44–46.

Australian Bureau of Statistics (2005b) 'Informal child care provided by grandparents', *Australian Social Trends 2005*, Cat. no. 4102.0, ABS, Canberra, 47–51.

Australian Bureau of Statistics (2005c) 'Recent fertility trends', *Australian Social Trends 2005*, Cat. no. 4102.0, ABS, Canberra, 23–27.

Australian Bureau of Statistics (2006) 'Education and training', *Measures of Australia's Progress*, Cat. no. 1370.0, ABS, Canberra, 41–8.

Australian Bureau of Statistics (2007a) *2006 Census QuickStats: Australia*, ABS, Canberra.

Australian Bureau of Statistics (2007b) *Basic Community Profile, Australia*, 2006 Census community profile series (Table B22), Cat. no. 2100.0, ABS, Canberra.

Australian Bureau of Statistics (2007c) 'Family and community: national summary living arrangements', *Australian Social Trends 2007*, living arrangements statistics (no. 14), Cat. no. 4102.0, ABS, Canberra, 34–42.

Australian Bureau of Statistics (2007d) Labour force historical time series, Australia, 1966 to 1984 – participation rates by age and martial status, 1966 to 1977, Cat. no. 6204.0.55.001, ABS, Canberra.

Australian Bureau of Statistics (2007e) 'One parent families', *Australian Social Trends 2007*, Cat. no. 4102.0, ABS, Canberra, 48–53.

Australian Bureau of Statistics (2007f) 'Women's experiences of partner violence', *Australian Social Trends 2007*, Cat. no. 4102.0, ABS, Canberra, pp. 200–204.

Australian Bureau of Statistics and Australian Institute for Health and Welfare (2008) *The health and welfare of Australia's Aboriginal and Torres Strait Islander peoples 2008*, Cat. no. 4704.0, AIHW Cat. no. IHW 21, ABS and AIHW, Canberra.

Australian Bureau of Statistics (2008a) *Births, Australia, 2007*, Cat. no. 3301.0, ABS, Canberra.

Australian Bureau of Statistics (2008b) 'Births' in Chapter 7, Population, *Year Book Australia 2008*, Cat. no. 1301.0, ABS, Canberra, 179–218.

Australian Bureau of Statistics (2008c) 'Education and Training' Chapter 12 in *Year Book Australia 2001*, Cat. no. 1301.0, ABS, Canberra, 375–400.

Australian Bureau of Statistics (2008d) 'Recent increases in Australia's fertility', *Year Book Australia 2008*, Cat. no. 1301.0, ABS, Canberra, 202–5.

Australian Bureau of Statistics (2008e) 'Work: national summary', *Australian social trends 2008*, Cat. no. 4102.0, ABS, Canberra, pp. 112–114.

Australian Bureau of Statistics (2009a) *Average Weekly Earnings, Australia, November 2008*, Cat. no. 6302.0, ABS, Canberra.

Australian Bureau of Statistics (2009b) *Labour Force, Australia, Spreadsheets, Jan 2009*, [Table 03: Labour force status by Sex], Australia, Cat. no. 6202.0, ABS, Canberra.

Australian Housing and Urban Research Institute (2004) *Housing Futures in an Ageing Australia*, Research and policy bulletin, AHURI, Melbourne.

Australian Women's Coalition (2005) *The Caring Sandwich, Caring for the Young and Old – The Price Women Play*, AWC. Online. Available HTTP: <http://www.awcaus.org.au/sandwich/sandwich-project%20report.pdf> (accessed 23 June 2007).

Badcock, B. and Beer, A. (2000) *Home Truths, Property Ownership and Housing Wealth in Australia*, Melbourne: Melbourne University Press.

Baker, M. (2001) *Families, Labour and Love: Family Diversity in a Changing World*, Sydney: Allen and Unwin.

Barnes, A. (2001) *Low Fertility: A Discussion Paper*, Occasional paper no. 2, Department of Family and Community Services, Canberra.

Beer, A. and Faulkner, D. (2009) *21st Century Housing Careers and Australia's Housing Future*, Australian Housing and Urban Research Institute Final Report no. 128, Melbourne.

Beer, A., Faulkner, D. and Gabriel, M. (2006) *21st Century Housing Careers and Australia's Housing Future: Literature Review*, Australian Housing and Urban Research Institute National Research Venture 2: 21st Century housing careers, research paper 1, Melbourne.

Beer, A., Kearins, B. and Pieters, H. (2007) 'Housing affordability and planning in Australia', *Housing Studies*, 22(1): 11–24.

Berry, M., Dalton, T., and Nelson, A. (2009) *Mortgage Default in Australia: Nature, Causes and Social and Economic Impacts*, Australian Housing and Urban Research Institute Positioning Paper No.114, Melbourne.

Brinsden, C. (2009) 'Australia suffering record wealth loss', *Sydney Morning Herald*, 15 April.

Broomhill, R. and Sharp, R. (2005) 'The changing male breadwinner model in Australia: a new gender order?', *Labour and Industry*, 16(1):103–27.

Cass, B. (1991) *The Housing Needs of Women and Children*, Discussion Paper presented to the National Housing Strategy, Australian Government Publishing Service, Canberra.

Cass, B. (1998) 'The social policy context', in P. Smyth and B. Cass, (eds) *Contesting the Australian Way: States, Markets and Civil Society,* Cambridge: Cambridge University Press, 38–54.

References

Castles, F. (1998) 'The really big trade off: home ownership and the welfare state', *Acta Politica*, 33(1):5–19.

Centrelink (c2007) *Information You Need to Know About Your Claim for Age Pension.* Online. Available HTTP: http://www.centrelink.gov.au/internet/internet.nsf/forms/ci006. htm (accessed 25 July 2009).

Chamberlain, C. and MacKenzie, D. (2008) *Counting the Homeless 2006*, Australian Census Analytic Program, Cat. no. 2050.0, Australian Bureau of Statistics, Canberra.

Chung, D., Kennedy, R., O'Brien, B., Wendt, S., with assistance from Cody, S. (2000) *Home Safe Home: The Link Between Domestic and Family Violence and Women's Homelessness*, Partnerships Against Domestic Violence, WESNET and the Department of Families, Community Services and Indigenous Affairs. Online. Available HTTP: <www.wesnet. org.au/publications/reports/0011HomeSafeHome.pdf> (accessed 24 August 2007).

Clare, R. (2001) 'Women and superannuation', paper presented to the Ninth Annual Colloquium of Superannuation Researchers, University of New South Wales, Sydney, July. Online. Available HTTP: <http://www.superannuation.asn.au/ArticleDocuments/116/ women&super.pdf>.(accessed 8 June 2007).

Clare, R. (2004) 'Why can't a woman be more like a man? – gender differences in retirement savings', paper presented to the Association of Superannuation Funds of Australia 2004 National Conference and Super Expo, Super: saving 4 the nation, Adelaide convention centre, 10–12 November.

Clare, R. (2008) *The Age Pension, Superannuation and Australian Retirement Incomes*, Association of Superannuation Funds of Australia Research and Resource Centre, Sydney, NSW, December 2008.

Commonwealth of Australia (2008) *The Road Home, A National Approach to reducing Homelessness*, Homelessness Taskforce, Department of Families, Housing, Community Services and Indigenous Affairs, Commonwealth of Australia, Canberra, December 2008.

Commonwealth of Australia (2009a) *Australia's Paid Parental Leave Scheme, Supporting Working Australian Families*, Australian Government, Canberra.

Commonwealth of Australia (2009b) *National Housing Supply Council*, Department of Families, Housing, Community Services and Indigenous Affairs, Canberra. Online. Available HTTP: http://www.fahcsia.gov.au/sa/housing/progserv/affordability/Pages/ NationalHousingSupplyCouncil.aspx (accessed 17 August 2009).

de Vaus, D., Gray, M., Qu, L. and Stanton, D. (2007) *The Consequences of Divorce for Financial Living Standards in Later Life*, Australian Institute of Family Studies research paper no. 38, AIFS, Melbourne.

Department of Families, Housing, Community Services and Indigenous Affairs (2008a) *Making Housing Affordable Again*, DFaHCSIA, Government of Australia, Canberra. Online. Available HTTP: <http://www.facs.gov.au/internet/facsinternet.nsf/housing/ affordable_housing.htm> (accessed 24 June 2008).

Department of Families, Housing, Community Services and Indigenous Affairs (2008b) *National Rental Affordability Scheme Technical Discussion Paper*, DFaHCSIA, Government of Australia, Canberra. Online. Available HTTP: <http://www.facs.gov.au/ housing/nras/p1.htm> (accessed 27 June 2008).

Department of Families, Housing, Community Services and Indigenous Affairs (2009) *Nation Building – Economic Stimulus Plan, Social Housing Initiative*, DFaHCSIA Government of Australia, Canberra. Online. Available HTTP: <http://www.fahcsia.gov.au/internet/ facsinternet.nsf/housing/nbjp_factsheet.htm> (accessed 9 April 2009).

Department of Family and Community Services (Australian Government) (2005) *Annual Report 2004–05*, DFaHCSIA. Online. Available HTTP: <http://www.facsia.gov.au/annualreport/2005/part2/output2-1.html> (accessed 22 September 2008).

Department of Health and Ageing (2006) *The Report on the Findings and Recommendations of the National Speakers Series, a Community for All Ages, Building the Future*, Australian Government, Canberra.

Doughney, J., Pyke, J., Lyon, A., Leahy, M. and Rea, J. (2004) *Lifelong Economic Wellbeing for Women, Summary Paper: What Women Want*, summary paper of report commissioned by the Security4Women consortium, Online. Available HTTP: <http://www.security4women.com/documents/What%20Women% 20Want%20Summary%20July%202004.pdf> (accessed 8 June 2007).

Drago, R., Sawyer, K., Sheffler, K., Warren, D. and Wooden, M. (2009) *Did Australia's Baby Bonus Increase the Fertility Rate?*, Melbourne Institute Working Paper, Melbourne.

Equal Opportunity for Women in the Workforce Agency (2009) *Milestones*, EOfWWA, Australian Government. Online. Available HTTP: <http://www.eowa.gov.au/About_Equal_Opportunity/Where_Are_We_Now/Milestones.asp> (accessed 12 April 2009).

Family Assistance Office (2009) *Family Assistance Office Guide to Payments*, Australian Government, Canberra.

Faulkner, D., Tually, S., Baker, E. and Beer, A. (2007) *Report on the Outcomes of Focus Groups for the South Australian Ageing Atlas: Ageing and its Implications for Social and Planning Policy*, Report for Planning SA, Adelaide.

Flatau, P., Hendershott, P., Watson, R. and Wood, G. (2004) *What Drives Australian Housing Careers? An Examination of the Role of Labour Market, Social and Economic Determinants*, Australian Housing and Urban Research Institute Final Report No. 68, Melbourne.

Gilding, M. (1991) *The Making and Breaking of the Australian Family*, Allen and Unwin, Sydney.

Hall, T. (2007) *Where Have All the Gardens Gone? An Investigation into the Disappearance of Backyards in the Newer Australian Suburb*, Urban Research Program Research Paper 13, Griffith University, Brisbane.

Harding, A., Lloyd, R. and Greenwell, H. (2001) *Financial Disadvantage in Australia 1990–2000: The Persistence of Poverty in a Decade of Growth*, The Smith Family and National Centre for Social and Economic Modelling, The Smith Family, Camperdown.

Harmer, J. (2008) *Pension Review Background Paper*, Department of Families, Housing, Community Services and Indigenous Affairs, Commonwealth of Australia, Canberra.

Harmer, J. (2009) *Pension Review Report*, Department of Families, Housing, Community Services and Indigenous Affairs, Commonwealth of Australia, Canberra.

Herd, D., Ward, M. and Seeger, B. (2003) 'Included by design: a national strategy for accessible housing for all', Paper presented to the National Housing Conference, 26–28 November, Adelaide.

House of Representatives Standing Committee on Expenditure (1982) *In a Home or at Home: Accommodation and Home Care for the Aged*, Report from the House of Representatives Standing Committee on Expenditure, Australian Government Publishing Service, Canberra.

Hugo, G. (1986) *Australia's changing population: trends and implications*, Oxford University Press, Melbourne.

Hulse, K. and Saugeres, L. (2008) *Home life, work and housing decisions: a qualitative analysis*, Research paper no. 7, Australian Housing and Urban Research Institute National Research Venture 3: Housing assistance and non-shelter outcomes, Melbourne.

Human Rights and Equal Opportunity Commission (2007), *Its about time: women, men, work and family*, Final paper 2007, HREOC, Sydney. Online. Available HTTP: <http://www.hreoc.gov.au/sex_discrimination/its_about_time/docs/its_about_time_2007.pdf> (accessed 24 August 2007).

Jain, S. (2007) 'Lifetime marriage and divorce trends', *Australian social trends 2007*, Cat. no. 4102.0, Australian Bureau of Statistics, Canberra, 43–46.

Kippen, R. (2006) 'The rise of the older mother', *People and Place*, 14(3): 1–11.

Kroehn, M., Hutson, K., Faulkner, D. and Beer, A. (2007) *The housing careers of persons with a disability and family members with care responsibilities for persons with a disability*, report of focus groups, research as part of Australian Housing and Urban Research Institute National Research Venture 2: 21st century housing careers and Australia's housing future, AHURI Southern Research Centre, Adelaide.

Kryger, T. (2009) *Home ownership in Australia–data and trends*, Parliamentary Library Research Paper no. 21, Department of Parliamentary Services, Parliament of Australia, Canberra.

Lloyd, R., Harding, A. and Payne, A. (2004) 'Australians in poverty in the 21st century', paper prepared for the 33rd Conference of Economists, 27–30 September, National Centre for Social and Economic Modelling, Canberra.

McDonald, P. and Baxter, J. (2004) *Trends in home ownership rates in Australia: the relative importance of affordability trends and changes in population composition*, Australian Housing and Urban Research Institute final report No. 56, Melbourne.

McDonald, P. and Merlo, R. (2002) *Housing and its association with other life outcomes*, Australian Housing and Urban Research Institute final report No. 26, Melbourne.

Mace, R. (n.d.) 'About universal design', Center for Universal Design, North Carolina State University, Online. Available HTTP: <http://www.design.ncsu.edu/cud/about_ud/about_ud.htm> (accessed 30 June 2008).

Manne, A. (2001) 'Women's preferences, fertility and family policy: the case for diversity', *People and Place*, 9(4): 6–25.

Martin, J. and Richmond, C. (1968) 'Working women in Australia', in *Anatomy of Australia*, Sun Books: Melbourne, pp. 196–222.

Mission Australian (2007) 'Sydney's bed shortage crisis for homeless women', News release, 6 August 2007. Online. Available HTTP: <http://www.missionaustralia.com.au/news/media-releases/42-media-releases/193-sydney-bed-shortage-crisis-for-homeless-women> (accessed 22 September 2007).

Murphy, J. (2002) 'Breadwinning: accounts of work and family life in the 1950s', *Labour and Industry*, 12(3): 59–75.

National Housing Supply Council (2009) *National Housing Supply Council, state of supply report, report 2008*, Commonwealth of Australia, Canberra.

Nolan, M. (2003) 'The high tide of a labour system: The Australasian male breadwinner model', *Labour and Industry*, 13(3): 73–92.

Pocock, B. (1999) 'Equal pay thirty years on: the policy and practice', *The Australian Economic Review*, 32(3): 279–85.

Pocock, B. and Masterman-Smith, H. (2006) *Work Families and Affordable Housing*, CWL discussion paper 2/06, Centre for Work + Life, Hawke Research Institute for Sustainable Societies, University of SA, Adelaide, June 2006. Online. Available HTTP: <http://

www.unisa.edu.au/hawkeinstitute/cwl/documents/WorkAffordableHousingDP2.pdf> (accessed 6 June 2007).

Probert, B. (2002) '"Grateful slaves" or "self-made women": a matter of choice or policy?', Clare Burton Memorial Lecture, *Australian Feminist Studies*, 17(37): 7–17.

Productivity Commission (2008) *Paid Parental Leave: Support for Parents with Newborn Children, Draft Inquiry Report*, Australian Government Productivity Commission, Canberra.

Queensland Department of Housing (2008) *About the Pathways Shared Equity Loan*, DoH. Online. Available HTTP: <http://www.housing.qld.gov.au/loans/home/loans/shared/index.htm> (accessed 30 June 2008).

Robinson, C. and Searby, R. (2006) *Accommodation in Crisis: Forgotten Women in Western Sydney*, UTS shopfront monograph series no. 1, University of Technology, Sydney. Online. Available HTTP: <epress.lib.uts.edu.au/dspace/bitstream/2100/51/6/Accommodation+in+Crisis+WEBversion+April+07.pdf> (accessed 26 August 2007).

Security4Women and Boulden, K. (2004) *Economic Security for Women*, policy research report, May 2004, S4W. Online. Available HTTP: <http://www.security4women.com/documents/Policy%20Paper_May%202004.pdf> (accessed 8 June 2007).

Senate Community Affairs References Committee Secretariat (2004) *A Hand Up Not a Hand Out: Renewing the Fight Against Poverty, Report on Poverty and Financial Hardship*, SCARC, Commonwealth of Australia, Canberra.

Sheehan, G. (2002) 'Financial aspects of the divorce transition in Australia: recent empirical findings', *International Journal of Law, Policy and the Family*, 16(1):95–126.

Sheridan, T. and Stretton, P. (2004) 'Mandarins, ministers and the bar on married women', *The Journal of Industrial Relations*, 46(1): 84-101.

Summers, A. (2002) *Damned Whores and God's Police*, 4th edn, Penguin, Victoria.

Swan, W. and Macklin, J. (2009) 'Secure and sustainable pension reform: simpler and more flexible pension system', joint press release (no. 057) by the Treasurer of the Commonwealth of Australia and Minister for Families, Housing, Community Services and Indigenous Affairs. Online. HTTP: <http://www.treasurer.gov.au/DisplayDocs.aspx?doc=pressreleases/2009/057.htm&pageID=&min=wms&Year=&DocType=0> (accessed 15 August 2009).

Tually, S. (2008) *Understanding the Housing Careers of People Who Have Divorced, Families, Those Who Have Left Home Ownership and Public Tenants in the 21st Century*, Project E Report, Australian Housing and Urban Research Institute Southern Research Centre, Adelaide.

Tually, S., Beer, A., and Faulkner, D. (2007) *Too Big to Ignore: Future Issues for Australian Women's Housing, 2006–2025*, report prepared for the Women's Housing Caucus of SA, September.

Tually, S., Faulkner, D., Cutler, C., and Slatter, M. (2008) *Women, domestic And Family Violence and Homelessness: A Synthesis Report*, report prepared for the Office for Women, Department of Families, Housing, Community Services and Indigenous Affairs, August.

UK Department for Communities and Local Government, Department of Health and Department for Work and Pensions (2008) *Lifetime homes, Lifetime Neighbourhoods: A National Strategy for Housing in an Ageing Society*, DfCaLG, London.

Urban Development Institute of Australia (2007) *An industry Report into Affordable Homeownership in Australia*, UDIA National. Online. Available HTTP: <http://www.udia.com.au/resource/Part%201.pdf> (accessed 8 June 2008).

References

Ward, M. (2005) 'Universal housing design: it just makes good sense', Paper presented to the National Housing Conference, 27–28 October, Perth. Online. Available HTTP: <http://www.anuhd.org/publications/It_just_makes_good_sense.doc> (accessed 22 August 2007).

Weeks, W. and Oberin, J. (2004) *Women's Refuges, Shelters, Outreach and Support Services in Australia: From Sydney Squat to Complex Services, Challenging Domestic and Family Violence*, Report for the Office for Women, Department of Family and Community Services, Australian Government, Canberra.

Wilson, K., Pech, J. and Bates, K. (1999) *Parents, the labour force and social security*, Department of Family and Community Services Policy Research Paper No 2, Department of Family and Community Services, Commonwealth of Australia, Canberra.

Winter, I. and Stone, W. (1999) *Reconceptualising Australian Housing Careers*, Working Paper No. 17, Australian Institute of Family Studies, Melbourne.

Yates, J. (1991) *Australia's Owner Occupation Housing Wealth and its Impact on Income Distribution*, Reports and proceedings no. 92, Social Policy Research Centre, Sydney.

Yates, J. and Gabriel, M. (2006) *Housing Affordability in Australia*, research paper no. 3, Australian Housing and Urban Research Institute National Research Venture No. 3: Housing affordability for lower income Australians, Sydney Research Centre and Southern Research Centre, AHURI, Melbourne.

Yates, J., Wulff, M. and Reynolds, M. (2004) *Changes in the Supply of and Need for Low Rent Dwellings in the Private Rental Market*, Australian Housing and Urban Research Institute Final Report No. 61, AHURI, Melbourne.

Yates, J. and Milligan, V. with Berry, M., Burke, T., Gabriel, M., Phibbs, P., Pinnegar, S. and Randolph, B. (2007) *Housing Affordability: A 21st Century Problem*, Australian Housing and Urban Research Institute final report no. 105, AHURI, Melbourne.

4 Women and housing affordability in the United States

Abramovitz, M. (1988) *Regulating the Lives of Women: Social Welfare Policy from Colonial Times to the Present* Boston, MA: South End Press.

Amott, T. (1988) 'Working for Less: Single Mothers in the Workplace. in E. Mulroy (ed.) *Women as Single Parents: Confronting Institutional Barriers in the Courts, the Workplace, and the Housing market* (pp. 99–122). Dover, MA: Auburn House/Greenwood Press

Applied Research Center (2009) 'Race and Recession Report' http://www.arc.org/content/view/726/136 retrieved 15 December 2009.

Belsky, E. and Drew, R.B. (2007) 'Taking Stock of the Nation's Rental Housing Challenges and a Half-Century of Public Policy Responses'.RR07-1. Paper presented at Revisiting Rental Housing: A National Policy Summit. Joint Center for Housing Studies, Harvard University, Cambridge, MA

Birch, E. (1985) 'The Unsheltered Woman: Definitions and Needs.' In Eugenie Birch (ed.) *The Unsheltered Woman: Women and Housing in the 1980s* (pp. 21-46). New Brunswick, NJ: Center for Urban Policy Research.

The Boston Globe (2009) 'New Formula Shows More Live in Poverty', October 21.

Boushey, H., Fremstad, S., Gragg, R., and Waller, M. (2007) *Understanding Low-Wage Work in the United States. The Mobility Agenda: A Special Initiative of Inclusion*. Washington, DC: Center for Economic Policy and Research

Cohen, C. and Phillips, M. (1997) 'Building Community: Principles for Social Work Practice in Housing Settings', ... *Social Work* 42(5): 471–82.

Cohen, C., Mulroy, E., Tull, T., White, C., and Crowley, S. (2004) 'Housing Plus Services: Supporting Vulnerable Families in Permanent Housing', *Child Welfare* LXXXIII(5): 509-528.

deSouza-Briggs, X. (ed.) (2005) *The Geography of Opportunity: Race and Housing Choice in Metropolitan America*. Washington, DC: Brookings Institution Press.

Ehrenreich, B. (2001) *Nickel and Dimed: On (Not) Getting By in America*. New York: Henry Holt.

English, A., Hartmann, H., and Hegewisch, A. (2009) *Unemployment Among Single Mother Families*. IWPR #C369. Washington, DC: Institute for Women's Policy Research.

Figueira-McDonough, J. and Sarri, R. (2002) 'Increasing Inequality: The Ascendancy of Neoconservatism and Institutional Exclusion of Poor Women'. In Josephina Figueira-McDonough and Rosemary Sarri (eds) *Women At the Margins: Neglect, Punishment, and Resistance* (pp. 5–30) New York: Haworth Press.

Gilderbloom, J. and Applebaum, R. (1988) *Rethinking Rental Housing*. Philadelphia, PA: Temple University Press.

Hartmann, H., Sorokina, O., and Williams, E. (2006). *The Best and Worst Sate Economies for Women*. IWPR No. R334. Washington, DC: Institute for Women's Policy Research.

Housing Plus Services (2002) *Housing Plus Services Typology*. Washington, DC: Committee of the National Low Income Housing Coalition.

Institute for Women's Policy Research (2009) *The Gender Wage Gap: 2008*. IWPR #C350. Washington, DC: Institute for Women's Policy Research.

Joint Center for Housing Studies at Harvard University (2008) *The State of the Nation's Housing, 2008* Cambridge, MA: Joint Center for Housing Studies of Harvard University.

Joint Center for Housing Studies of Harvard University (2009) *The State of the Nation's Housing 2009*. Cambridge, MA: Joint Center for Housing Studies of Harvard University.

Jones-Deweever, A and Hartmann, H. (2006) 'Abandoned Before the Storms: The Glaring Disaster of Gender, Race, and Class Disparities in the Gulf'. In Chester Hartman and Gregory Squires (eds.). *There is No Such Thing As A Natural Disaster: Race, Class, and Hurricane Katrina* (pp. 85–102). New York: Routledge

Kotlowitz, A. (1991) *There Are No Children Here: A story of Two Boys Growing Up in the Other America*. New York: Doubleday Publishing Co.

MacQuarrie, B. (2009) 'For These Women Veterans, A Home To Call Their Own'. *The Boston Globe*. October 31, 2009, p. A1

McAdoo, H. (2002) 'The Storm Is Passing Over: Marginalized African American Women'. In Josefina Figueira-McDonough and Rosemary Sarri, (eds) *Women At the Margins: Neglect, Punishment, and Resistance* (pp. 87–102). New York: Haworth Press.

McKernan, S. and Sherraden, M. (2008) *Asset Building and Low Income Families*. Washington, DC: The Urban Institute Press.

Markman, J. (2009) 'Rescued Child Prostitutes Not Getting Needed Help'. *The Boston Globe*. December 13, 2009, p. A2.

Mulroy, E.A. (1988) 'The Search for Affordable Housing'. In Elizabeth Mulroy (ed.) *Women As Single Parents: Confronting Institutional Barriers in the Courts, the Workplace, and The Housing Market* (pp. 123–160). Westport, CT: Auburn House/Greenwood Press.

Mulroy, E.A. (1991). Mixed Income Housing in Action. *Urban Land* May 1991 2-7.

Mulroy, E. A., (1995) *The New Uprooted: Single Mothers in Urban Life*. Westport, CT: Auburn House/Greenwood Press

Mulroy, E. A. (2002) 'Low-Income Women and Housing: Where Will They Live?' In Josephina. Figueira-McDonough & Rosemary Sarri, (eds) *Women At The Margins: Neglect, Punishment, and Resistance* (pp. 151-168). New York: Haworth Press.

National Low Income Housing Coalition (2002) 'Typology of Housing Plus Services Programs'. Housing Plus Services Committee. Washington, DC. http://www.nlihc.org/template/page.cfm?id=43. Retrieved Dec. 15, 2002.

National Low Income Housing Coalition (2005). 'Hurricane Katrina's Impact On Low Income Housing Units Estimated 302,000 Units Lost Or Damaged'. Research Note #05-02. Washington, DC: National Low Income Housing Coalition. Sept. 22.

Pelletiere, D. (2007) 'American Community Survey Estimate Shows Larger National, State Affordable Rental Housing Shortage's. Research Note #07-01 National Low Income Coalition. Washington, DC.

Pelletiere, D. (2009) *Renters in Foreclosure: Defining the Problem, Identifying Solutions*. Washington DC: National Low Income Housing Coalition.

Pelletiere, D. and Waldrip, K. (2008) 'Renters and the Housing Credit Crisis'. *Poverty & Race* 17(4): 3–7.

Polikoff, A. (1978) *Housing the Poor: The Case for Heroism*. Cambridge, MA: Ballinger.

Ross, M., Sattelmeyer, S., Waller, M. (2008). *Employment and Housing Mobility: Promising Practices for the Twenty-First Century Economy*. Washington, DC: The Mobility Agenda.

Salzman, J. (2009) 'Treatment Units For Mentally Ill Inmates On Hold'. *The Boston Globe*. November 10, 2009, p. A1

Schmitt, J. (2008) *Unions and Upward Mobility for Women Workers*. Washington, DC: Center for Economic and Policy Research.

Schmitt, J. and Warner, K. (2009) *The Changing Face of Labor, 1983–2008*. Washington, DC: Center for Economic and Policy Research.

Schwartz, A. (2006) *Housing Policy in the United States*. New York: Routledge

Shipler, D. (2004) *The Working Poor: Invisible in America*. New York: Knopf.

Spader, J. (2008) Subprime's Footprint. *Shelterforce* 30(2): 38–46.

Squires, G. (2008) 'Scapegoating Blacks for the Economic Crisis'. *Poverty & Race* 17(6): 34.

Turner, M., Popkin, S. and Rawlings, L. (2009) *Public Housing and the Legacy of Segregation*. Washington, DC: The Urban Institute Press.

Waldrip, K., Pelletiere, D. and Crowley, S (2008) *Out of Reach 2007–2008: The Wait For a Home Grows Longer*. Washington D.C: National Low Income Housing Coalition.

Wilson, W. J.(1987) *The Truly Disadvantaged: The Inner City, the Underclass, and Public Policy*. Chicago, IL: University of Chicago Press.

5 Social change and housing systems

Allen, A., Barlow, J., Leal, J., Maloutas, T., and Padovani, L. (2004) *Housing & Welfare in Southern Europe*, Oxford: Blackwell Publishing.

Balchin, P. (1996) *Housing Policy in Europe*, London: Routledge.

Barceló, C. (2006) "Housing Tenure and Labour mobility: a comparison across european countries", Working Paper No. 0603. Madrid: Banco de España. Available at http://www.bde.es/webbde/Secciones/Publicaciones/PublicacionesSeriadas/DocumentosTrabajo/06/Fic/dt0603e.pdf . Visited on 30th October 2009.

Bonvalet, C., Laflamme, V., and Arbonville, D. (eds) (2009) *Family and Housing*, Oxford: The Bardwell Press.

Bosch, J. (2006) *El problema de la vivienda en España desde una perspectiva de género: análisis y propuestas para su desarrollo.* Fundación Alternativas. Available online at www.falternativas.org/content/download/5897/168151/version/2/file/9563_13-06-06_Estudios%252020.pdf. Visited on 14 November 2009.

Cortés, L. (1998) Malestar urbano y cuestión residencial, in El malestar urbano en la gran ciudad, Madrid: Talasa. pp. 79–89.

Crouch, C. (1999) *Social Change in Western Europe*, Oxford: Oxford University Press.

Esping-Andersen, G. (1990) *The Three Worlds of Welfare Capitalism.* Cambridge: The Policy Press.

Esping-Andersen, G. (1999) *Social Foundations of Postindustrial Economies*, Oxford: Oxford University Press.

Esping-Andersen, G. (2002) *Why Do We Need a New Welfare State?,* Oxford: Oxford University Press.

Eurostat (2005) Eurostat Database. Population and Social Conditions, Living Conditions and Welfare. Available at http://epp.eurostat.ec.europa.eu/portal/page/portal/income_social_inclusion_living_conditions/data/main_tables. Visited on 2nd November 2009.

Eurostat (2008) 'The life of women and men in Europe: a statistical portrait'. Available online at http://ec.europa.eu/social/main.jsp?langId=en&catId=681&newsId=240&furtherNews=yes.

Ferrera, M. (1996) The 'Southern Model' of welfare in social Europe, *Journal of European Social Policy*, 6 (1), pp.17–37.

Flaquer, L. (2002) 'Family policy and the maintenance of the traditional family in Spain', in A. Carling, S. Duncan and R. Edwards (eds), *Analysing Families Morality and Rationality in Policy and Practice*, London: Routledge.

Hidalgo, A., Pérez Camarero, S., and Calderón, M. J. (2007) *La discriminación salarial de la mujer: una década a examen.* Madrid: Instituto de la Mujer.

Leal, J. (1997) 'Emancipación y vivienda', in R. Vergés (ed), *La edad de emancipación de los jóvenes,* Serie Urbanitas, Barcelona: Centre de Cultura Contemporània de Barcelona.

—— (2005) 'Desigualdad residencial y sistema de bienestar en España' in J. Ruiz-Huerta (ed.), *Políticas públicas y distribución de la renta.* Fundación BBVA.

Leibfried, S. (1992) 'Towards a European welfare state?', in C. Jones (ed.), *New Perspectives on the Welfare State in Europe*, London: Routledge.

Maclennan, D., Muellbauer, J., and Stephens, M. (1998) 'Asymmetries in housing and financial market institutions and EMU', *The Oxford Review of Economic Policy*, 14:3(Autumn), pp. 54–80.

Marcuse, P., and van Kempen, R. (2000) *Globalizing Cities: A New Spatial Order?*, Oxford: Wiley-Blackwell.

Mignone, E. (2005) 'Urban social change: a socio-historical framework of analysis' in Y. Kazepov (ed.), *Cities of Europe, Changing contexts: Local Arrangements, and the Challenge to Urban Cohesion*, Oxford: Blackwell Publishing.

Ministry of Labour and Social Security (2006) *Directory of Labour Statistics and Social Affairs 2006.* Available at http://www.mtin.es/estadisticas/anuario2006/welcome.htm. Visited on 14th November 2009.

Molina, I. (2006) 'Estudios de espacio y género: desde la cuenta de cuerpos hasta las intersecciones del poder', in I. Molina (ed.), *Rompiendo Barreras: género y espacio en el campo y la ciudad,* Santiago de Chile: Editorial El Tercer Actor.

References

Moreno Mínguez, A. (2005) 'Empleo de la mujer y familia en los regímenes de bienestar del sur de Europa en perspectiva comparada. Permanencia del modelo de varón sustentador', *Revista Española de Investigaciones Sociológicas*, 112: 127–59.

Moreno Mínguez, A (2008) 'El reducido empleo femenino en los estados del bienestar del Sur de Europa: Un análisis comparado', *Revista Internacional De Sociología*, LXVI(50, May-August): 129–62.

Naldini, M. (2003) *The Family in the Mediterranean Welfare States*, London: Frank Cass.

National Institute of Statistics (INE) (several years) Active Population Survey - Encuesta de Población Activa (EPA). Available at http://www.ine.es/jaxi/menu. do?type=pcaxis&path=%2Ft22/e308_mnu&file=inebase&L=1. Visited on 2nd November 2009.

National Institute of Statistics (INE) (several years) Population and Housing Census. Available at http://www.ine.es/en/inebmenu/mnu_cifraspob_en.htm. Visited on 16th November 2009.

National Institute of Statistics (INE) (2006) Household Budget Survey. Available at http:// www.ine.es/jaxi/menu.do?type=pcaxis&path=%2Ft25/p458&file=inebase&L=1 . Visited on 27th November 2009.

National Institute of Statistics (INE) (several years) Living conditions survey. Available at http://www.ine.es/jaxi/menu.do?type=pcaxis&path=%2Ft25/p453&file=inebase&L=1. Visited on 30th November 2009.

Navarro, V. (2000), *Neoliberalismo y Estado del Dienestar*, Madrid: Ariel Sociedad Economia.

O'Connor, J. (1996) 'From women in the welfare state to gendering welfare state regimens', *Current Sociology*, 44(2): 1–24.

OECD (2005) *Economic Survey of Spain 2005: Stabilising the Housing Market*, Paris, OECD Publications. Available online at http://www.oecd.org/dataoecd/53/3/34586052. pdf. Accessed 30 November 2009.

Pajares, M. (2009) *Inmigración y mercado de trabajo: Informe 2009*. Madrid, National Immigration Observatory.

Pareja-Eastaway, M. (2009) 'The effects of the Spanish housing system on the settlement patterns of immigrants', *Tijdschrift voor economische en sociale geografie*, 100(4) 519–34.

Pareja-Eastaway, M., and San Martin, I. (2000) 'The importance of housing systems in safeguarding social cohesion in Europe', Part A. (unpublished). SOCOHO.

Pareja-Eastaway, M., and San Martin, I (2002), 'The tenure imbalance in Spain: the need for social housing', *Urban Studies* 39(2): 283–95.

Pareja-Eastaway, M., and San Martin, I (2003) *The Importance of Housing Systems in Safeguarding Social Cohesion*. SOCOHO Final report.

Pareja-Eastaway, M., and Sánchez-Martínez, M. T. (2009) 'European rental markets: regulation or liberalization? The Spanish case', in P. Arestis, P. Mooslechner and K. Wagner (eds), *Housing Market Challenges in Europe and the United States: Any Solutions Available,* Basingstoke: Palgrave Macmillan.

Sainsbury, D. (1999) *Gender and Welfare State Regimes*, Oxford: Oxford University Press.

Sánchez-Martínez, M. T. (2002) *La política de vivienda en España: Análisis de sus efectos redistributivos*, Granada: Ediciones de la Universidad de Granada.

Sociological Research Center (CIS) (2005) 2620 Report. Latinobarómetro (VIII). Available at http://www.cis.es/cis/opencm/ES/1_encuestas/estudios/listaMuestras.jsp?orden=4&d esc=&estudio=5158&cuestionario=5471&pagina=1. Accessed on November 7 2009.

Taltavull, P. (ed.) (2000) *Vivienda y familia*, Madrid: Fundación Argentaria.

Valiente, C. (1998) 'Género, mercado de trabajo y estado de bienestar: el caso de España', *Sociología del Trabajo*, 32: 53–79.

6 Women's housing in Sweden

AKU (September 2009), Statistics Sweden's monthly statistics on the labour force (www. scb.se)

Almqvist, Annika (2004), *Drömmen om det egna huset. Från bostadsförsörjning till livsprojekt* [The Dream of a House of One's Own. From Housing Provision to Life Project]. Uppsala: Uppsala Universitet.

Bengtsson, B., Annaniassen, E., Jensen, L., Ruonavaara, H. and Sveinsson, J. R., (2006), *Varför så olika? Nordisk bostadspolitik i jämförande historiskt ljus* [Why so Different? Nordic Housing Policies in Comparative, Historical Light]. Malmö: Égalité.

Bernhardt, E., Gähler, M. and Goldscheider, F. (2005), 'Childhood Family Structure and Routes Out of the Parental Home in Sweden.' *Acta Sociologica,* 48 (2): 99–116.

Brå [National Council for Crime Prevention] (2007), *Nationella trygghetsundersökningen 2006. De första resultaten om utsatthet, trygghet och förtroende* [The National Safety Survey. The First Results on Exposure, Safety and Confidence]. Rapport 2007:14. Stockholm: Brottsförebyggande rådet.

Brå [National Council for Crime Prevention] (2008), *Otrygghet och segregation. Bostadsområdets betydelse för allmänhetens otrygghet och oro för brott* [Unsafety and Segregation. The Impact of the Residential Area for Public Unsafety and Fear of Crime]. Rapport 2008:16. Stockholm: Brottsförebyggande rådet.

Engberg, E. (2005), *I fattiga omständigheter* [In Poor Conditions]. Umeå: Demografiska databasen.

Eriksson, E. (1990), *Den moderna stadens födelse. Svensk arkitektur 1890–1920* [The Birth of the Modern City. Swedish Architecture 1890–1920]. Stockholm: Ordfronts förlag.

Esping-Andersen, G. (1990), *The Three Worlds of Welfare Capitalism.* Cambridge: Polity Press.

EU Commission (2005), *Commission decision on the application of Article 86(2) of the Treaty to State aid in the form of public service compensation granted to certain undertakings entrusted with the operation of services of general economic interest.* Brussels. Press release July 2005.

Franzén, M. (1992), *Den folkliga staden. Söderkvarter i Stockholm mellan krigen* [The Popular City. The South End in Stockholm Between the Wars]. Lund: Arkiv förlag.

Fritzell, Johan, Gähler, Michael and Nermo, Magnus (2007), 'Vad hände med 1990-talets stora förlorargrupper?' [What Happened to the Loser Groups of the 1990s?]. *Socialvetenskaplig tidskrift*, 14(2–3): 110–33.

Gardberg Morner, C. (2003), *Självständigt beroende. Ensamstående mammors försörjningsstrategier* [Autonomous Dependence. Lone Mothers' Subsistence Strategies]. Doctoral thesis. Göteborg Studies in Sociology No 18. Göteborg: Department of Sociology, Göteborg University.

Gähler, M. (2001), 'Bara en mor – ensamstående mödrars ekonomiska levnadsvillkor i 1990-talets Sverige' [Only a Mother – Single Mothers' Economic Living Conditions in Sweden of the 1990s].' In Bergmark, Åke (ed.), *Ofärd i välfärden* [Faring Badly in the Welfare] SOU 2001:54. Stockholm: Fritzes.

References

Knutagård, M. (2009), *Skälens fångar. Hemlöshetsarbetets organisering, kategoriseringar och förklaringar* [The Prisoners of the Reasons. Organisation, Categorisations and Accounts within Homelessness Work]. Malmö: Égalité.

Lauster, N. T. and Fransson, U. (2006), 'Of Marriages and Mortgages: The Second Demographic Transistion and the Relationship between Marriage and Homeownership in Sweden.' *Housing Studies*, 21 (6): 909–27.

Listerborn, C. (2002), Trygg stad. Diskurser om kvinnors rädsla i forskning, policyutveck-ling och local praktik. [Safe City. Discourses on Women's Fear in Research, Policy Development and Lokal Practices]. Doctoral thesis in Architecture. Göteborg: Chalmers University.

Löfstrand, C. (2005), *Hemlöshetens politik. Lokal policy och praktik* [The Politics of Homelessness. Local Policy and Practice]. Malmö: Égalité.

Löfstrand, C. and Thörn, C. (2004), 'The Construction of Gender and Homelessness in Sweden'. *Open House International Journal*, 29 (2): 6–13.

Magnusson, L. and Turner, B. (2008), 'Municipal Housing Companies in Sweden – Social by Default'. *Housing, Theory and Society* 25 (4): 275–96.

Migration B., monthly statistics, http://www.migrationsverket.se/info/1894.html.

Myrdal, A. and Myrdal, G. (1934 [1997]), *Kris i befolkningsfrågan* [Population Crisis]. Nora: Nya Doxa.

Myrdal, G. (1944) *An American Dilemma. The Negro Problem and Modern Democracy*. New York: Harper & Brothers.

NBHBP (National Board of Housing, Building and Planning – Boverket) (2008), *Hyreskontrakt via kommunen* [Rental Leases Through the Municipality]. Karlskrona: Boverket.

NBHBP (National Board of Housing, Building and Planning – Boverket) (2009), *Bostadsmarknaden 2009–2010. Med slutsatser från bostadsmarknadsenkäten 2009* [The Housing Market 2009–2010. With Conclusions from the Housing Market Survey 2009]. Karlskrona: Boverket.

NBHW (National Board of Health and Welfare – Socialstyrelsen) (2006), *Social rapport 2006* [Social Report 2006]. Stockholm: Socialstyrelsen.

NBHW (National Board of Health and Welfare – Socialstyrelsen) (2009), *Vuxna personer med missbruksproblem och övriga vuxna – insatser år 2008* [Adult Persons with Substance Abuse Problems and Other Adult People. Measures Taken during 2008]. Stockholm: Socialstyrelsen.

Nilsson, J. Olof (1994), *Alva Myrdal: en virvel i den moderna strömmen* [Alva Myrdal: An Eddy in the Modern Stream]. Stockholm: Brutus Östlings förlag Symposion.

Nordisk Familjebok (1888). (Encyclopedia)

Popoola, M. (1999), *Trångt i Herrgårdsmiljö. Rapport om trångboddhet på Herrgården* [Cramped-in Herrgården. Report on Overcrowding in Herrgården]. Research report Forskningsrapport MAH/IMER/FR99/001-SE. Malmö: Malmö Högskola.

Regnér, M. (2006), *'Familjebilder. Om klientfamiljer, kontaktfamiljer och idealfamiljer'* [Notions of the Family. On Client Families, Contact Families and Ideal Families]. Doctoral thesis. Göteborg: Department of Social Work, Göteborg University.

Regnér, M. and Johnsson, Lisbeth (2007), 'The "ordinary" family as a resource for single parents – on the Swedish contact family service'. *European Journal of Social Work*, 10 (3): 319–36.

Rosengren, A. (2003), *Mellan ilska och hopp. Om hemlöshet, droger och kvinnor* [Between Anger and Hope. On Homelessness, Drugs, and Women]. Stockholm: Carlssons.

Sahlin, I. (1998), *The Staircase of Transition*. Brussels: FEANTSA.

Sahlin, I. (2001), *Access to Housing for the Excluded*. National Report from Sweden to the European Observatory on Homelessness. Brussels: FEANTSA.

Sahlin, I. (2005), *Access to Decent Housing for Immigrants and Ethnic Minorities*. National Report from Sweden to the study on Policy Measures for Housing for Immigrants and Ethnic Minorities. Göteborg: Department of sociology, Göteborg University.

Sahlin, I. (2008), 'De uppstudsiga kvinnorna på Stora fattighuset' [The Obstinate Women in the Great Poorhouse]. In S. Hans and E. Marie-Anne (eds), *Villkorandets politik* [The Policy of Conditioning]. Malmö: Égalité.

Sahlin, I. and Thörn, Catharina (1999), *Women, Exclusion and Homelessness*. National Report from Sweden to the Europen Observatory on Homelessness. Brussels: FEANTSA.

Schmidt, L. H. and Kristensen, J. E. (1986), *Lys, luft og renlighed. Den moderne socialhygiejnes fødsel* [Light, Air and Cleanliness. The Birth of the Modern Social Hygiene]. Viborg: Akademisk forlag.

Sheiban, H. (2002), *Den ekonomiska staden. Stadsplanering i Stockholm under senare hälften av 1800-talet* [The Economic City. Urban Planning in Stockholm During the Latter Half of the Nineteenth Century].Lund: Arkiv.

Social Insurance (2008), *Family Policy in Sweden*. Stockholm: Försäkringskassan.

Social Insurance, statistics, 2009 http://statistik.forsakringskassan.se/rfv/html/BOB_5_1_2009.html.

SOU 1935:2, *Lån och årliga bidrag av statsmedel för främjande av bostadsförsörjning för mindre bemedlade barnrika familjer jämte därtill hörande utredningar* [Loans and Yearly State Contributions for the Promotion of Housing Provision for Poor Families with Many Children and Associated Investigations]. Report by the Housing-Social Committee.

SOU 1945:63, *Allmänna riktlinjer för den framtida bostadspolitiken. Förslag till låne- och bidragsformer* [General Guidelines for the Future Housing Policy. Suggestions on Forms of Loans and Contributions]. Final Report by the Housing-Social Committe, Part I.

SOU 1947:26, *Saneringen av stadssamhällenas bebyggelse* [Demolition of Urban Community Buildings] Final Report by the Housing-Social Committe, Part II. Stockholm: Socialdepartementet.

Statistics Sweden, data bases, press releases and short reports (www.scb.se).

Statistics Sweden (2008), *Women and Men. Fact and Figures 2008*. Stockholm: Statistics Sweden.

Statistics Sweden (2009), *Bostads- och byggnadsstatistisk årsbok 2009* [Yearbook of Housing and Building Statistics 2009]. Stockholm: Statistics Sweden.

Statistics Sweden (2010), *Women and Men in Sweden. Facts and Figures 2010*. Stockholm: Statistics Sweden.

Thörn, C. (2001), '(In)visibility and shame: the stigma of being a woman and homeless in Sweden'. In Edgar, Bill and Doherty, Joe (eds), *Women and Homelessness in Europe*. Bristol: Policy Press.

Thörn, C. (2004), *Kvinnans plats(er) – bilder av hemlöshet* [A Woman's Place(s) – Images of Homelessness]. Stockholm: Égalité.

Wallengren, H. (1994), *Hyresvärden. Maktrelationer på hyresmarknaden i Malmö 1880–1925* [The Landlord. Power Relations on the Rental Market in Malmö 1880–1925]. Ystad: Mendocino.

Woolf, V. (1929 [1981]), *A Room of One's Own*. Orlando: Harcourt Inc.

7 Women, housing and citizenship in Great Britain

Blair, A. (1997) *The Third Way: New Politics for the New Century,* London: Fabian Society.

Cabinet Office (2002) *Ethnic Minorities in Britain,* HMSO.

Cabinet Office (2003) *Ethnic Minorities and the Labour Market: Final Report Strategy Unit,* London.

Campbell, B. (1993) *Goliath, Britain's Dangerous Places,* London: Methuen

Castles, S. and Kosack, G. (1973) *Immigrant Workers and Class Structure in Western Europe* .London: Harper and Row.

Christie, H. (2000) 'Mortgage arrears and gender inequalities', *Housing Studies* 15(6) 877–905.

Clapham, D., Kemp, S. and Smith, S. (1990) *Housing and Social Policy,* London: Macmillan.

CML (2000) 'Characteristics of mortgage lending in 1999: results from the survey of mortgage lenders', *Housing Finance* 46: 13–19.

CML (2010) 'Mortgage arrears and possessions declined in fourth quarter', Council of Mortgage Lenders 11 February 2010 http://www.cml.org.uk/cml/media/press/2541 (accessed 24 March 2010).

Crompton, R. (ed) (1999) *Restructuring Gender Relations and Employment: The Decline of the Male Breadwinner,* Oxford: Oxford University Press.

Daly, M. and Lewis, J. (2000) The concept of social care and the analysis of contemporary welfare states, *British Journal of Sociology* 51(2): 281–98.

DCLG (2007) *Homes for the Future: More Affordable, More Sustainable,* The Government's 2007 Green Paper: CM 7191 London: HMSO.

Dench, S., Aston, J., Evans, C., Meger, N., Williams, M. and Williamson, R. (2002) *Key Indicators of Women's Position in Britain,* Women and Equality Unit: London.

Dunleavy (1981) *The politics of mass housing in Britain 1945-1975: Study of corporate power and professional influence in the welfare state,* Oxford: Clarendon Press.

Dunleavy, P. (1984) 'The limits to local government', in M. Boddy and C. Fudge (eds) *Local Socialism? Labour Councils and the New Left Alternatives,* London: Macmillan.

Dunn, R., Forrest, R., and Murie, A. (1987) 'The geography of council house sales in England – 1979–1985', *Urban Studies* 24(1): 47–59.

EHS (2010) *Headline Report 2008-09.* Department for Community and Local Government, HMSO.

Eisenstein, Z. (1979) *Capitalist Patriarchy and the Case for Socialist Feminism.* New York: Monthly Review Press.

Equal Opportunities Commission (2002) *Women and Men in Britain: Management,* EOC.

Forrest, R. and Kennett, P. (1994) 'Regimes of exclusion and housing', paper presented at European Network For Housing Research Workshop on Housing and Social Integration and Exclusion, Copenhagen, May 16.

Forrest, R. and Murie, A. (1986) 'Marginalisation and subsidized individualism: the sale of council housing in the restructuring of the British welfare state', *International Journal of Urban and Regional Research* vol 10 no 1 pp46-65.

Gilroy, R. and Woods, R. (1994) *Women and Housing,* London: Routledge

Government Equalities Office (2009) *Tackling the Gender Pay Gap. Factsheet,* London: HMSO

Government Equalities Office (2010a) *Diversity in the Boardroom – a Guide for Business and Board Ready Candidates in the UK,* London: HMSO.

Government Equalities Office (2010b) *Improving Women's Lives. Factsheet,* London: HMSO

Griggs, J. (2010) *Examining the Role of Grandparents in Families at Risk of Poverty,* London: Grandparents Plus and the Equality and Human Rights Commission

Hay, C. (1992) 'Housing policy in transition: from the post-war settlement towards a "Thatcherite" hegemony', *Capital and Class* 46(Spring): 27–64.

Henderson, J. and Karn, V. (1987) *Race, Class and State Housing: Inequality and the Allocation of Public Housing in Britain,* Aldershot: Gower

ILO (2009) *Gender Equality at the Heart of Decent Work*, Report V International Labour Conference 98th Session, Geneva, June.

ILO (2010) *Women in Labour Markets: Measuring Progress and Identifying Challenges*, Geneva: ILO.

Innes, S. and Scott, G. (2003) 'After I've done the Mum things: women, care and transitions', *Sociological Research Online* 8(4). http://www.socresonline.org.uk/8/4/innes.html (accessed 3 March 2010).

Izuhara, M. and Kennett, P. (2003) *Interim Report: Women and Material Assets in Britain,* Tokyo: Institute for Research on Household Economics.

Kerr, M. (1988) *The Right To Buy: A National Survey of Tenants and Buyers of Council Homes,* London: HMSO.

Land, H. (2009) 'The 1970s: the beginning of the demise of the british male breadwinner model', paper presented at the European Societies at Work in Transformation: Comparative and Transnational Perspectives in Great Britain, Sweden and Germany during the 1970s, London, 26–28 November.

Lewis, J. (2001) 'The decline of the male breadwinner model: the implications for work and care', *Social Politics* 8(2): 152–70.

Lissenburgh, S. (2000) Gender Discrimination in the Labour Market. *PSI Discussion Paper 3. Evidence from the BHPS and EIB Surveys*. London: Policy Studies Institute.

Malpass, P. and Murie, A. (1987) *Housing Policy and Practice,* Basingstoke: Macmillan Education.

Modood, T., Berthoud, R., Lakey,. J., Nazroo, J., Smith, P., Virdee, S. and Beishon, S. (1997) *Ethnic Minorities in Britain: Diversity and Disadvantage,* London: Policy Studies Institute.

NHPAU (2008) *Impact of Worsening Affordability on Demand for Social and Affordable Housing: Tenure Choice and Household Formation,* Fareham: National Housing and Planning Advice Unit.

NHPAU (2009) *Affordability: More Than Just a Housing Problem*, Fareham: National Housing and Planning Advice Unit.

ONS (1982) *Social Trends* London: HMSO.

ONS (2001a) *Living in Britain: Results from the 2000 General Household Survey*, London: HMSO.

ONS (2001b) *UK Labour Force Survey Spring Quarters Historical Supplement*, London: HMSO from Izuhara and Kennett (2003) p. 12.

ONS (2009a) *Housing in England 2007–08. A Report Principally from the 2007–08 Survey of English Housing,* London: Department of Communities and Local Government, HMSO.

ONS (2009b) *Social Trends 38* HMSO: London.

ONS (2010) *Social Trends 39 2009,* HMSO: London.

Rex, J. and Tomlinson, S. (1979) *Race, Community and Conflict,* Oxford: Oxford University Press.

Smith, J. (2005) 'Housing, Gender and Social Policy' in P. Sommerville and N. Sprigings (eds) *Housing and Social Policy. Contemporary themes and critical perspectives,* London: Routledge.

Ungerson, C. (1983) 'Why do women care?' in J. Finch and D. Groves (eds) *A labour of love: Women, work and caring,* London: Routledge and Kegan Paul.

Walby, S. (1989) 'Theorising patriarchy', *Sociology* 23: 213–34.

Wilcox, S. (2001) *Housing Finance Review 2001/2002,* Chartered Institute of Housing and the Council of Mortgage Lenders/Joseph Rowntree Foundation, London.

Wong, C., Gibb, K., McGreal, S., Hincks, S., Kingston, R., Leishman, C., Brown, L. and Blair, N. (2009) *Housing and Neighbourhood Monitor UK-Wide Report.* York: Joseph Rowntree Foundation.

8 Moving beyond the standard family model

Bureau of Statistics (2005) 'Population Census, Households', http://www.stat.go.jp/english/data/kokusei/2005/kihon1/00/04.htm.

Cabinet Office (2004) 'Public Opinion Survey', Tokyo.

Cabinet Office (2005) 'Public Opinion Survey', Tokyo.

Esping-Andersen, G. (1997) 'Hybrid or Unique? The Japanese Welfare State Between Europe and America'. *Journal of European Social Policy,* 7(3):179–89.

Ezawa, A., and Fujiwara, C. (2005) 'Lone Mothers and Welfare-to-Work Policies in Japan and the United States', Journal of Sociology and Social Welfare 32(4): 41–63.

Finch, J., Hayes, L., Mason, J., and Wallis, L. (1996) *Wills, Inheritance and Families,* Oxford, Clarendon Press.

Genda, Y. (2001) *Shigoto no Naka no Aimai no Fuan* [The vague uneasiness of work], Tokyo:Chou Korou Shinsha.

Haruka, Y. (2002) *Kaigo no ren' ai* [Elderly Care and Romantic Love], Tokyo, Chikuma Shobou.

Hinokidani, M. (2007) 'Housing, family and gender', in Y. Hirayama and R. Ronald (eds) *Housing and Social Transition in Japan*, London, Routledge.

Hirayama, Y. (2007) 'Reshaping the housing system: homeownership as a catalyst for social transformation', in Y. Hirayama and R. Ronald (2007) *Housing and Social Transition in Japan*, London: Routledge.

Hirayama, Y., and Izuhara, M. (2008) 'Women and Housing Assets in Context of Japan'sHome Owning Democracy', *Journal of Social Policy*, 37(4): 641–60.

Hirayama, Y. and Ronald, R. (2008) 'Baby Boomers, Baby Busters and the Lost Generation: Generational Fractures in Japan's Homeowner Society', *Urban and Policy Research,* 26(3) 325–342.

Honma, Y. (1980) *Mai Homu Gemu* [My Home Game], Tokyo, Otsuki Shoten.

IPSSR (2008) Institute of Population and Social Security Research, http://www.ipss.go.jp/index-e.asp (accessed August 26 2010).

Iwama, A. (2008) *Jyosei no Syugyo to Kazoku no Yukue: Kakusa Syakai nonakano Henyo* [Women's Work and Future of Family: Changes in Disparity Society], Tokyo, Tokyo University Press.

Izuhara, M. (2002) 'Care and Inheritance: Japanese and English Perspectives on the 'Generational Contract''. *Ageing and Society*, Vol 22, p 61–77.

Kawata, N. (2007) 'Single People in Context of Japan's Housing System', European Network of Housing Research Conference, Sustainable Urban Areas, Seoul, South Korea, August 2007.

Kondo, D. (1990) *Crafting Selves: Power, Gender, and Discourses of Identity in a Japanese Workplace*, Chicago, University of Chicago Press.

Kitagawa, K. (2002) *Dining Kitchen wa Koushite Tanjyo sita: Jyosei Kenchikuka dai-ichigo Hamaguchi Miho ga Mezasitamono* [Creation of the Dining Kitchen: Aspirations of the First Japanese Female Architect – Miho Hamaguchi], Tokyo, Gihodo Press.

Koyano, W. (1996) 'Filial Piety and Intergenerational Solidarity in Japan'. *Australian Journal on Ageing*, 15(2): 51–6.

Matsumoto, M. (1998) 'Seijin mikonsha no Tokyo kennai niokeru kyoju jittai' [Housing conditions of unmarried people in the Tokyo metropolitan area] *Sogo Toshi Kenku* [Comprehensive Urban Studies] 66: 79–92.

MHLW (2001) *Kokumin Seikatsu Kiso Chousa,* Tokyo [Basic Survey on the Life of People in Japan].

MHLW (2003) *Chingin Kozo Kihon Tokei Chousa,* Tokyo [Basic Statistical Survey on the Wage Structure in Japan], http://www.mhlw.go/jp.

MHLW (2005a) *Mi Shakai fukushi: seikatsu,* Tokyo, [Social Welfare and Public Assistance].

MHLW (2005b) Ministry of Health Labour and Welfare, Wage Structure Survey, Labor Statistics, Tokyo, http://www.mhlw.go.jp/english/database/db-l/index.html.

MHLW (2006) *Heisei 18 nendo zenkoku boshi setai tou chousa kekka houkoku,* Tokyo, [Results of the 2006 National Survey on Lone Mother and Other Households].

MIAC (2008), *Statistical Handbook of Japan*, Tokyo. Statistical Training and Research Institute.

Ministry of Construction (1995) *Minkan Juutaku Kensetsu Shikin Jittai Chousa* [Survey on the Financial Situation in Private home Construction]. Tokyo, Ministry of Construction.

Miura, A. (2005) *Karyu Shakai* [Low Class Society], Tokyo, Kobunsha.

MLIT (2005) Ministry of Land Infrastructure and Transport, Toshi Hakusho, Tokyo, (Government White Paper on Land).

Moriizumi, Y. (2003) 'Target saving by renters for housing purchase in Japan', *Journal of Urban Economics*, 53: 494509. http://www.sciencedirect.com/science?_ob=MiamiImageURL&_imagekey=B6WMG-48FSWH1-6-1&_cdi=6934&_user=496085&_pii=S009411900300010X&_check=y&_orig=search&_coverDate=05%2F31%2F2003&view=c&wchp=dGLbVtz-zSkWA&md5=655a3a6334a350af39bdd62074864741&ie=/sdarticle.pdf.

Morikawa, M., Sasatani, H., Nagata, S., Yamanoi., Yamaguchi, M. and Saito, A. (2007) 'Preventative care or preventing needs? rebalancing long-term care between government and service users in Japan', The Fourth Annual East Asian Social Policy Research Network International Conference, Tokyo, October 2007.

Morishima, M. (1988) 'Confucianism as a Basis for Capitalism', in Okimoto, D. I. and Rohlem, T. P. (eds) *Inside the Japanese System: Readings on Contemporary Society and Political Economy*. Stanford University Press, pp 36–38.

Nakano, L. (2010) 'Working and Waiting for an "Appropriate Person": How Single Women Support and Resist Family in Japan', in R Ronald and A Alexi (eds) *Home and Family in Japan: Continuity and Change*, London, Routledge, pp 131–151.

Nakano, L., and Wagatsuma, M. (2004) 'Mothers and Their Unmarried Daughters: An Intimate Look at Generational Change', in G. Mathews and B. White (eds) *Japan's Changing Generations: Are Young People Creating a new Society?* London, Routledge.

Nishikawa Y. (2004) *Sumai to Kazoku wo Meguru Monogatari: Otoko no Ie, Onna no Ie, Seibetsu no Nai Heya* [A Tale about House and Family: House for Men, House for Women and Room without Sexual distinction], Tokyo, Shyueishya Press.

Ochiai, E. (1994) *21-seiki kazoku e* [Toward a Twenty first Century Family] Tokyo, Yuuhikaku.

Oi, T., Toyofuku, Y., and Oizumi, E. (2007) 'Recent changes in housing markets and housing affordability', paper presented to Asia Pacific Network for Housing Research, Transformations in Housing, Urban Life and Public Policy, South Korea, Seoul National University, August.

Recruit, Co., Ltd., 2005, *Shutoken Shinchiku Manshon Keiyakusha Doko Chosa* [Research on New Condominium Purchasers in the Capital Metropolitan Area] Tokyo, Recruit Co.

Sakata, K., and McKenzie, C.R. (2009) 'The impact of divorce precedents on the Japanese divorce rate', *Mathematics and Computers in Simulation, 79*(9) pp. 2917–2926.

Sand, J. (2003) *House and Home in Modern Japan: Architecture, Domestic Space and Bourgeois culture, 1880-1930*, Cambridge, MA, Harvard University Press.

Shinada, T. (2007) *Kaji to Kazoku no Nichijyo Seikatsu: Naze Syufu wa Hima ni Naranakattanoka* [Domestic duties and Daily Life of Family: Why Housewives Could Not Get The Time Off], Tokyo, Gakubunshya.

Ueno, C. (ed.) (1982) *Syufu Ronso wo Yomu 1, 2* [Reading Arguments about Housewife: Part 1 and 2], Tokyo, Keiso-Press.

Uzuhashi, T. K. (2001) 'Japan: bidding farewell to the welfare society', in P. Alcock and G. Craig (eds) *International Social Policy*, Basingstoke, Palgrave.

Vogel, E.F. (1979) *Japan as Number One: Lessons for America*. New York: Harper.

Watson, S. (1986) 'Women and Housing or Feminist Housing Analysis', *Housing Studies*, 1: 1–10.

Yamada, M. (1999) *Parasaito Shinguru no Jidai* [The Age of the Parasite Singles], Tokyo: Chikuma Shobou.

Yamaguchi, K. (2008) 'Measures for Narrowing Male–Female Wage Gap: Support for Work Life Balance', *Nihon Kezai Shinbun*, 16 June.

Yamanaka, E. (1988) *Nihon Kindai Kokka no Seiritsu to 'ie' Seido* [The Establishment of the Modern State of Japan and the Family System], Tokyo, Nihon Hyouronsha.

Yui, Y (2004) 'Daitoshi niokeru shingeru josei no manshon konyo to sono haikei' [Condominum purchase by single women in large cities] in Yui, Y., Kiyama, H. Wakabayashi, Y. and Nakazawa, T. (eds) *Hataraku josei no toshi kukan* [Urban Space and Working Women], Tokyo, Kokin Shouten.

9 Neo-liberalization and the invisibility of women's housing problems in Taiwan

Bih, H. D. (1996). 'Married women's living experiences'. *Indigenous Psychological Research in Chinese Societies, 6*, 300–52 (in Chinese).

Chang, Y. H. and Chi, L. (1991). 'The change of household types in Taiwan'. *Thought and Words: Journal of the Humanities and Social Science, 29*(4), 85–113 (in Chinese).

Chao, A. (2005). 'Moving house: The relational–materialistic aspect of queer cultural citizenship'. *Taiwan: A Radical Quarterly in Social Studies, 57*, 41–85 (in Chinese).

Chen, J. Y. (2006). 'A home of 'her' own: Home formation and lived experience of single women'. Unpublished masters thesis. Graduate Institute of Building and Planning, National Taiwan University, Taipei (in Chinese).

Chen, S. M. (2000). 'A study of households' housing adjustment decisions and location choice in Taipei: Discussion of female decision-making effect'. Unpublished doctoral dissertation, Department of Land Economics, Chengchi University, Taipei (in Chinese).

Chen, Y. C. (1990). 'The motivations of the transfer behavior between generations'. Unpublished masters thesis, Graduate Institute of Economics, National Taiwan University, Taipei (in Chinese).

Chen, Y. L. (2005). 'Provision for collective consumption: Housing production under neoliberalism'. In R. Y. W. Kwok (ed.), *Globalizing Taipei: The Political Economy of Spatial Development*. London: Routledge.

Chen, Y. L. (2006). 'Housing and single mothers in the KMT regime of Taiwan, 1949–2000'. *Geography Research Forum, 26*, 93–114.

Chen, Y. L. and Li, W. D. (forthcoming). 'Neo-liberalism, the developmental state and housing policy in Taiwan'. In B. G. Park, A. Saito, and R. C. Hill (Eds.), *Locating Neoliberalism in East Asia: Neoliberalizing Spaces in Developmental States*. Studies in Urban and Social Change Series. London: Blackwell.

Chen, Y. S. (2006) 'Big changes of family types in Taiwan'. *China Times*, July 2, p. A6 (in Chinese).

Cheng, L. and Hsiung, P. C. (1993) 'Women, export-oriented growth, and the state: The case of Taiwan'. *Taiwan: A Radical Quarterly in Social Studies, 14*, 39–76 (in Chinese).

Cheng, L. C. (2001). 'Poverty feminization and social relief policies'. *Annual Journal of Social Education, 49*, 13–18 (in Chinese).

Cheng, L. C. and Chang, H. J. (2004). *Research on the Survey, Analysis and Suggestion of the Problem of the Homeless*. Taipei: Department of Social Affairs, Ministry of the Interior (in Chinese).

Cheng, N. J. (2006). Masters Thesis, 'Social exclusion and social welfare policy: Case study on low income female single-parent families in Hsinchu City'. Graduate Institute of Public Policy, Feng Chia University, Taichung (in Chinese).

Chou, W. C. (2005). Conference paper, 'New Strategies to promote women's labor participation rate and quality of human resources'. October 2005 Central Taiwan Conference of Human Resources. http://www.ccunix.ccu.edu.tw/~shlin/Gender%20 and%20work/increase%20female%20human%20resource.pdf

CPA (Construction and Planning Agency) (2006). *The Journal of the Ministry of the Interior, Summer 2006*. Taiwan: Ministry of the Interior (in Chinese).

DBASTCP (Department of Budget, Accounting and Statistics, Taipei City Government) (2006). *Major statistical index by sex in Taipeu City*. (in Chinese) Taipei: Taipei City Government.

DGBAS (Directorate-General Budget, Accounting and Statistics) (2003). *Special Analysis on National Statistics*, June 14, 2003. Taiwan: Executive Yuan (in Chinese).

DGBAS (Directorate-General Budget, Accounting and Statistics) (2006a). *Budget on Social Security Expenditure*. Taiwan: Executive Yuan (in Chinese).

DGBAS (Directorate-General Budget, Accounting and Statistics) (2006b). *The transformation of Family Structure*. Taiwan: Executive Yuan (in Chinese).

DGBAS (Directorate-General Budget, Accounting and Statistics) (2007). *The General Report on Gender 2007*. Taiwan: Executive Yuan (in Chinese).

References

DGBAS (Directorate-General Budget, Accounting and Statistics) (2008a). *The General Report on Gender 2008*. Taiwan: Executive Yuan (in Chinese).

DGBAS (Directorate-General Budget, Accounting and Statistics) (2008b). *Special Analysis on National Statistics*, March 6, 2003. Taiwan: Executive Yuan (in Chinese).

DGBAS (Directorate-General Budget, Accounting and Statistics) (2009). *R.O.C.—Human Resource Monthly Statistics*. Taiwan: Executive Yuan.

DSAMI (Department of Social Affairs, Ministry of the Interior) (2008). 'Households and persons of low-income families'. Available online, retrieved January 10, 2009 from http://sowf.moi.gov.tw/stat/month/m3-01.xls (in Chinese)

DSATPC (Department of Social Affairs, Taipei City Government) (2008). *The Fourth Report of the Tenth City Council Meeting*. September 2008. Available online, retrieved January 10, 2009 from http://www.bosa.tcg.gov.tw/e/e1000.asp?uid=18 (in Chinese)

Hsieh, C. T. (2002). Single-parent family and its change in Taiwan: 1990 and 2000 Census data in comparison. *NTU Social Work Review, 6*, 1–33 (in Chinese).

Hu, Y. H. (1995). *Three Generation Households: Myths and Traps*. Taipei: Chuliu (in Chinese).

Huang, L. (2006). 'A world without strangers? Taiwan's new households in the nexus of China and Southeast Asia relations'. *International Development Planning Review, 28*(4), 447–73.

Institute for Physical Planning and Information. (2009). *Housing Demand Survey of the Fourth Quarter 2008*. Taiwan: Construction and Planning Agency, Ministry of the Interior (in Chinese).

Lan, P. J. and Wu, C. L. (2005) 'Gender and families in transformation: Female minority and immigrant caretakers'. In J. H. Wang and Y. H. Chang (eds), *Agglomerating the Vitality of Taiwan*. Taipei: Chuliu (in Chinese).

Lee, A. (2004). *In the Name of Harmony and Prosperity. Labor and Gender Politics in Taiwan's Economic Restructuring*. Albany, NY: State University of New York Press.

Lee, Y. J. and Ku, Y. W. (2003). 'Another welfare world? a preliminary examination of the developmental welfare regime in East Asia'. *Taiwanese Journal of Sociology, 31*, 189–241 (in Chinese).

Li, T. I. (2007). 'Lesbians "doing family" in Taiwan'. Unpublished masters thesis. Graduate Institute of Sociology, National Taiwan University, Taipei (in Chinese).

Lin, C. J. (2007). 'Identity differences among women in patrilineal families: A cross-generational comparison of the division of domestic labor of the middle-class working women'. *Taiwan: A Radical Quarterly in Social Studies, 68*, 1–73 (in Chinese).

Lin, W. Y. (1995). *Survey and Analysis of the Problems of the Homeless*. Taipei: Research, Development, and Evaluation Commission, Executive Yuan (in Chinese).

Lu, C. Y. (2008). *The Analysis on the Draft of Housing Law and Policy Recommendation*. Guozheng pinglun [National Policy Foundation Commentary]. 2008.9.11 (in Chinese) Taipei, Taiwan: National Policy Foundation.

Ministry of the Interior. (1989). *Survey on Women's Living Conditions*. Taipei, Taiwan: Ministry of Interior.

Peng, C. W. and Wang, C. Y. (2005) 'The determinants of homeownership rates across different cities and counties'. *Journal of Taiwan Land Research 8*(2), 1–20.

Peng, Y. W. (2007). 'Women's movements and politics'. In S. L. Huang and M. H. You (eds), *Gender dimensions in Taiwanese society*. Taipei: Chuliu (in Chinese).

238

Saegert, S. and Clark, H. (2006) 'Opening doors: What a right to housing means for women'. In R. G. Bratt, M. E. Stone and C. Hartman (eds), *A Right to Housing: Foundation for a New Social Agenda*. Philadelphia, PA: Temple University Press.

Statistics Bureau, 2009. *National Statistics, ROC (Taiwan)*. Available online http://www.stat.gov.tw/ct.asp?xItem=12934&ctNode=517. Acessed: August 29 2010.

Tsai, Y. S. (2006). 'The division of household labor in Taiwan lesbian family'. Unpublished masters thesis. Department of Sociology, Soochow University, Taipei (in Chinese).

Wang, J. T. (2007) 'Expenditure of social welfare'. Available online, retrieved January 10, 2009 from http://www.ios.sinica.edu.tw/TSCpedia/index.php/%E7%A4%BE%E6%9C %83%E7%A6%8F%E5%88%A9%E6%94%AF%E5%87%BA (in Chinese)

Wolfe, M. (1992). 'Invisible women in invisible places: Lesbians, lesbian bars, and the social production of people/environment relationships'. *Architecture and Behaviour,* 8(2), 137–157.

Wong, J. (2004). *Healthy Democracies: Welfare Politics in Taiwan and South Korea*. New York: Cornell University Press.

Wu. C. A. (1999). 'Research on homeless women: The meanings of home and experiences of living in Taipei City'. Unpublished masters thesis. Graduate Institute of Building and Planning, National Taiwan University, Taipei (in Chinese).

Wu, S. S. (2004). 'The transformation of Taiwan's welfare system: The challenges of democratization and globalization'. Unpublished masters thesis, Department of Sociology, Donghai University, Taichung (in Chinese).

Yi, C. C. (2008).' The continuity and change of patriarchal family system: The family sociology in Taiwan, 1960–2000'. In Shieh, G. S. (ed.), *Interlocution: A thematic history of Taiwanese sociology, 1945–2005*. Taipei: Socio (in Chinese).

10 A gender study of housing rights of women in urban China

ACWF News (2008) 'Gender composition of household heads in families in cities and rural areas, 2005', Available online at People's Daily Online http://acwf.people.com.cn/ GB/99061/136280/137016/8231144.html (in Chinese).

Chan, K. W. (1997) 'Feminism: Urban and housing problem beyond traditional perspective', in Chan, Kam Wah, Woo, Man Lung, Yu, Wai Kam and Li, Chi Fai, *Urban and Housing in Hong Kong: An Introduction to Urban Sociology*, Hong Kong: Joint Publishing (HK) Co. Ltd. (in Chinese). 陳錦華 (1997) "女性主義：突破傳統的角度看城市與房屋問題"，陳錦華、胡文龍、余偉錦、李志輝(編)香港城市與房屋：城市社會學初探，香港：三聯出版社。

Chan, K. W. and Chan, F. Y. (2003) 'Inclusion or Exclusion? Housing Battered Women in Hong Kong*', Critical Social Policy*, 23(4): 526–46.

Chen, J. (2006) 'Rate of private ownership of housing units is not equal to the rate of home ownership', *China Real Estate*, (10): 17.

Du S.-T. (2005) 'Research on gender differences of architecture and space', *Journal of Shandong University of Architecture and Engineering*, 20(1) 25–9 (in Chinese). 都胜君 (2005) "建築與空間的性別差異研究"，山東建築工程學院學報，第2005第1期，25-29頁。

Economic Daily (2001) 'Cities in China: which city has the best conditions for economic development?', 18 October (in Chinese).

Fu, Y. (2005) '25 Indexes for building China into a middle-income country, 27 square metres set as average housing size per person", People's Daily Online, retrieved 9 December. Http://finance.sina.com.cn/g/20051209/16292187022.shtml.

Lan, P.-C. (2003) 'Maid or madam? Filipina migrant workers and the continuity of domestic ', *Labor*, Gender & Society 17(2): 187–208.

Lan, P.-C. (2004) Why do women agonize women? The triangular relationship of migrant domestic workers, *Taiwanese Sociology*, 8(December): 43–97 (in Chinese).

Lan, P.-C. (2005) 'The stratified other: recruitment, training and racialization', *Taiwanese Journal of Sociology*, 34(June): 1–57 (in Chinese).

McDowell, L. (2006) *Gender, Identity and Place: Understanding Feminist Geography* (Chinese translation), translated by Up Tai-ling and Wang Zhi-hong, Taiwan: National Institution for Compilation and Translation, (in Chinese). Linda McDowell (2006) 徐苔玲,王志弘譯,性別、認同與地方——女性主義地理學概說,台灣:國立編譯館譯。

Perry, E. J. (2005) 'What the Chinese working class is experiencing today is unprecedented', Preface in Yu Jian-rong, *Conditions of the Working Class in China*", 2005, Hong Kong: Ming Jing Publishing House (in Chinese).

Tang, J. (2006), 'An exploration on gender space theory in architecture"', *Sichuan Architecture*, 12: 60–5 (in Chinese). 唐静 (2006),建築中的性別空間理論研究初探,四川建築, 第12期, 60-65頁。

Wang, M.-A. (2007) 'Space politics in the family', *Oriental Art*, 6: 12–21 (in Chinese). 汪民安 (2007), 家庭的空間政治,東方藝術,第6期P12-21,

Wang, J. and Zhou, F. (2007) 'Women's rights, space, city', *Chinese and Overseas Architecture*, 7: 39–40 (in Chinese). 王建,周凡 (2007) "女權空間城市",中外建築, 第7期, 39-40頁。

Xu, A.-Q. and Zhang, Jie-hai (2003) 'Welfare of the single parents as subjects: Chinese interpretative model', *Sociological Study*, 2003(04), pp. 85–97 (in Chinese).

Xue N.-l. and Hao Yang (2006), 'Gender analysis of marital property in China', *Collection of Women's Studies*, December, S2(77): 37–41 (in Chinese). 薛寧蘭,邵陽 (2006) "中國夫妻財產制的社會性別分析———以離婚夫妻財產分割為側重", 婦女研究論叢, 12月增刊總第77期, 37-41頁。

Zhao, L. and Wang, J. (2008), 'The comparative study on the urban social spatial polarization in China and foreign countries', *World Regional Studies*, 17(4): 59–65 (in Chinese). 趙亮,王婧 (2008) "國內外城市社會空間極化分異比較研究", 世界地理研究, 12期, 59-65頁。

11 Women and housing inequalities in Hong Kong

Castells, M., Goh, L. and Kwok R.Y.W. (1990) *The Shek Kip Mei Syndrome: economic development and public housing in Hong Kong and Singapore*, London: Pion.

Census and Statistics Department (2007) *Thematic Report: Persons from the Mainland Having Resided in Hong Kong for Less Than 7 Years – 2006 Population By-census*, Hong Kong: Hong Kong SAR Government.

Census and Statistics Department (2008a) *A Graphic Guide on Hong Kong's Development (1967–2007)*, Hong Kong: Hong Kong SAR Government.

Census and Statistics Department (2008b) *Thematic Report: Older Persons – 2006 Population By-census*, Hong Kong: Hong Kong SAR Government.

Census and Statistics Department (2009a) *Annual Digest of Statistics 2009 Edition*, Hong Kong: Hong Kong SAR Government.

Census and Statistics Department (2009b) *Women and Men in Hong Kong: Key Statistics 2009 edition*, Hong Kong: Hong Kong SAR Government.

Centadata (2010) data provided by Centaline Property. Available online, retrieved 27 March 2010 from http://www.centadata.com/

Chan, K. W. (1997) *Social Construction of Gender Inequality in the Housing System: Housing experience of women in Hong Kong,* Aldershot: Ashgate.

Chan, K. W. (2000) 'Prosperity or inequality: deconstructing the myth of home ownership in Hong Kong', *Housing Studies*, 15(1): 28-43.

Chan, K. W. (forthcoming) 'Women and housing organizations', in Smith, Susan (ed.) *International Encyclopedia of Housing and Home*, London: Elsevier.

Chan, K. W. and Chan, F. Y. (2003) 'Inclusion or exclusion? Housing battered women in Hong Kong', *Critical Social Policy*, 23(4): 526–46.

Chan, K. W. and Lee, J. (2003) 'Autonomy or dependence? Housing and living arrangement of the elderly in Hong Kong', *Indian Journal of Gerontology*, 17(1 & 2): 59–76.

Chiu, R. L. H.(2007) 'Planning, land and affordable housing in Hong Kong', *Housing Studies*, 22(1): 63–81.

Chui, E. W.T. (2002) 'Housing welfare services in Hong Kong for new immigrants from China: Inclusion or exclusion', *Asian and Pacific Migration Journal*, 11(2): 221–45.

Fung, K. K. and Forrest, R. (2002) 'Institutional mediation, the Hong Kong residential housing market and the Asian financial crisis', *Housing Studies*, 17(2): 189–207.

Hochschild, A. R. (1990) *The Second Shift*, New York: Avon Books.

Hong Kong Consumer Council (1996) *How Competitive is the Private Residential Market? – Report on the Private Residential Property Industry in Hong Kong*, Hong Kong: Hong Kong Consumer Council.

Hong Kong Housing Authority (2009) *Hong Kong Housing Authority Annual Report 2008/09*, Hong Kong: Hong Kong Housing Authority.

Hopkinson, L. and Lao, M. M.L. (2003) *Rethinking the Small House Policy*, Hong Kong: Civic Exchange. Available online, retrieved 31 March 2010 from http://www.civic-exchange.org/eng/upload/files/200309_RethinkSmallPolicy.pdf.

Law, K.-Y. and Lee, K.-M. (2006) 'Citizenship, economy and social exclusion of mainland Chinese immigrants in Hong Kong', *Journal of Contemporary Asia*, 36(2): 217–42.

Lee, J. (1994) 'Affordability, home ownership and the middle class housing crisis in Hong Kong', *Policy and Politics*, 22(3): 179–89.

Lee, C. K. (2000) 'Public Discourses and collective identities: emergence of women as a collective actor in the women's movement in Hong Kong', in Chui, Stephen W.K. and Lui, Tai Lok (eds) *The Dynamic of Social Movement in Hong Kong*, Hong Kong: Hong Kong University Press.

Lee, W. K. M. (2004) 'Ethnic and gender relations in Hong Kong: The work experiences of recent mainland Chinese immigrant women', *Asian and Pacific Migration Journal*, 13(2): 233–53.

Leung, L. C. (2004) 'Engendering citizenship', in Ku, Agnes S. and Pun, Ngai (eds) *Remaking Citizenship in Hong Kong: Community, Nation And The Global City*, London and New York: RoutledgeCurzon.

Leung, L.i C. and Chan, K. W. (1998) 'The new opium war: welfare dependency of lone mothers in Hong Kong', *Hong Kong Journal of Social Work*, 32(2): 117–29.

Task Force on Population Policy (2003) *Report of the Task Force on Population Policy*, Hong Kong: Hong Kong SAR Government. Available online, retrieved 31 March 2010 from www.info.gov.hk/info/population/eng/index.htm.

Yu, S. W. K. (1997) 'The Hong Kong government's strategy for promoting home ownership: An approach to reducing the decommodifying effect of public housing services' *International Journal of Urban and Regional Research*, 21(4): 537–53.

12 Conclusion

Christie, H. (2000) Mortgage arrears and gender inequalities, *Housing Studies* 15(6): 877–905

Dowling, R. (1998) Gender, class and home ownership: placing the connections, *Housing Studies* 13(4): 471–86.

Pascall, G. and Sung, S. (2007) Gender and East Asian welfare states: from Confucianism to gender equality? Paper presented at Fourth Annual East Asian Social Policy research network (EASP) International Conference, 20–21 October.

Smith, S. (2005) States, markets and an ethic of care, *Political Geography* 24(1): 1–20.

Index

Index